Lecture Notes in Computer Science　　6834

Commenced Publication in 1973
Founding and Former Series Editors:
Gerhard Goos, Juris Hartmanis, and Jan van Leeuwen

T0236056

Klaus-Dieter Schewe
Bernhard Thalheim (Eds.)

Semantics in Data and Knowledge Bases

4th International Workshop
SDKB 2010
Bordeaux, France, July 5, 2010
Revised Selected Papers

 Springer

Volume Editors

Klaus-Dieter Schewe
Software Competence Center Hagenberg and
Johannes-Kepler-University Linz
Softwarepark 21, 4232 Hagenberg, Austria
E-mail: kd.schewe@scch.at; kd.schewe@faw.jku.at

Bernhard Thalheim
Christian-Albrechts-University Kiel
Department of Computer Science
Olshausenstr. 40, 24098 Kiel, Germany
E-mail: thalheim@is.informatik.uni-kiel.de

ISSN 0302-9743   e-ISSN 1611-3349
ISBN 978-3-642-23440-8   e-ISBN 978-3-642-23441-5
DOI 10.1007/978-3-642-23441-5

Springer Heidelberg Dordrecht London New York

Library of Congress Control Number: 2011934960

CR Subject Classification (1998): H.2, H.4, H.3, I.2.4, C.2.4, F.4.1

LNCS Sublibrary: SL 3 – Information Systems and Application, incl. Internet/Web
and HCI

Typesetting: Camera-ready by author, data conversion by Scientific Publishing Services, Chennai, India

Printed on acid-free paper

Springer is part of Springer Science+Business Media (www.springer.com)

Preface

This volume contains six papers presented at the 4th International Workshop on Semantics in Data and Knowledge Bases, which was co-located with ICALP 2010 and organized in Bordeaux in July 2010. These papers were carefully revised and extended after the workshop and subjected to a thorough reviewing process.

The first two workshops under the initial name "Semantics in Databases" took place in Rež, Czech Republic, in 1995 and Dagstuhl, Germany, in 2001, the third workshop on "Semantics in Data and Knowledge Bases" was co-located with EDBT 2008 and organized in Nantes, France, in 2008. The proceedings of the first three workshops were published by Springer in the LNCS series, volumes 1358, 2582 and 4925.

The SDKB workshop series tries to bring together researchers in the areas of data and knowledge bases who work on aspects of semantics. In particular, the workshop presents original contributions demonstrating the use of logic, discrete mathematics, combinatorics, domain theory and other mathematical theories of semantics for database and knowledge bases, computational linguistics and semiotics, and information and knowledge-based systems.

The SDKB 2010 call for papers sought research papers concentrating on the following research topics:

- Formal models for data and knowledge bases
- Integrity constraints maintenance and dependency theory
- Formal methods for data and knowledge base design
- Reasoning about data and knowledge base dynamics
- Adaptivity for personalized data and knowledge bases
- View-centered data- and knowledge-intensive systems
- Information integration in data and knowledge bases
- Knowledge discovery in data and knowledge bases
- Validation and verification of data and knowledge base designs
- Formal linguistics for data and knowledge bases
- Logical and mathematical foundations of semantics
- Semantics in data- and knowledge-intensive applications

The papers in this volume reflect a variety of approaches to semantics in data and knowledge bases:

Waseem Akhtar, Álvaro Cortés Calabuig and Jan Paredaens deal with the problem of dependencies, which is a core area of database theory and has been widely studied in the context of relational databases. Here, the authors approach functional and equality-generating dependencies in the context of RDF. They highlight the key problem of RDF being impredicative, which makes it hard for a straightforward generalization of relational techniques. In the paper it is shown that for RDF, functional dependencies form a proper subclass of equality-generating dependencies. For the latter ones a sound and complete axiomatization is achieved, but unfortunately, the corresponding problem for functional dependencies is still open. For the implication problem the article presents a solution by means of an adapted chase procedure.

Nicole Bidoit-Tollu sheds light on the relationship between schemata and optimization for queries and updates, in the case of XML focusing on XML schema, XQuery and the corresponding update facility XUF. By exploiting static type analysis it is shown how types rank before constraints for XML data processing.

Hendrik Decker investigates the case of possibly inconsistent databases, and asks for which queries one might obtain answers with integrity nonetheless. A key contribution of the paper is a semantic definition of what constitutes integrity for query answers. This is done by analyzing causes that explain the answer. Integrity is defined by the existence of a cause that does not overlap with any cause for integrity violation.

Stephen J. Hegner investigates view updates looking at complementary views, which embody information not in the view at hand and permit the reconstruction of the entire database. As in general there are many such complements, the question is to characterize and construct optimal ones. In this paper this is solved for a class of relational views by exploiting unique decompositions within a semi-lattice of views.

Attila Sali demonstrates interesting relationships between databases and coding theory. The starting point is the question of minimal Armstrong instances for certain dependencies. This is first investigated for branching dependencies leading to a new metric space and contributions to error-correcting codes. A second scenario concerns functional dependencies, in particular keys in the case of bounded domains, where Armstrong instances give rise to q-ary codes.

Qing Wang presents an axiomatization for a multi-modal logic for a variant of abstract state machines that have been proven to capture database transformations in general with bounded non-determinism. The key idea is to use update sets and multisets explicitly in the logic. As these are finite, the logic can be kept first-order.

We want to thank the authors for their contributions to this volume. We are grateful to the members of our Program Committee for their detailed reviews for both the preliminary workshop papers and the revised conference papers. We are thankful to the ICALP organizers for the venue and the organization of the workshop. Our thanks go especially to René Noack for his support of the organization.

June 2011

Klaus-Dieter Schewe
Bernhard Thalheim

SDKB 2010 Program Committee

Pablo Barcelo, Chile
Christoph Beierle, Germany
Nicole Bidoit-Tollu, France
Egon Börger, Italy
Stefan Brass, Germany
Andrea Cali, Italy
Lois Delcambre, USA
Thomas Eiter, Austria
Victor Felea, Romania
Flavio Ferrarotti, New Zealand
Marc Gyssens, Belgium
Edward Hermann Haeussler, Brazil
Sven Hartmann, Germany
Stephen Hegner, Sweden
Gabriele Kern-Isberner, Germany
Sebastian Link, New Zealand
Sebastian Maneth, Austràlia
Carlo Meghini, Italy
Wilfred Ng, Hong Kong
René Noack, Germany
Jaroslav Pokorny, Czech Republic
Peter Revesz, USA
Klaus-Dieter Schewe, Austria (Co-chair)
Attila Sali, Hungary
Dietmar Seipel, Germany
Leticia Tanca, Italy
Bernhard Thalheim, Germany (Co-chair)
Alex Thomo, Canada
Riccardo Torlone, Italy
Thomas Triplet, Canada
Junhu Wang, Australia
Qing Wang, New Zealand
Jef Wijsen, Belgium

Table of Contents

About Semantics

Klaus-Dieter Schewe[1] and Bernhard Thalheim[2]

[1] Software Competence Center Hagenberg, Hagenberg, Austria
[2] Christian-Albrechts-University Kiel, Department of Computer Science, Kiel, Germany
kd.schewe@scch.at, thalheim@is.informatik.uni-kiel.de

Abstract. This introductory article presents the workshop organisers' view on semantics, the intentions of the SDKB workshop series, and a brief account on what has been achieved in the field. Previous SDKB volumes survey different approaches to semantics in database research and discuss research on database semantics. Most of these research questions are still open.

1 Knowledge Bases Supported by Database Technology

Semantics is the study of meaning, i.e. how meaning is constructed, interpreted, clarified, obscured, illustrated, simplified, negotiated, contradicted and paraphrased [22]. It has been treated differently in the scientific community, e.g., in the area of knowledge bases and by database users.

- The scientific community prefers the treatment of 'always valid' semantics based on the mathematical logic. A constraint is valid if this is the case in any correct database.
- Database modellers often use a 'strong' semantics for several classes of constraints. Cardinality constraints are based on the requirement that databases exist for both cases, for the minimal and for the maximal case.
- Database mining is based on a 'may be valid' semantics. A constraint is considered to be a candidate for a valid formula.
- Users usually use a weak 'in most cases valid' semantics. They consider a constraint to be valid if this is the usual case.
- Different groups of users use an 'epistemic' semantics. For each of the group its set of constraints is valid in their data. Different sets of constraints can even contradict.

Semantics is currently one of the most overused notions in modern computer science literature. Its understanding spans from synonyms for structuring or synonyms for structuring on the basis of words to precise defined semantics. This partial misuse results in a mismatch of languages, in neglecting formal foundations, and in brute-force definitions of the meaning of syntactic constructions.

Designing a database application means to specify the structure, the operations, the static semantics and the dynamic semantics. The aim is to find a full specification or at least to find a specification which leads to a database structure on which operating is simple.

Structuring of databases is based on three interleaved and dependent semiotic parts [9,19]:

K.-D. Schewe, and B. Thalheim (Eds.): SDKB 2010, LNCS 6834, pp. 1–22, 2011.

Syntactics: Inductive specification of database structures based on a set of base types, a collection of constructors and an theory of construction limiting the application of constructors by rules or by formulas in deontic logics. In most cases, the theory may be dismissed. Structural recursion is the main specification vehicle.

Semantics: Specification of admissible databases on the basis of static integrity constraints describes those database states which are considered to be legal. If structural recursion is used then a variant of hierarchical first-order predicate logics may be used for description of integrity constraints.

Pragmatics: Description of context and intension is based either on explicit reference to the enterprise model, to enterprise tasks, to enterprise policy, and environments or on intensional logics used for relating the interpretation and meaning to users depending on time, location, and common sense.

1.1   Knowledge Bases - Do We Have a Need for That?

Human often meet a situation in which additional information, knowledge or at least fact are urgently demanded. This knowledge on demand is however not uniquely determined. It depends on the user, the current user situation, the data on hand, the background, the policies of data providers, etc.

Example 1 (knowledge base demand).
   Let us consider the large variety for knowledge demand of people after the Iceland EyJafjallajokull Glacier volcano eruption on March 20, 2010:

- How long this situation will influence travel in Europe? Remember that the last Eyjafjallajokull eruption lasted for two years, and it is possible that this one will do the same. How weather conditions such as the anti-cyclone situation influence on ash spread?
- What are the contents of ash? Could particles of rock, glass and sand clog up aircraft engines? What are the fears of the effect of volcanic ash on plane engines? Are there other components on aircraft that are equally sensitive to particles? Is driving more dangerous than flying through ash? As flights resume, how dangerous is it to fly through a volcanic ash cloud? Are the airlines right with their requirement to resume flights on manual control by pilots depending on visibility? Which safety tests showed that the engines could cope in areas of low-density ash?
- Why mathematical simulations have been used for decision making? Why mathematics has partially failed in making predictions?
- How the weather changes can be explained after the volcano eruption? Why scientist were incorrect in their prediction for the weather impact? (The European summer in 2010 was far colder than any prediction could foresee. This summer seems to be a counterexample for the climate change discussion. Watching the enormous plumes of dust and ash rising from Eyjafjallajokull, it is hard to imagine that this almost week-long eruption would not have any effect on weather and climate. But scientist expected that there is no change.)
- What is the economical impact of such eruptions in general and of this eruption in special? What is the impact of the eruption for North Sea fishery, for industry, for tourism, etc.?

- What are the passengers rights for stranded passengers or cancellations? What are the best sources of advice? How I can cope with my personal situation? E.g., who gets priority on seats now flights are running again?
- Why icelanders enjoy their volcanos?
- How clouds depends on volcanos and flights? Jet contrails are effectively acting as cirrus clouds, reflecting solar energy in the day, acting as a blanket by night.
- Is there any correlation to other climate change drivers such as sun activity? What are the implications of ionospheric plasma bubbles? To what extent are sunspot activities related to economic cycles?

This small list can be extended in many directions and illustrates the variety of knowledge that is necessary to satisfy the demand of people.

The example shows that we need different data, concepts, explanations, theories, and information. In general, knowledge system environments must support the following kinds:

- state-of-the art, -affairs, -knowledge, -science;
- deficiencies, missing or withhold facts;
- background, scientific explanations, science, potential theories, analysis;
- cross links, bindings;
- associations;
- facts with quality properties, full or partial picture;
- predictions, possible tactics and strategies for the future;
- restrictions, generalisation;
- analogies;
- history beside news;
- ways to cope with and the outcome for the future;
- consequences;
- links with headlines and quality assessment.

This list of knowledge pieces or chunks that must be provided can be categorized by the utility that the knowledge provides as follows:

Orientation knowledge allows to cope with the situation, to explain, and to survey the history, the scenario, the facts, the summarisation or generalisation and the overall view.

Tacit or action knowledge is based on practices, technics, methods, and strategies. It provides rules, procedures, check lists, principles, strategies, law, regulations, comments to regulations in order to manage situations.

Explanation knowledge gives reasons, arguments for explanation of claims or arguments or assertions or recommendations (what, why,, ...).

Sources knowledge links to knowledge on data sources (meta knowledge) such as knowledge on archives, references to communication, or cross links.

Activity knowledge supports working, adaptation or processing, operating on analogies, and coping with errors.

1.2   The Notion of Knowledge

The notion of knowledge[1] is one of overused terms. Knowledge bases literature often lack in a precise definition of the notion of knowledge, e.g., [5] avoids to define the notion of knowledge. Knowledge has two sides. It is knowledge in general defined by a noun from one side and the knowledge by a user expressed by the verb 'to know' from the other side.

Knowledge as sustainable, potentially durable and verifiable grounded consensus:
   The required information can be qualified as knowledge, if the information

1. is consensus with a world and a community,
2. is based on postulates or principles that create the fundament for the knowledge,
3. is true according to a certain notion of 'truth',
4. is reusable in a rule system for new information,
5. is long-lasting and existing for a long time,
6. has an effect and is sustaining within a society, community or world, and
7. is not equivalent to other information that can be generated with the aid of facts or preliminary information in the particular inventory of knowledge by a rule system.

Knowledge as the state of information of a user: Different kinds of 'to know' are:
1. The state or fact of knowing.
2. Familiarity, awareness, or understanding gained through experience or study.
3. The sum or range of what has been perceived, discovered or learned.
4. Learning; erudition: teachers of great knowledge.
5. Specific information about something.
6. Carnal knowledge.

---

[1] The definition provided by the Encyclopedia Britannica [12] considers two 'Janus' meanings beside the obsolete 'cognizance' and the archaic 'sexual intercourse':
(I) as the fact of knowing something:
(Ia1) the fact or condition of knowing something with familiarity gained through experience or association;
(Ia2) acquaintance with or understanding of a science, art, or technique;
(Ib1) the fact or condition of being aware of something;
(Ib2) the range of one's information or understanding;
(Ic) the circumstance or condition of apprehending truth or fact through reasoning or cognition;
(Id) the fact or condition of having information or of being learned;
(II) the body of things known about or in science:
(IIa) the sum of what is known: the body of truth, information, and principles acquired by mankind;
(IIb) a branch of learning (synonyms of knowledge: learning, erudition, scholarship) meaning what is or can be known by an individual or by mankind.
We prefer this approach over the approach taken by the Wikipedia community who distinguishes between communicating knowledge, situated knowledge, partial knowledge, scientific knowledge and know-how or know-what or know-why or know-who knowledge.

We conclude therefore that within the scope of the Knowledge-Centered Web, it is necessary to deliver knowledge as enduring, justified and true consensus to users depending on context, users demands, desiderata and intention, whereby these aspects are supported by social facets, the environment, the profile, tasks and life cases of the users. Life cases, portfolios and tasks constitute the information demand of every users. The information demand of users requires a special content quality. It results in the requested knowledge, which is also depending on the understanding and motivation of users. So, the requested knowledge of users is a composition of understanding, and information demand, whereby the information demand is an aggregated component of life cases, motivation, intention and quality.

1.3 The Knowledge Delivery Task for Knowledge Bases

The knowledge delivery task of the knowledge bases is defined as:
Deliver the knowledge the user really needs through (1) concepts at the educational level level of the user that are illustrated and extended by (2) content which is quality content depending on the external and internal quality of the aggregated data (media object suite) and that are depicted by (3) topics in the language, in the culture and in the application portfolio of the user.

Therefore, knowledge delivery and acquaintance for the user is user-oriented and life-case-based content, concepts and topics.

1.4 The Quality Characteristics of Knowledge

It is surprising that the literature treat knowledge as a 100 % quality criterion. We can however distinguish between

validated knowledge that satisfiable within a scope of axioms and derivation rules (application domain), within a certain generality and has validity and timelineness,
verified and correct knowledge based on axioms and rules within a proof system that can be verified within a finite time, obey a correctness criteria (depending on profiles) and has some known interaction with other knowledge, and finally
sustainable and enduring knowledge that has a lifespan beyond volatile data and is torpid for a certain lifespan,
quality knowledge defined by the quality of use (understandability, learnability, operability, attractiveness, appropriatedness), by the external quality (privacy, ubiquity, pervasiveness, analysability, changeability, stability, testability), and by the internal quality (accuracy, suitability, interoperability, robustness, self-contained/independence).

We additionally may consider the user dimension. In this case the following requirements are added:

Potentially useful knowledge depends on a user, group or community or a culture and satisfies a number of quality criteria in dependence in the knowledge demand of these users.

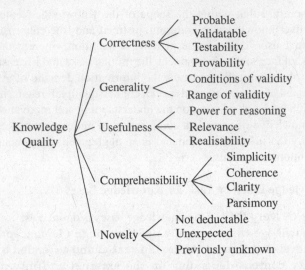

Fig. 1. Facets of Knowledge Quality

Ultimately understandable knowledge depends on the cognitive abilities of users, groups or communities.

These quality characteristics result is differences of the value of knowledge for the user. Quality is thus characterised by certain main characteristics. These characteristics can be ordered within the following tree in Figure 1.

We may also observe that these quality characteristics are of different *value* and *importance* depending on the needs of the user. We may differentiate knowledge depending on

- the role of the user such as learner, teacher, scientist, writer, etc.,
- the application area such as sciences, engineering, daily life,
- the timeliness of the information depending on the needs,
- the background necessary for transferring the data to the users information space, the users recognition and perception abilities, the users attention and interest, the users processing abilities, and the users abilities to integrate the data into his or her information space.

For instance the quality characteristics of of very different importance. Compare for instance the following two opposite evaluations

1.5   Typical Pitfalls of Knowledge Management and Their Solution by Database Techniques

Data are the main source for information and knowledge in research projects. They are used for deduction and exploration of hypotheses, for validation of hypotheses, for support of theories, and for illustration of behaviour or prediction of future behaviour. Their quality properties have been neglected for a long time. At the same time, modern data management allows to handle these problems. We compare the critical findings in the sequel with resolution techniques that can be applied to overcome the crucial pitfalls of data management in environmental sciences.

Economist:

Scientist:

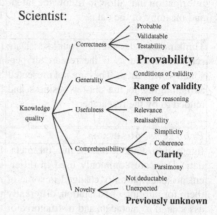

Problems observed	Their handling and resolution
Neglection of evolution: Data(base) models and databases can be versioned, shared, and reused. Each phase can lead to refining previous decisions, understandings, and changes due to external influences.	Database tools are designed to facilitate refinement and traceability. They support roundtrip modelling, comparison and merging, versioning, universal naming, and denormalisation mapping.
Invisible or missing models: Data that deliver project value must be accessible, understandable, and sharable. Models need to be available in an easily searchable manner.	Database modelling can help a project team ensure that appropriate data are available. Typical solutions on the basis of models are data reporting, repository management, and common dictionary.
Missing exchange of understanding: Data and data models developed within one team are not communicated to other teams. These teams have an unclear and inconsistent view on the data. They use however these data within their understanding.	Interactive 'intranets' based on common repository management support structured collaboration based on guidance and documentation, explicit communication of goals, benefits and deficiencies, and maintenance of metadata.
Thinking that models are only about data structuring: Data(base) models are restricted to the conceptual or logical schemata. The additional DBMS information is not well kept.	Data management includes metadata import and export, traces of data evolution, tools for usage tracking, export and import integration, macros for development of reports and scripts, and attachment generation.
Throwing data structures 'over the wall': Data structures are seen as early decisions without continuous change and deployment management. Data used at a later stage are kept prone to errors.	Data management generates and modifies data massives and ensures that there is a consistent link between the data and their history. It also includes changes within the structure and ensures that changes stay true to the original intent of the first structuring decisions.

Forgetting about the sizzle: Data should be clear and understandable in a collaboration. Often, they are not accompanied with information that allow to follow the intent and meaning of the data.	Data management can assist the data provider for presenting the data in the right form, the right format, the right size and structuring, at the right moment and under consideration of the user's information demand. The macro features extend and customise data delivery to meet the demand.
Thinking of data sets as "your" set: Data sets are treated as if the researcher personally owns them. They are not presented as belonging to the cluster business and tended to by the researcher.	Data set should be seen as corporate assets to be managed by a partnership within collaborating groups. Support can be generically provided for open sharing, for access to those who want it, offering metadata on how to understand the data and making every effort to deploy them clear and understandable.
Problems observed	*Their handling and resolution*
Integration without insight into the metadata: Data are commonly used in different projects, partially changed in some of them for purging or adaptation, differently associated to metadata and restructured or partially selected or aggregated. Their integration leads to data sets with high redundancy and data conflicts.	Entity resolution, record matching and data cleansing techniques support integration of data based on common sources. History tracking for data sets allows to trace back the data to their origin. Data sets can be extended by profiles. Computed data can be marked as such. Aggregation of data must be recorded as well as other data generating computations.

1.6 Typical Data Analysis Problems for Knowledge Discovery

Algorithms are typically used for the solution of data mining and analysis tasks. An algorithms also has an application area, application restrictions, data requirements, results at certain granularity and precision. These problems must be systematically tackled if we want to rely on the results of mining and analysis. Otherwise analysis may become misleading, biased, or not possible. Therefore, we explicitly treat properties of mining and analysis.

Data are the main source for information in data mining and analysis. Their quality properties have been neglected for a long time. At the same time, modern data management allows to handle these problems. We compare the critical findings of [10] with resolution techniques that can be applied to overcome the crucial pitfalls of data mining in environmental sciences reported there.

Problems observed [10]	*Their handling and resolution*
A large variety of competing algorithms and tools have been developed. Their advantages and specific application areas are not yet made explicit.	The development of an advisory system that supports selection and that help for the most appropriate selection might resolve this difficulty. The analysis of algorithms is necessary in advance.
Each of the algorithms has its specific data quality requirements.	We either improve the data quality or advice not to use the algorithm or only with special care.
The interpretation of results obtained by analysis is crucial for understanding analysis.	The user must be informed what has been achieved and what was not achievable.
The formation of best fitting hypotheses and concepts is still rather art than science.	The user is supported by explicit modelling of the triad of concepts, hypotheses, and data spaces.

The detection of new hypotheses and the selection of appropriate data is very difficult.	The user can be supported for orientation in the triad spaces and during drilling down into the data.
Visualisation of results is still rather difficult due to the specifics of the visualisation method and of the structure of the visualisation space.	Representation theory has developed approaches transformation of spaces to forms, e.g., abstract algebraic structures are represented using geometry.
The results of mining and analysis are open for misinterpretation and drawing wrong conclusions as long as the analysis properties of algorithms are not well understood.	The main properties of algorithms must provided together with the results obtained by these algorithms.
Data in analysis tasks are often missing, (partially) duplicated, partially wrong, partially (mis)corrected, and/or biased. Therefore, nobody can entirely rely on them.	Classical extrapolation, cleansing, control techniques developed for analysis, handling of complex functions and statistics can be applied if properties of data are known. Data identification techniques resolve redundancy of data.
Data are provided with wrong formats, wrong or mixed granularity, are isolated or are given only by partially integrated data massives.	Data modelling provides solutions for migration of legacy data into new data massives, for integration of data from heterogeneous resources, for extraction of data of interest by views and for abstractions of data.
Data massives are partially dense and huge at the same when mainly sparse data are used. This imbalance results in strange behaviour of algorithms.	Modern database modelling provides a number of techniques for extrapolation of data and for abstraction of data to other data sets. At the same time web information systems technology provides techniques for gardening of data.
Data massives are often unrelated to each other, not annotated, and have missing (geo & time) references.	Metadata injection, data modelling techniques and database integration techniques resolve these problems and provide additional information for new analysis tasks.
Data are of varying granularity and of various levels of detail. Micro-, meso- and macro-data are related to each other with an explicit association schema.	Integrated model suites with explicit association schemata among the different levels of detail and corresponding metadata for translation of data and semantics allow consistent handling of data of various levels of detail.
Data sets have their own hidden dependencies among dimensions of the data. Additionally turbulences and non-linear dependencies within the data are observed.	Data abstraction techniques support reduction to essential substructures and abstraction from substructures that are dependent from the main structures. Synergetics allows to separate dimensions into control and order dimensions.

2 Foundation of Knowledge Systems by Knowledge Chunks

Knowledge can be characterised through (1) its content, (2) its concepts, (3) its annotations or topics, and (4) its understanding by the user. Knowledge pieces cannot be considered in an isolated form. For this reason we imagine to use knowledge chunks as a suite of knowledge pieces consisting of content, concepts, topics and information. These dimensions are interdependent from each other. Figure 2 displays the knowledge space.

2.1 Content and Media Types: The Data Dimension

Content is complex and ready-to-use data. Content is typically provided with functions for its use. Content can be defined n the basis of *media types*. Content management systems are information systems that support extraction, storage and delivery of complex data.

Content in its actual definition is any kind of information that is shared within a community or organization. In difference to data in classical database systems content usually refers to aggregated macro data which is complex structured. Structuring of content can be distinguished:

- The structure of the aggregated micro data is preserved but micro data was combined to build larger chunks of information. Examples are scientific data sets such as time series of certain measurements. There is a common (or even individual) structuring and meaning for each sampling vector but the compound of all sampling vectors adds additional semantics.
- The structure of content is only partially known. A typical example is the content of Web pages: structuring is known up to a certain level of detail which may also be varying within one instance.
- Content may be subsymbolic, such as pictures, videos, music or other multimedia content.

Aggregation of content usually takes place by combining reusable fragments provided by different sources in different formats such as texts, pictures, video streams or structured data from databases. Content is subject to a content life cycle which implies a persistent change process to the content available in a content management system (CMS).

The more generic ones agree in a major paradigm: the separation of data management and presentation management. Data management reflects the process of supporting content creation, content structuring, content versioning, and content distribution while presentation management grabs the data for delivering it to the user in various ways. Only content which is generated following this separation can be easily shared, distributed, and reused.

Following new trends and developments in Web technologies, e.g., in the context of Web 2.0 or the Semantic Web the automated processing of content becomes more and more important. Because content represents valuable assets it may be reused in different contexts (*content syndication*) or has to remain accessible for a long time.

The semistructured or even unstructured nature of content requires annotations to enable search facilities for content. Expressing semantics in a machine interpretable way has been under investigation since the early days of artificial intelligence, see e.g., [18] for a survey of knowledge representation techniques such as logical theories, rule-based systems, frames or semantic nets. Today systems handle semantical descriptions as metadata describing certain content instances. There are different ways for associating data and metadata:

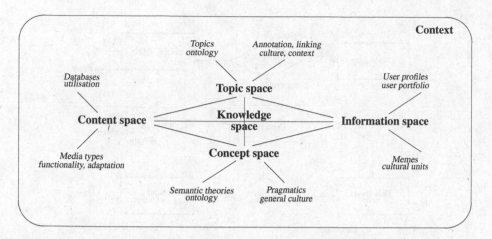

Fig. 2. The four dimensions of the knowledge space surrounded by the context dimension: (1) data dimension through content; (2) foundation dimension through concepts; (3) language dimension through topics; (4) user dimension through information; (5) context of data (content) or theories (concept) or user (information) or carrier/language (topic)

- A conceptual, logical, or physical *schema* is defined and instances are created according to this schema. This is the usual way for classical databases. The modelling language strongly restricts the capabilities of this description facility. Common languages such as Entity-Relationship Modelling or UML focus on structural properties with support of selected integrity constraints.
- Defining a schema is not applicable (or only in a restricted way) to semistructured or unstructured content. For that reason content instances are annotated. An annotation is a triple (S, P, O) where S denotes the subject to be annotated, P a predicate denoting the role or purpose of this annotation, and O the object (or resource) which is associated with S. The vocabulary for annotations is organized in ontologies and thesauri. A typical language for expressing annotations in the context of the Semantic Web is the Resource Description Framework (RDF, [21]) while the Web Ontology Language OWL ([20]) may be used to express semantic relationships between the concepts and resources used for annotation. There exist myriads of ontologies and parameter definitions for different application domains such as the Dublin Core parameters [1]) for editorial content.

2.2 Concepts and Theories: The Foundation Dimension

Concepts are the basis for knowledge representation. They specify our knowledge what things are there and what properties things have. Concepts are used in everyday life as a communication vehicle and as a reasoning chunk. Concepts can be based on definitions of different kinds. Therefore our goal for the development of knowledge bases can only be achieved if the content definition covers any kind of content description and goes beyond the simple textual or narrative form.

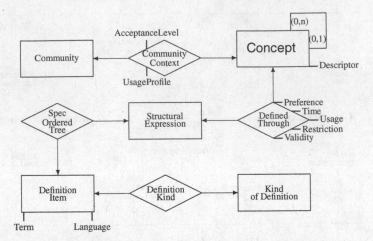

Fig. 3. The main schema for Concept Definition and Formation

A general description of concepts is considered to be one of the most difficult tasks. We analysed the definition pattern used for concept introduction in mathematics, chemistry, computer science, and economics. This analysis resulted in a number of discoveries:

- Any concept can be defined in a variety of ways. Sometimes some definitions are preferred over others, are time-dependent, have a level of rigidity, are usage-dependent, have levels of validity, and can only be used within certain restrictions.
- The typical definition frame we observed is based on definition items. These items can also be classified by the kind of definition. The main part of the definition is a tree-structured structural expression of the following form

SpecOrderedTree(StructuralTreeExpression
                (DefinitionItem, Modality(Sufficiency, Necessity),
                Fuzziness, Importance, Rigidity,
                Relevance, GraduationWithinExpression, Category))) .

- Concepts typically also depend on the application context, i.e. the application area and the application schema. The association itself must be characterised by the kind of association.

Concepts are typically hierarchically ordered and can thus be layered. We assume that this ordering is strictly hierarchical and the concept space can be depicted by a set of concept trees. A concept is also dependent on the community that prefers this concept. A concept is also typically given through an embedding into the knowledge space. The schema in Figure 3 displays the general structure for content definition. This schema also covers all aspects discussed in [8]. A concept has typically a manyfold of definitions. Their utilisation, exploration and application depend on the user (e.g. the education profile), the usage, and context.

Example (concept of mathematical set): *A set can be given by an enumeration of its elements, by inductive definition of its elements, by an algorithm for the construction of the set, or by explicit description of the properties of the set. Which of the definitions is more appropriate depends on the application domain.*

These set definitions are based on the principle of extensionalism: Two sets are equal if they contain the same elements. We might also use sets that are not based on this principle.

2.3 Topics and Ontologies: The Language Dimension

Content and concepts may be enhanced by **topics** that specify the pragmatic understanding of users.

Semantic annotation in current content management systems is usually restricted to preselected ontologies and parameter sets. Rich conceptual data models are only available in more sophisticated systems. Because most generic CMS are focused on Web content management semantic annotation is usually restricted to editorial parameters. Specialized content management systems which are adapted to certain application domains incorporate preselected and tailored ontologies. Especially for XML-based content there exist several annotation platforms which incorporate semantical annotation either manually or semi-automatically; see [11] for a survey on available platforms.

Automated processing of semantical metadata is usually restricted to search facilities, e.g., searching for the author of an article. Because ontologies are preselected for most systems a full-featured reasoning support is usually not available. Especially for OWL ontologies there are reasoning tools based on description logics such as Racer ([3]) or FaCT which enable T-box (but also A-box) reasoning about semantic relationships between annotation concepts.

Applying generic semantical annotation and classical reasoning facilities to content management suffers from several drawbacks:

– Content as aggregated macro data is only partially analysable. The purpose of metadata is the description of properties which cannot be concluded from the data itself. The very simple annotation frame of (S, P, O) triples does not allow one to express complex properties. For that reason this information has to be kept in the underlying ontology by defining appropriate concepts. The support of user-specific concepts increases the size of the ontology significantly and makes reasoning support even harder. Ad hoc definitions of user-specific concepts is not supported in this annotation model.
– Annotation with respect to arbitrary ontologies implies general purpose reasoning support by the system. Reasoning for even simple languages suffers from its high computational complexity (e.g., NEXPTIME for the restricted OWL-DL dialect, [6]). Dealing with high worst-case complexities implies a small size of input data but this is a contradiction to expressible ontologies and the definition of content as complex structured macro data. Especially the size of content instances is a crucial factor because A-box reasoning is a critical point for automated content processing [4].

But there are advantages, too:

– Usually, it is possible to distinguish between different points of view on content instances. Not every property is important while looking from every point of view.

The macro data may encapsulate and hide properties from its aggregated micro data. Reasoning about the properties of the compound can be separated from the properties of the elements as well as the properties of interconnections between content instances.

- Typical application scenarios determine important properties and suggest evaluation strategies. So ontologies may be decomposed to enable a contextualized reasoning, e.g., on the basis of Local Model Semantics ([2]). Local reasoning may rely on a language that is just as expressive as needed in this context. Contexts relying on less expressive languages may support automated reasoning while contexts relying on more expressive languages may be used for manually interpreted information. Soundness and completeness of the reasoning process are not of primary interest as long as the reasoning result is acceptable in the application domain.
- The separation between annotations relying on common knowledge, user-specific annotations and (especially) usage-specific annotations reduces the size of incorporated ontologies significantly.
- If semantic annotations themselves are given a more sophisticated internal structure reasoning can be adapted to the requirements of the application domain.

The major disadvantage of current semantic description in content management is the treatment of knowledge over content instances as metadata on a secondary level in a strongly restricted language. In the following sections we will introduce a data model for content which handles the semantic part on the same level as the content itself and gives additional structure to the semantic description. Content chunks are semantically enriched content instances. They are based on the notion of a schema for content chunks to incorporate typical functionality of content management systems such as content generation, content delivery, or content exchange.

2.4 Information and Memes: The User Dimension

There are several definitions for information[2]. We categorize these notions:

---

[2] In general, information is

- raw data and
- well-formed and meaningful data
- that   (1) has been verified to be accurate and timely relative to its context,
        (2) is specific and organized for a purpose,
        (3) is presented within a context that gives it meaning and relevance, and which
        (4) leads to increase in understanding and decrease in uncertainty.

This notion extends the GDI notion (General Definition of Information). "Well-formed" means that the raw data are clustered together correctly, according to the rules (syntax) that govern the chosen system, code or language being analysed. Syntax is understood broadly, as what determines the form, construction, composition or structuring of something. "Meaningful" means that the data must comply with the meanings (semantics) of the chosen system, code or language in question. We refer to [17] for different kinds of semantics. However, let us not forget that semantic information is not necessarily linguistic. For example, in the case of the manual of the car, the illustrations are such as to be visually meaningful to the reader.

- The first category of these definitions is based on the mathematical notion of entropy. This notion is independent of the user and thus inappropriate in our project context.
- The second category of information definitions bases information on the data a user has currently in his data space and on the computational and reasoning abilities of the user. Information is any data that cannot be derived by the user. This definition is handy but has a very bad drawback. Reasoning and computation cannot be properly characterised. Therefore, the definition becomes fuzzy.
- The third category is based on the notion of information utility. Business information systems understand information as data that have been shaped into a form that is meaningful, significant and useful for human beings. These data satisfy an information demand and can be understood by this group. Typical data represent information about significant people, places, and things within an organisation or in the environment surrounding it.
- The fourth category is based on the general language understanding of information [12]. Information is either the communication or reception of knowledge or intelligence. Information can also defined as
  - knowledge obtained from investigation, study, or instruction, or
  - intelligence, news or
  - facts and data.
  Information can also be the act of informing against a person.
  Finally information is a formal accusation of a crime made by a prosecuting officer as distinguished from an indictment presented by a grand jury.

All these definitions are too broad.

We are thus interested in a definition that is more appropriate for the internet age (*anthroposophic* understanding) in extension of the GDI notion of information.

Information as processed by humans,

- is carried by *data*
- that is perceived or noticed, selected and organized by its receiver,
- because of his subjective human interests, originating from his instincts, feelings, experience, intuition, common sense, values, beliefs, personal knowledge, or wisdom,
- simultaneously processed by his cognitive and mental processes, and
- seamlessly integrated in his recallable knowledge.

The value of information lies solely in its ability to affect a behavior, decision, or outcome. A piece of information is considered valueless if, after receiving it, things remain unchanged. For the technical meaning of information we consider the notion used in information theory.

Therefore, information is directed towards pragmatics, whereas content may be considered to highlight the syntactical dimension. If content is enhanced by concepts and topics, then users are able to capture the meaning and the utilisation of the data they receive. In order to ease perception we use *metaphors*. Metaphors may be separated into those that support perception of information and into those that support usage or functionality.

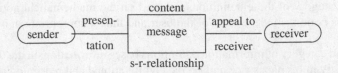

Fig. 4. Dimensions of understanding messages

Users are reflected by actors that are abstractions of groups of users. Pragmatics and syntactics share data and functions. The functionality is provided through functions and their representations. The web utilisation space depends on the technical environment of the user. It is specified through the layout and the playout. Layout places content on the basis of a data representation and in dependence of the technical environment. Playout is based on functionality and function representations, and depends on the technical environment.

The *information transfer* from a user A to a user B depends on the users A and B, their abilities to send and to receive the data, to observe the data, and to interpret the data. Let us formalise this process. Let s_X denote the function user by a user X for data extraction, transformation, and sending of data. Let r_X denote the corresponding function for data receival and transformation, and let o_X denote the filtering or observation function. The data currently considered by X is denoted by D_X. Finally, data filtered or observed must be interpreted by the user X and integrated into the knowledge K_X a user X has. Let us denote by i_X the binary function from data and knowledge to knowledge. By default, we extend the function i_X by the time t_{i_X} of the execution of the function.

Thus, the data transfer and information reception (or briefly information transfer) is formally expressed it by

$$I_B = i_B(o_B(r_B(s_A(D_A))), K_B, t_{i_X}).$$

In addition, time of sending, receiving, observing, and interpreting can be taken into consideration. In this case we extend the above functions by a time argument. The function s_X is executed at moment t_{s_X}, r_X at t_{r_X}, and o_X at t_{o_X}. We assume $t_{s_A} \le t_{r_B} \le t_{o_B} \le t_{i_B}$ for the time of sending data from A to B. The time of a computation f or data consideration D is denoted by t_f or t_D, respectively. In this extended case the information transfer is formally expressed it by

$$I_B = i_B(o_B(r_B(s_A(D_A, t_{s_A}), t_{r_B}), t_{o_B}), K_B, t_{i_B}).$$

The notion of information extends the dimensions of understanding of message displayed in Figure 4 to a web communication act that considers senders, receivers, their knowledge and experience. Figure 5 displays the multi-layering of communication, the influence of explicit knowledge and experience on the interpretation.

The *communication act* is specified by

– the communication message with the content or content chunk, the characterisation of the relationship between sender and receiver, the data that are transferred and may lead to information or misinformation, and the presentation,

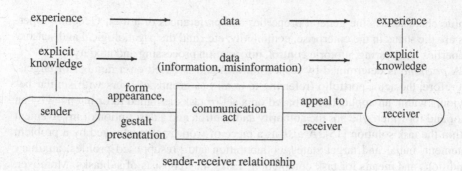

sender-receiver relationship

Fig. 5. Dimensions of the communication act

– the sender, the explicit knowledge the sender may use, and the experience the sender has, and
– the receiver, the explicit knowledge the receiver may use, and the experience the receiver has.

We approach the analysis of knowledge system usage as the first important part of storyboarding pragmatics. Knowledge system usage analysis consists of three parts:

1. *Life cases* capture observations of user behaviour in reality. They can be used in a pragmatic way to specify the story space. The work on life cases was reported in a previous publication [16].
2. *User models* complement life cases by specifying user and actor profiles, and actor portfolios. The actor portfolios are used to get a better understanding of the tasks associated with the knowledge system. The work on user models was reported in a previous publication [14].
3. *Contexts* complement life cases and user models by characterising the situation in which a user finds him/herself at a certain time in a particular location. We classify various aspects of contexts related to actors, storyboard, system and time, which make up the context space, then analyse each of these aspects in detail. This is formally support by lifting relations.

User modelling is based on the specification of *user profiles* that address the characterisation of the users, and the specification of *user portfolios* that describe the users' tasks and their involvement and collaboration on the basis of the mission of the knowledge system [13].

To characterize the users of a knowledge system we distinguish between *education*, *work* and *personality* profiles. The education profile contains properties users can obtain by education or training. Capabilities and application knowledge as a result of educational activities are also suitable for this profile. Properties will assigned to the work profile, if they can be associated with task solving knowledge and skills in the application area, i.e. task expertise and experience as well as system experience. Another part of a work profile is the interaction profile of a user, which is determined by his frequency, intensity and style of utilization of the knowledge system. The personality profile characterises the general properties and preferences of a user. General properties are the status in the enterprise, community, etc., and the psychological and sensory properties like hearing, motoric control, information processing and anxiety.

A *portfolio* is determined by responsibilities and is based on a number of targets. Therefore, the actor portfolio (referring to *actors* as groups of users with similar behaviour) within an application is based on a set of tasks assigned to or intended by an actor and for which s/he has the authority and control, and a description of involvement within the task solution [15]. A *task* as a piece of work is characterized by a problem statement, initial and target states, collaboration and presupposed profiles, auxiliary conditions and means for task completion. Tasks may consists of subtasks. Moreover, the task execution model defines what, when, how, by whom and with which data a task can be accomplished. The result of executing a task should present the final state as well as the satisfaction of target conditions.

For task completion users need the right kind of data, at the right time, in the right granularity and format, unabridged and within the frame agreed upon in advance. Moreover, users are bound by their ability to verbalise and digest data, and their habits, practices, and cultural environment. To avoid intellectual overburdening of users we observe real applications before the system development leading to *life cases* [16]. Life cases help closing the pragmatic gap between intentions and storyboarding. They are used to specify the concrete life situation of the user and characterise thus a bundle of tasks the user should solve. Syntax and semantics of life cases have already been well explored in [13].

In addition, each user has an *information portfolio*, which specifies the information needs as well as the information entered into the system. We do not model the information portfolio as part of a user, but instead of this we will model the information "consumed" and "produced" with each more detailed specification of a user request.

2.5   Context Dimension Characterisation and Adaptation of Knowledge Delivery by Context

Taking the commonly accepted meaning a context [7] characterises the situation in which a user finds him/herself at a certain time in a particular location. In this sense context is usually defined only statically referring to the content of a database. Only very few attempts have been made so far to consider context of scenarios or stories.

More generally, we consider context as everything that surrounds a utilisation situation of a knowledge system by a user and can throw light on its meaning. Therefore, context is characterised by interrelated conditions for the existence and occurrence of the utilisation situation such as the external environment, the internal state, location, time, history, etc. For knowledge systems we need to handle the mental context that is based on the profile of the actor or user, the storyboard context that is based on the story leading to a situation, the data context that is based on the available data, the stakeholder context, and the collaboration context. These different kinds of contexts have an influence on the development of the storyboard and must thus be considered for the development of the knowledge system.

We distinguish the following facets of context [14,16,13]:

Actor context: The knowledge system is used by actors for a number of tasks in a variety of involvements and well understood collaboration. These actors impose their quality requirements on the knowledge system usage as described by their security and privacy profiles. They need additional auxiliary data and auxiliary functions. The variability of use is restricted by the actor's context, which covers the actor's specific tasks and specific data and function demand, and by chosen involvement, while the profile of actors imposes exceptions. The involvement and collaboration of actors is based on assumptions of social behaviour and restrictions due to organisational decisions. These assumptions and restrictions are components of the actor's context.

Storyboard context: The meaning of content and functionality to users depends on the stories, which are based on scenarios that reflect life cases and the portfolios of users or actors. According to the profile of these users a number of quality requirements such as privacy, security and availability must be satisfied. The actor's scenario context describes what the actor needs to understand in order to efficiently and effectively solve his/her tasks in the actual portfolio. The actor's determine the policy for following particular stories.

System context: The knowledge system is developed to support a number of intentions. The purposes and intents lead to a number of decisions on the knowledge system architecture, the technical environment, and the implementation. The knowledge system architecture has an impact on its utilisation, which often is only implicit and thus leads to not understandable systems behaviour. The technical environment restricts the user due to restrictions imposed by server, channel and client properties. Adaptation to the current environment is defined as context adaptation to the current channel, to the client infrastructure and to the server load. At the same time a number of legal decisions based on regulations, laws and business rules have been incorporated into the knowledge system.

Temporal context: The utilisation of a scene by an actor depends on his/her history of utilisation. Actors may interrupt and resume their activities at any moment of time. As they may not be interested in repeating all previous actions they have already successfully completed, the temporal context must be taken into account. Due to availability of content and functionality the current utilisation may lead to a different story within the same scenario.

Provider context: Providers are characterised by their mission, intentions, and specific policies. Additionally, terms of business may be added. Vendors need to understand how to run the knowledge system economically. Typical parts of this context are intentions of the provider, themes of the website, mission or corporate identity of the site, and occasion and purpose of the visits of actors. Thus, providers may require additional content and functionality due to their mission and policy. They may apply their terms of business and may require a specific layout and playout.

Based on this information, the knowledge system is extended by provider-specific content and functionality. The storyboard may be altered according to the intentions of the provider, and life cases may be extended or partially supported. Provider-based changes to portfolios are typical for knowledge systems in e-government and e-business applications.

Developer context: The knowledge system implementation depends on the capability of the developer. Typically we need to take into account the potential environment, e.g. hard- and software, communication channels, the information systems that are to be incorporated, especially the associated databases, and the programming environment developers use.

Organisational and social context: The organisation of task solutions is often already predetermined by the application domain. It follows organisational structures within the institutions involved. We captured a part of these structures already on the basis of the portfolio and modelled it by collaboration. The other pars form the organisational context. Collaboration of partners consists of communication, coordination, and cooperation. Cooperation is based on cooperativity, i.e. the disposition to act in a way that is best helpful for the collaboration partners, taking their intentions, tasks, interests and abilities into account. At the same time, collaboration is established in order to achieve a common goal. Actors choose their actions and organise them such that their chances of success are optimised with respect to the portfolio they are engaged in. Additionally, the social context may be taken into account, which consists of interactive and reactive pressures. Typical social enhancements are socially indicated situations such as welcome greetings, thanking, apologising, and farewell greetings.

Most systems today do not support adaptivity and user orientation. Information as processed by humans is perceived in a very subjective way. As for a knowledge system, the determining factor whether the user can derive advantage from the content delivered is the user's individual situation, i.e. the life case, user model and context. The same category of information can cause various needs in different life cases.

Not any user can deal with any kind of content. For the casual user or the novice other content has to be delivered than for experts. The common knowledge system doesn't reflect the user's situation and neglects the user's specific needs. As a result, the user is spammed with information which is predominantly out of focus. The abundance of information also makes it impossible to separate useful from for the user useless content. Any by the absence of meta data unspecified information reduces the usability of World Wide Web on the whole.

Furthermore, users are limited

- in their abilities for verbalisation,
- in their abilities for digestion of data and
- by their habits, practices and cultural environment.

These limitations may cause intellectual overburdening of users. Most systems that require sophisticated learning courses for their exploration and utilization did not consider these limitations and did not cope with real life situations. The approach we use for avoiding overload is based on observation of real applications before developing the knowledge system.

User typically request or need various content depending on their situation, on material available, on the actual information demand, on data already currently available and on technical equipment and channels on hand. Therefore, we need a facility for content adaptation depending on the context of the user. Content matching and adaptation may be thus considered as one of the 'grand' challenges of modern internet.

To meet this challenge, the information has to be matched against the particular needs of the user [14,16,13]. Since the thinkable combinations of user life cases, user models and context [7] are indefinitely, the definition of life cases [16] has to be determined for the content and matched against the users situation. For a knowledge system, there should be not only concrete definitions of which content is applicable for which life case. To avoid making useful content useless by presenting it in an inappropriate way to the user, knowledge systems have also to consider the user's specific profile and context. By processing this data, the knowledge system should provide different views of information and the appropriate media types for presenting their knowledge to various audiences.

The implicit goals of content management and content delivery are:

- to meet all the information (contextual) requirements of the entire spectrum of users in a given application area;
- to provide a "natural" and easy-to-understand structuring of the information content;
- to preserve the designers entire semantic information for a later redesign;
- to achieve all the processing requirements and also a high degree of efficiency in processing;
- to achieve logical independence of query and transaction formulation on this level;
- to provide a simple and easily to comprehend user interface family.

Acknowledgement. The work of Klaus-Dieter Schewe was supported by the European Fund for Regional Development as well as the State of Upper Austria for the project *Vertical Model Integration* within the program "Regionale Wettbewerbsfähigkeit OÖ 2007-2013".

References

1. Dublin Core Metadata Initiative. Dublin Core (June 2007), http://dublincore.org/
2. Ghidini, C., Giunchiglia, F.: Local models semantics, or contextual reasoning = Locality + compatibility (April 2000), http://citeseer.ist.psu.edu/481285.html
3. Haarslev, V., Möller, R.: Racer: An OWL reasoning agent for the semantic web. In: Proceedings of the International Workshop on Applications, Products and Services of Web-based Support Systems, in Conjunction with the 2003 IEEE/WIC International Conference on Web Intelligence,? Halifax, Canada, October 13, pp. 91–95 (2003)
4. Haarslev, V., Möller, R., Wessel, M.: Description Logic inference technology: Lessions learned in the trenches. In: Horrocks, I., Sattler, U., Wolter, F. (eds.) Proc. International Workshop on Description Logics (2005)
5. Hinkelmann, K., Wache, H. (eds.) Fifth Conference Professional Knowledge Management: Experiences and Visions, Solothurn, Switzerland, March 25-27. LNI, vol. 145. GI (2009)
6. Horrocks, I., Patel-Schneider, P.F., van Harmelen, F.: From SHIQ and RDF to OWL: The making of a web ontology language. Journal of Web Semantics 1(1), 7–26 (2003)
7. Kaschek, R., Schewe, K.-D., Thalheim, B., Zhang, L.: Integrating context in modelling for web information systems. In: Bussler, C.J., Fensel, D., Orlowska, M.E., Yang, J. (eds.) WES 2003. LNCS, vol. 3095, pp. 77–88. Springer, Heidelberg (2004)

8. Murphy, G.L.: The big book of concepts. MIT Press, Cambridge (2001)
9. Paredaens, J., Bra, P.D., Gyssens, M., Gucht, D.V.: The structure of the relational database model. Springer, Berlin (1989)
10. Pilkey, O.H., Pilkey-Jarvis, L.: Useless Arithmetic: Why Environmental Scientists Cant't Predict the Future. Columbia University Press, New York (2006)
11. Reeve, L., Han, H.: Survey of semantic annotation platforms. In: SAC 2005, pp. 1634–1638. ACM Press, New York (2006)
12. Safra, J., Yeshua, I.: Encyclopædia Britannica. Merriam-Webster (2007)
13. Schewe, K.-D., Thalheim, B.: Usage-based storyboarding for web information systems. Technical Report 2006-13, Christian Albrechts University Kiel, Institute of Computer Science and Applied Mathematics, Kiel (2006)
14. Schewe, K.-D., Thalheim, B.: User models: A contribution to pragmatics of web information systems design. In: Aberer, K., Peng, Z., Rundensteiner, E.A., Zhang, Y., Li, X. (eds.) WISE 2006. LNCS, vol. 4255, pp. 512–523. Springer, Heidelberg (2006)
15. Schewe, K.-D., Thalheim, B.: Development of collaboration frameworks for web information systems. In: 20th Int. Joint Conf. on Artifical Intelligence, Section EMC 2007 (Evolutionary models of collaboration), Hyderabad, pp. 27–32 (2007)
16. Schewe, K.-D., Thalheim, B.: Life cases: A kernel element for web information systems engineering. In: Web Information Systems and Technologies. LNBIP, vol. 8. Springer, Heidelberg (2009)
17. Schewe, K.-D., Thalheim, B.: Semantics in data and knowledge bases. In: Schewe, K.-D., Thalheim, B. (eds.) SDKB 2008. LNCS, vol. 4925, pp. 1–25. Springer, Heidelberg (2008)
18. Sowa, J.: Knowledge Representation, Logical, Philosophical, and Computational Foundations. Brooks/Cole, a division of Thomson Learning, Pacific Grove, California (2000)
19. Thalheim, B.: Dependencies in relational databases. Teubner, Leipzig (1991)
20. W3C. Web Ontology Language Overview (February 2004), http://www.w3.org/TR/owl-features/
21. W3C RDF Core Working Group. Resource Description Framework (RDF) (2004), http://www.w3.org/RDF/
22. Wanner, P. (ed.): The Cambridge Encyclopedia of Language. Cambridge University Press, Cambridge (1987)

Constraints in RDF

Waseem Akhtar[1], Álvaro Cortés-Calabuig[2], and Jan Paredaens[2]

[1] Vrije Universiteit Brussel, Belgium
waseem.akhtar@vub.ac.be
[2] University of Antwerp, Belgium
{alvaro.cortes,jan.paredaens}@ua.ac.be

Abstract. RDF (Resource Description Framework) is a World Wide Web Consortium recommendation for specifying meta-data models on the web. RDF databases consist of triples in the form of subject-predicate-object, which are often conceptualized as defining a directed labeled graph. In this paper, we extend the basic model of RDF by introducing two types of integrity constraints, namely functional and equality generating constraints. Our formal framework is inspired and motivated by the importance of the corresponding constraints in the relational model. In the first part of the paper we present the formal notion of satisfaction for both types of constraints and introduce a mechanism to express functional constraints in terms of equality generating constraints, and we show that the converse is not possible. In the second part, we define an Armstrong-type scheme of rules for equality generating constraints and we prove that these rules form a sound and complete set. In addition, we present chase-like algorithms for both types of constraints that check whether a single constraint follows from a given set of constraints.

1 Introduction

The semantic web idea envisions the web as a large repository of semantic information that can be accessed and queried by both, machines and human beings. Unlike standard autonomous relational databases, data in semantic web repositories is meant to be linked to other data sources available on the web by means of universal identifiers (usually in the form of Uniform Resource Identifiers or URIs) and stored in schema-less repositories. Towards the instantiation and support of this vision, the World Wide Web Consortium (W3C) has proposed the recommendation of the RDF data model [25] and the SPARQL query language [30].

RDF documents (or databases) arrange data in simple triples of *subject*, *predicate* and *object*. Triples represent assertions about certain predefined domain consisting of *resources*. Resources are identified by URIs. RDF databases are often conceptualized as defining a directed labeled graph, where subjects and objects are nodes and the predicate represents a directed edge between the subject and the object. From a logical stand, the W3C defines RDF as "...[an] assertional logic, in which each triple expresses a simple proposition. This imposes a fairly strict monotonic discipline on the language, so that it cannot express

K.-D. Schewe, and B. Thalheim (Eds.): SDKB 2010, LNCS 6834, pp. 23–39, 2011.

closed-world assumptions, local default preferences, and several other commonly used non-monotonic constructs" [26]. While RDF databases consist of simple triples, they cannot be regarded as merely a ternary relation of the relational model. Indeed, in RDF there is only one set of triples; RDF triples are heterogeneous entities and as such semantically less structured than in the relational model. As a consequence the languages for RDF are more pattern-based than in the relational counterpart.

Integrity constraints are an important component of the relational database machinery. They are often defined as conditions that a database instance must satisfy at all times. In the relational model and also more recently in less structured data formats such as XML, integrity constraints have been extensively studied from both practical and theoretical perspectives. These studies include semantics of integrity constraints [27], update of incomplete databases [33], query optimization [9], consistent query answering [5], and semantics of locally incomplete databases with constraints [12]. The importance of integrity constraints has permeated database practice and nowadays their use is ubiquitous in all modern database management systems.

Two of the most relevant and well-studied relational constraints are functional [11] and equality generating dependencies [4]. The importance of these dependencies is that they provide relationships between attributes of a relation that determine some of its properties, and as such they play an important role on designing and normalizing databases. This led Armstrong [2] to the definition of his well-known set of rules (or axioms) for functional dependencies. Armstrong proved the rules to be complete, i.e. all the functional dependencies derived using the rules were indeed all the consequences of the original (given) set of dependencies. It has been further argued, for instance in [3], that a complete set of rules for databases dependencies provide a powerful tool for database designers that need, for instance, to check whether certain dependency is implicit in an initial set of dependencies.

In this paper, we introduce the aforementioned database dependencies into the RDF data model. Our main motivation for this work is to gain understanding and provide insights on the properties of the RDF paradigm as a data model in the presence of constraints. Towards this goal, we make the following contributions:

- We introduce the notions of **functional constraint and equality generating constraint** to the RDF data model. The semantics of these constraints is given in terms of embeddings over graphs. We show how to represent functional constraints as equality generating constraints, and we show that the converse is not always possible.
- **Deductive rules for RDF equality generating constraints.** We provide a set of deductive rules for equality generating constraints, and we show that these rules are independent, correct and complete. In addition, by means of a transformation algorithm we use these rules for generating functional constraints in a correct and complete fashion.
- **Chasing algorithms.** We introduce chasing algorithms for functional and equality generating constraints. These algorithms compute all the logical

consequences of a given initial set of constraints. Our algorithms are inspired by chase methods introduced by Saudi and Ullman [28] in the context of relational databases.

This paper is organized as follows. In Section 2, we formally introduce the two types of constraints we discuss in the paper, namely equality generating and functional constraints, define the notion of constraint satisfaction and provide a mechanism to translate functional into equality generating constraints. In Section 3, we introduce derivation rules for equality generating constraints and define a chasing algorithm to compute new constraints given an initial set of equality generating constraints. We conclude the paper in Sections 4 and 5 with a discussion of the related work and presenting possible future lines of research.

2 Functional Constraints (FCs) and Equality Generating Constraints (EGCs)

In this section, we introduce our basic framework of RDF. We start by extending the basic RDF data model with functional and equality generating constraints. Throughout this section and the rest of the paper we make references to Figure 1, which depicts an RDF database that stores information about publications, authors and characters of books. Subject and object are nodes of the graph, while edges represent predicates. For instance, triple $(Literaria, Sp, Magazine)$ states that subject $Literaria$ is a subproperty (Sp) of the object $Magazine$. Likewise, triple $(Paper, Sp, Journal)$ asserts that subject $Paper$ is a subproperty of the object $Journal$. Observe that, unlike the case of the relation model, a resource can be both a subject and a predicate. In Figure 1, it is the case that $Don\_Quixote$ is the predicate in triples $(Sancho, Don\_Quixote, Sanchica)$ and$(Sancho, Don\_Quixote, Rocinante)$, but the subject in $(Don\_Quixote, Sp, Book)$. Similarly, $Literaria$ is the predicate in triple $(Metaphysics, Literaria, Ethics)$, the object in triple $(NYTimes, Review, Literaria)$ and the subject in $(Literaria, Sp, Magazine)$. This is one of the distinctive features of the RDF data model which makes the definition of constraints into RDF not just a trivial migration of constraints from the relational domain.

In what follows, we use the following vocabulary:

- $\mathcal{U}$, is an infinite set of URI's;
- V, an infinite set of variables denoted by prefixing them by $.

V and $\mathcal{U}$ are pairwise disjoint.

We do not consider blank nodes in this paper. In addition, for the sake of simplicity, we do not make a distinction between URI's and literals.

Definition 1 (RDF-graph). *An* RDF-graph $\mathcal{G}$ *is a finite set of triples* (s, p, o), *subject, property, object,* $s, p, o \in \mathcal{U}$.

A *term* is an element of $V \cup \mathcal{U}$. Let t_1 and t_2 be two terms. $\phi_{t_2 \leftarrow t_1}$ denotes the function that is equal to the identity, except that $\phi_{t_2 \leftarrow t_1}(t_1) = t_2$. Let $\mathcal{K}$ be a

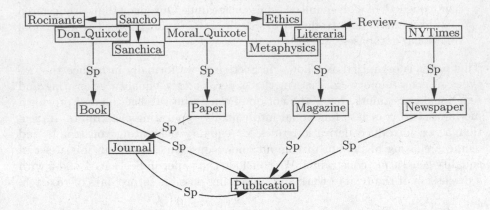

Fig. 1. RDF Graph representing information about different types of publications

set of triples of terms. We denote $\mathcal{U}_{\mathcal{K}}$ the set of URI's in $\mathcal{K}$ and denote $V_{\mathcal{K}}$ the set of variables in $\mathcal{K}$.

To formally introduce constraints we first need the following definition:

Definition 2 (Embedding of a set of triples of terms in an RDF-graph $\mathcal{G}$). *An embedding of a finite set S of triples of terms in an RDF-graph $\mathcal{G}$ is a total function $e : V_S \cup \mathcal{U} \to \mathcal{U}$, such that*

- $e(u) = u$, *for each $u \in \mathcal{U}$;*
- *If $(t_1, t_2, t_3) \in S$ then $(e(t_1), e(t_2), e(t_3)) \in \mathcal{G}$;*

Definition 3 (EGC). *An equality generating constraint is a pair (S, E), where*

- *S is a finite set of triples of terms;*
- *E is a finite set of equalities, each of the form $(t_1 = t_2)$, with $t_1, t_2 \in V_S \cup \mathcal{U}$.*

Definition 4 (EGC satisfaction). *An RDF-graph $\mathcal{G}$ satisfies the EGC (S, E), denoted by $\mathcal{G} \models (S, E)$, iff for every embedding e of S in $\mathcal{G}$ and every $(t_1 = t_2) \in E$ it holds that $e(t_1) = e(t_2)$.*

Example 1. Figure 1. satisfies:

- $\mathcal{C}_1 = (\{(Sancho, Don\_Quixote, \$y), (Don\_Quixote, Sp, \$t)\}, \{(\$t = Book)\})$
- $\mathcal{C}_2 = (\{(Book, Sp, \$y), (Journal, Sp, \$z)\}, \{(\$y = \$z)\})$

Figure 1. does not satisfy:

- $\mathcal{C}_3 = (\{(\$x, Sp, \$z), (\$z, Sp, \$u)\}, \{(\$u = Publication)\})$
- $\mathcal{C}_4 = (\{(\$x, Don\_Quixote, \$y)\}, \{(\$y = Sanchica)\})$
- $\mathcal{C}_5 = (\{(\$x, Sp, \$z), (\$v, \$u, \$x)\}, \{(\$u = Sp)\})$

Functional dependencies are arguably the most studied –from both theoretical and practical perspectives– types of integrity constraints in the database literature. Their application is common practice in modern database management

systems, as they indeed have been used as declarations of partial identification, functional coupling, semantic constraint specific for a given application,
and more (see [31] for a detailed description of the different kinds of functional
dependencies and their uses).

In the definition below we formally introduce the notion of functional constraint into the RDF data model. Although similar in spirit to their relational
counter parts, functional constraints in RDF have some distinctive features that
make them worth studying in their own merit. First, as in RDF the distinction
between relations and domain elements is somehow blurred, it is valuable and
sometimes necessary to express, for instance, that certain property functionally
determines its object; likewise, we may need to express that certain object –or
set of objects– functionally determines the relation to which they are related to.
And second, given the pattern-like nature of RDF documents, the need for identifying those pattern in order to define functional relations between its members
arises.

Using a similar syntax as with EGCs, we formally define functional constraints
in RDF:

Definition 5 (FC). *A functional constraint is a pair* $(S, L \rightarrow R)$*, where*

- S *is a finite set of triples of terms;*
- $L, R \subseteq V_S$.

In the following definition, two embeddings e and e' coincide on a variable $\$v$ iff
$e(\$v) = e'(\$v)$.

Definition 6 (FC satisfaction). *An RDF-graph* $\mathcal{G}$ *satisfies the FC* $(S, L \rightarrow R)$*, denoted by* $\mathcal{G} \models (S, L \rightarrow R)$ *, iff for every two embeddings of* S *in* $\mathcal{G}$ *that coincide on the variables of* L*, they also coincide on the variables of* R.

We denote a variable that occurs only once in S and does not occur in L nor in
R by $*$.

Example 2. Figure 1. satisfies:

- $\mathcal{C}_6 = (\{(\$x, Sp, \$y)\}, \{\$x\} \rightarrow \{\$y\})$
- $\mathcal{C}_7 = (\{(\$x, Sp, \$y), (\$y, Sp, \$z)\}, \{\$x, \$z\} \rightarrow \{\$y\})$

Figure 1. does not satisfy:

- $\mathcal{C}_8 = (\{(\$x, \$y, \$z), (\$y, Sp, \$y_1), (\$y_1, Sp, \$y_2)\}, \emptyset \rightarrow \{\$y_2\})$
  $= (\{(*, \$y, *), (\$y, Sp, \$y_1), (\$y_1, Sp, \$y_2)\}, \emptyset \rightarrow \{\$y_2\})$
- $\mathcal{C}_9 = (\{(Sancho, \$x, \$y), (\$x, Sp, \$z)\}, \emptyset \rightarrow \{\$z\})$
  $= (\{(Sancho, \$x, *), (\$x, Sp, \$z)\}, \emptyset \rightarrow \{\$z\})$
- $\mathcal{C}_{10} = (\{(\$x, Sp, \$y)\}, \{\$y\} \rightarrow \{\$x\})$
- $\mathcal{C}_{11} = (\{(\$x, Don\_Quixote, \$y)\}, \{\$x\} \rightarrow \{\$y\})$
- $\mathcal{C}_{12} = (\{(\$x, \$y, \$z)\}, \{\$x\} \rightarrow \{\$y\})$
- $\mathcal{C}_{13} = (\{(\$x, \$y, \$z)\}, \{\$y\} \rightarrow \{\$x\})$
- $\mathcal{C}_{14} = (\{(\$x, \$y, \$z), (\$y, Sp, \$y_1)\}, \{\$x\} \rightarrow \{\$y, \$y_1\})$
  $= (\{(\$x, \$y, *), (\$y, Sp, \$y_1)\}, \{\$x\} \rightarrow \{\$y, \$y_1\})$

The following notion of homomorphism, similar to the idea of an embedding, will serve us to translate FCs into EGCs.

Definition 7 (Homomorphism from a set of triples of terms in a set of triples of terms). *A homomorphism from a finite set of triples of terms S in a set of triples of terms S' is a total function $h : V_S \cup U_S \to V_{S'} \cup U_{S'}$, such that*

- $h(u) = u$, *for each* $u \in U_S$;
- *If* $(t_1, t_2, t_3) \in S$ *then* $(h(t_1), h(t_2), h(t_3)) \in S'$;

A homomorphism h can be extended in a natural way to a set of variables, a set of triples of terms and a set of equalities.

Let C_1 and C_2 be two sets of constraints, we say that C_1 *logically implies* C_2, denoted by $C_1 \models C_2$, iff every graph that satisfies all the constraints of C_1 also satisfies all the constraints of C_2. If the set C_1 or C_2 is a singleton, we write the constraint of that singleton, instead of that singleton.

Lemma 1. *Let S_1 and S_2 be two finite sets of triples and let h be a homomorphism from S_1 in S_2. $(S_1, L \to R) \models (S_2, h(L) \cap V_{S_2} \to h(R) \cap V_{S_2})$, but in general $(S_2, h(L) \cap V_{S_2} \to h(R) \cap V_{S_2}) \not\models (S_1, L \to R)$. $(S_1, E) \models (S_2, h(E))$, but in general $(S_2, h(E)) \not\models (S_1, E)$.*

Proof. Consider first the FC $C = (S_1, L \to R)$. Let G satisfy C and let e_1 and e_2 be two embeddings of S_2 in G that coincide on $h(L) \cap V_{S_2}$ and hence $e_1 \circ h$ and $e_2 \circ h$ are two embeddings of S_1 in G that coincide on L. So $e_1 \circ h$ and $e_2 \circ h$ coincide on R and e_1 and e_2 coincide on $h(R) \cap V_{S_2}$. On the other hand consider the FC $(\{(\$x, \$y, \$z)\}, \{\$x, \$y\} \to \{\$z\})$, $h(\$x) = \$x'$, $h(\$y) = \$x'$ and $h(\$z) = \$z'$. Clearly $\{(a, b, c), (a, b, d)\}$ satisfies $(h(\{(\$x, \$y, \$z)\}), h(\{\$x, \$y\} \to \{\$z\})) = (\{(\$x', \$x', \$z')\}, \{\$x'\} \to \{\$z'\})$ but $\{(a, b, c), (a, b, d)\}$ does not satisfy $(\{(\$x, \$y, \$z)\}, \{\$x, \$y\} \to \{\$z\})$.

Consider now the EGC $C = (S_1, E)$. Let G satisfy C and let e be an embedding of S_2 in G. $e \circ h$ is an embedding of S_1 in G and hence $e \circ h(\$x) = e \circ h(\$y)$ if $(\$x = \$y) \in E$, or if $(h(\$x) = h(\$y)) \in h(E)$. On the other hand consider the EGC $(\{(\$x, \$y, \$z)\}, \{(\$x = \$y)\})$, $h(\$x) = \$x'$, $h(\$y) = \$x'$ and $h(\$z) = \$z'$. Clearly $\{(a, b, c)\}$ satisfies $(h(\{(\$x, \$y, \$z)\}), h(\{(\$x = \$y)\})) = (\{(\$x', \$x', \$z')\}, \{(\$x' = \$x')\})$ but $\{(a, b, c)\}$ does not satisfy $(\{(\$x, \$y, \$z)\}, \{(\$x = \$y)\})$.

With the next theorem we prove that every functional constraint can be written as an equality generating constraint. The converse, however, is not always possible.

Theorem 1. *Every FC can be expressed by a EGC, but not vice-versa.*

Proof. Given $C = (S, L \to R)$. We will construct $C' = (S', E')$ such that $C \models C'$ and $C' \models C$.
G satisfies C iff for every two embeddings of S in G that coincide on the variables of L, they also coincide on the variables of R (1). G satisfies C' iff for every embedding e of S' in G and every $(t_1 = t_2) \in E'$ it holds that $e(t_1) = e(t_2)$ (2).

Let $h_1(\$x) = \$x$, for every $\$x \in L$ (3), $h_1(\$x) = \$x_1$ for every $\$x \in V_S - L$, $h_1(u) = u$ for every $u \in \mathcal{U}_S$ (4). Let $h_2(\$x) = \$x$, for every $\$x \in L$ (3), $h_2(\$x) = \$x_2$ for every $\$x \in V_S - L$, $h_2(u) = u$ for every $u \in \mathcal{U}_S$ (4). We extend the functions h_1 and h_2 to triples of terms and to sets of triples of terms.

We construct $\mathcal{C}' = (S', E')$ with $S' = h_1(S) \cup h_2(S)$ and $E' = \{(h_1(\$x) = h_2(\$x)) \mid \$x \in R\}$ (5). Clearly h_1 and h_2 are homomorphisms from S in S'. Suppose $\mathcal{G}$ satisfies $\mathcal{C}$ and consider an embedding e' of S' in $\mathcal{G}$. $e' \circ h_1$ is a total function $e' \circ h_1 : V_S \cup \mathcal{U}_S \rightarrow \mathcal{U}_\mathcal{G}$, and $e' \circ h_1$ is an embedding of S in $\mathcal{G}$. For analogous reasons $e' \circ h_2$ is an embedding of S in $\mathcal{G}$. By (3) $e' \circ h_1$ and $e' \circ h_2$ coincide on L, so by (1) they also coincide on R. Hence $e' \circ h_1(\$x) = e' \circ h_2(\$x)$ for all $\$x \in R$. By (5) for every $(t_1 = t_2) \in E'$ it holds that $e(t_1) = e(t_2)$, which implies (2) and hence $\mathcal{G}$ satisfies $\mathcal{C}'$.

On the other hand, suppose $\mathcal{G}$ satisfies $\mathcal{C}'$ and consider two embeddings e_1, e_2 of S in $\mathcal{G}$ that coincide on L (6). By (3) and (4) $e_1 \circ h_1^{-1} \cup e_2 \circ h_2^{-1}$ is a total function $e_1 \circ h_1^{-1} \cup e_2 \circ h_2^{-1} : V_{S'} \cup \mathcal{U}_{S'} \rightarrow \mathcal{U}_\mathcal{G}$. By (5) $e_1 \circ h_1^{-1} \cup e_2 \circ h_2^{-1}$ is an embedding of S' in $\mathcal{G}$. Hence by (2) for every $(t_1 = t_2) \in E'$ it holds that $(e_1 \circ h_1^{-1} \cup e_2 \circ h_2^{-1})(t_1) = (e_1 \circ h_1^{-1} \cup e_2 \circ h_2^{-1})(t_2)$. (5) induces that for every $\$x \in R$ holds $(e_1 \circ h_1^{-1} \cup e_2 \circ h_2^{-1})(h_1(\$x)) = (e_1 \circ h_1^{-1} \cup e_2 \circ h_2^{-1})(h_2(\$x))$. This induces that $e_1(\$x) = e_2(\$x)$ and by (6) this implies (1) and hence $\mathcal{G}$ satisfies $\mathcal{C}$.

The converse does not hold. Indeed, consider the EGC $\mathcal{C} = (S, E)$ with $S = \{(\$x, \$y, \$z)\}$ and $E = \{(\$x = \$y)\}$. It cannot be expressed by an FC since the graph $\{(a, b, c)\}$ does not satisfy $\mathcal{C}$ but it satisfies all FCs.

3   Deriving Equality Generating Constraints and Functional Constraints

In this section we answer two questions regarding reasoning tasks with RDF constraints: (1) whether a single EGC is logically implied by a given set of EGCs and (2) whether it is possible to define a complete set of deductive axioms to derive all the EGCs that are logically implied by a given set of EGCs.

3.1   Chasing Algorithm for EGCs

The next chasing algorithm takes as input a given set of EGCs and another EGC and checks whether the latter is logically implied by the given set. Our algorithm is inspired by the chase method of Sadri and Ullman [28] used in the relational model context.

Input:
A set of EGCs $\{(S_i, E_i) \mid 1 \leq i \leq n\}$ and an EGC (S, E).
Output:
Does it hold that $\{(S_i, E_i) \mid 1 \leq i \leq n\} \models (S, E)$?
Algorithm:

1. Consider the function ϕ_0 that is defined on V_S, such that $\phi_0(\$x) = x_0$, $x_0 \notin \mathcal{U}_S$, being different URI's. Let $\overline{\mathcal{G}} = \phi_0(S)$.

2. Repeat the following as long as possible : If there exists an (S_i, E_i) with $1 \leq i \leq n$ and an embedding f of S_i in $\overline{\mathcal{G}}$ with $f(\$x) \neq f(\$y)$ for some $(\$x = \$y) \in E_i$, equalize $f(\$x)$ and $f(\$y)$ in $\overline{\mathcal{G}}$. Equalizing is done by:
   - replacing all occurrences of the URI $f(\$x)$ by the URI $f(\$y)$ if $f(\$x) \in \phi_0(V_S)$;
   - replacing all occurrences of the URI $f(\$y)$ by the URI $f(\$x)$ if $f(\$x) \notin \phi_0(V_S)$ and $f(\$y) \in \phi_0(V_S)$;
   - stopping the algorithm with the result that $\{(S_i, E_i) \mid 1 \leq i \leq n\} \models (S, E)$ if $f(\$x), f(\$y) \notin \phi_0(V_S)$.

3. $\{(S_i, E_i) \mid 1 \leq i \leq n\} \models (S, E)$ iff $\overline{\mathcal{G}}$ satisfies (S, E).

Theorem 2. *The algorithm above is correct.*

Proof.
Suppose first that the algorithm does not stop in step 2. We have to prove that for the final value of $\overline{\mathcal{G}}$ holds $\{(S_i, E_i) \mid 1 \leq i \leq n\} \models (S, E)$ iff $\overline{\mathcal{G}}$ satisfies (S, E) (1).
Since, by step 2 we have $\overline{\mathcal{G}}$ satisfies $\{(S_i, E_i) \mid 1 \leq i \leq n\}$, (1) holds from left to right.

Conversely, suppose that $\overline{\mathcal{G}}$ satisfies (S, E) and consider an arbitrary graph $\mathcal{G}$ that satisfies $\{(S_i, E_i) \mid 1 \leq i \leq n\}$. We have to prove that $\mathcal{G}$ satisfies (S, E). Therefore we take an arbitrary embedding e of S in $\mathcal{G}$. First we shall prove that the following two conditions are invariants of the algorithm:

- there is a function $\chi : \mathcal{U}_{\overline{\mathcal{G}}} \to \mathcal{U}_{\mathcal{G}}$ such that $\chi(l) = l$ for all $l \in \mathcal{U}_S \cup \mathcal{L}_S$ and such that χ maps the triples of $\overline{\mathcal{G}}$ into triples of $\mathcal{G}$ (2);
- there is an embedding $\overline{e}$ of S in $\overline{\mathcal{G}}$ with $e = \chi \circ \overline{e}$ (3).

Let us construct χ and $\overline{e}$ for the $\overline{\mathcal{G}}$ after step 1 : $\chi(x_0) = e(\$x)$ for every $\$x \in V_S$ and $\chi(l) = l$ for every $l \in \mathcal{U}_S \cup \mathcal{L}_S$ and $\overline{e} = \phi_0$. So (2) and (3) hold after step 1. Consider now step 2. Step 2 stops, since each time it is executed the number of subscripted URI's in $\overline{\mathcal{G}}$ decreases by 1. Let by induction $\chi : \overline{\mathcal{G}} \to \mathcal{G}$ such that $\chi(l) = l$ for all $l \in \mathcal{U}_S \cup \mathcal{L}_S$ and consider f as in step 2. So we have that $\chi \circ f$ is an embedding of S_i in $\mathcal{G}$. We have that $f(\$x) \neq f(\$y)$ for the $(\$x, \$y)$ of step 2, but since $\chi \circ f(\$x) = \chi \circ f(\$y)$ we can do the proposed equalization. We adjust $\overline{e}$ in a natural way such that (3) still holds. This proves that (2) and (3) are invariants. Since $\overline{\mathcal{G}}$ satisfies (S, E), we deduce that $\mathcal{G}$ satisfies (S, E) from (3).

Suppose now the algorithm stops in step 2. By induction we still have (2). $\chi \circ f$ is an embedding of S_i in $\mathcal{G}$. Furthermore $\chi \circ f(\$x) \neq \chi \circ f(\$y)$ since $f(\$x) \neq f(\$y)$ and $f(\$x)$ and $f(\$y)$ both belonging to $\mathcal{U}_S$. That means that for every graph $\mathcal{G}$ for which there is an embedding of S in $\mathcal{G}$, there is always an embedding that has a different value for $\$x$ and for $\$y$. So the graphs that satisfy the premises of
$(\forall i, 1 \leq i \leq n : \mathcal{G}$ satisfies $(S_i, E_i)) \Rightarrow \mathcal{G}$ satisfies (S, E) will have no embedding of S and hence $\mathcal{G}$ satisfies (S, E).

Example 3. Let

$$(S_1, E_1) = (\{(a, \$y, \$y), (\$u, \$t, \$w)\}, \{(\$u = \$y)\})$$
$$(S_2, E_2) = (\{(a, \$x, \$y)\}, \{(\$x = \$y)\})$$
$$(S_3, E_3) = (\{(a, \$y, b), (\$z, \$u, \$v)\}, \{(\$y = \$u)\})$$

and $(S, E) = (\{(a, \$u, \$v), (b, \$w, \$z)\}, \{(b = \$w)\})$.
Does it hold that $\{(S_i, E_i) \mid 1 \le i \le 3\} \models (S, E)$?
Now follows the sequence of the intermediate values of $\overline{\mathcal{G}}$:

1. $\overline{\mathcal{G}} = \{(a, u_0, v_0), (b, w_0, z_0)\}$;
2. • $\overline{\mathcal{G}} = \{(a, v_0, v_0), (b, w_0, z_0)\}$, applying (S_2, E_2);
   • $\overline{\mathcal{G}} = \{(a, b, b), (b, w_0, z_0)\}$, applying (S_1, E_1);
   • $\overline{\mathcal{G}} = \{(a, b, b), (b, b, z_0)\}$, applying (S_3, E_3);
   • now $\mathcal{G}$ satisfies all $(S_i, E_i), 1 \le i \le 3$
3. $\overline{\mathcal{G}}$ also satisfies (S, E), hence $\{(S_i, E_i) \mid 1 \le i \le 3\} \models (S, E)$

With the following example we illustrate the algorithm when the chasing process stops in step 2.

Example 4. Let
$(S_1, E_1) = (\{(\$x, \$y, \$z)\}, \{(\$x = \$y)\})$ and
$(S, E) = (\{(a, b, \$u)\}, \{(\$u = a)\})$.
Does it hold that $(S_1, E_1) \models (S, E)$?

1. $\overline{\mathcal{G}} = \{(a, b, u_0)\}$;
2. • There is only one embedding of S_1 in $\overline{\mathcal{G}}$. As it is not possible to equalize a and b, since they are constants, the chasing process necessarily stops in step 2. Indeed, $(S_1, E_1) \models (S, E)$, since for every graph $\mathcal{G}$ that satisfies (S_1, E_1) it is not possible to find an embedding of $\{(a, b, \$u)\}$.

3.2 Deductive Rules

In this section we proceed to the definition of the deductive rules for deriving EGCs.

Let $\mathcal{EC}$ be an arbitrary set of ECs. We define in a syntactical way, by Rules 0-8 when $\mathcal{EC} \vdash (S, E)$, and we prove that this set of rules is sound, independent and complete.
The rules that define $\vdash$ are :

Rule 0 : $\mathcal{EC} \vdash (S, E)$, for every $(S, E) \in \mathcal{EC}$;
Rule 1 : $\mathcal{EC} \vdash (S, \{(t = t)\})$, for every finite set S of triples of terms and $t \in V_S \cup U_S$;
Rule 2 : $\mathcal{EC} \vdash (S, \{(t_1 = t_2)\})$ implies $\mathcal{EC} \vdash (S, \{(t_2 = t_1)\})$;
Rule 3 : $\mathcal{EC} \vdash (S, \{(t_1 = t_2), (t_2 = t_3)\})$ implies $\mathcal{EC} \vdash (S, \{(t_1 = t_3)\})$;
Rule 4 : $\mathcal{EC} \vdash (S, E)$ and $E_1 \subseteq E$ implies $\mathcal{EC} \vdash (S, E_1)$;
Rule 5 : $\mathcal{EC} \vdash (S, E_1)$ and $\mathcal{EC} \vdash (S, E_2)$ implies $\mathcal{EC} \vdash (S, E_1 \cup E_2)$;

Rule 6 : $\mathcal{EC} \vdash (S, E)$ and h is a homomorphism from S in S_1 implies $\mathcal{EC} \vdash (S_1, h(E))$;

Rule 7 : $\mathcal{EC} \vdash (S, \{(t = t')\})$ and $\mathcal{EC} \vdash (\phi_{t \hookrightarrow t'}(S), E)$ implies $\mathcal{EC} \vdash (S, E)$;

Rule 8 : $\mathcal{EC} \vdash (S, \{(a = b)\})$ for $a, b \in \mathcal{U}_S$ and $a \neq b$ implies $\mathcal{EC} \vdash (S, E)$ for all possible E.

Lemma 2. *Let* $\phi_{t_k \hookrightarrow t'_k, \ldots, t_1 \hookrightarrow t'_1} = \phi_{t_k \hookrightarrow t'_k} \circ \phi_{t_{k-1} \hookrightarrow t'_{k-1}, \ldots, t_1 \hookrightarrow t'_1}$, *for* $k > 1$ *and for* $\forall i, 1 < i \leq k, \forall j, 1 \leq j < i (t_i \neq t'_j \neq t'_i)$.
The following holds:
$\mathcal{EC} \vdash (S, \{(t_1 = t'_1), \ldots, (t_k = t'_k)\})$ *and* $\mathcal{EC} \vdash (\phi_{t_k \hookrightarrow t'_k, \ldots, t_1 \hookrightarrow t'_1}(S), E)$ *implies* $\mathcal{EC} \vdash (S, E)$.

Proof. For $k = 1$ this is Rule 7. Let $k > 1$ and let $\mathcal{EC} \vdash (S, \{(t_1 = t'_1), \ldots, (t_k = t'_k)\})$ and $\mathcal{EC} \vdash (\phi_{t_k \hookrightarrow t'_k, \ldots, t_1 \hookrightarrow t'_1}(S), E)$. By Rule 4 we know that $\mathcal{EC} \vdash (S, \{(t_1 = t'_1), \ldots, (t_{k-1} = t'_{k-1})\})$ (1) and $\mathcal{EC} \vdash (S, \{(t_k = t'_k)\})$. Since $\phi_{t_{k-1} \hookrightarrow t'_{k-1}, \ldots, t_1 \hookrightarrow t'_1}$ is a homomorphism we have by Rule 6 that $\mathcal{EC} \vdash (S, \{(t_k = t'_k)\})$ implies $\mathcal{EC} \vdash \phi_{t_{k-1} \hookrightarrow t'_{k-1}, \ldots, t_1 \hookrightarrow t'_1}(S), \{(t_k = t'_k)\}$.
But by Rule 7

$$\mathcal{EC} \vdash (\phi_{t_{k-1} \hookrightarrow t'_{k-1}, \ldots, t_1 \hookrightarrow t'_1}(S), \{(t_k = t'_k)\})$$

and $\mathcal{EC} \vdash (\phi_{t_k \hookrightarrow t'_k, \ldots, t_1 \hookrightarrow t'_1}(S), E)$ implies $\mathcal{EC} \vdash (\phi_{t_{k-1} \hookrightarrow t'_{k-1}, \ldots, t_1 \hookrightarrow t'_1}(S), E)$ (2). ¿From (1) and (2) we deduce by induction that $\mathcal{EC} \vdash (S, E)$.

We say a set of deductive rules is *sound* if $\mathcal{EC} \vdash (S, E)$ implies $\mathcal{EC} \models (S, E)$, and *complete* if the inverse holds. A set of deductive rules is *independent* if no single rule can be removed from the set without loosing completeness.

Theorem 3. *The set of deductive rules 0-8 are sound, independent and complete.*

Proof.
Soundness:
We have to prove that $\mathcal{EC} \vdash (S, E) \Rightarrow \mathcal{EC} \models (S, E)$. We will prove this for each rule. Rules 0-5 are trivially sound, as a consequence of the definition of ECs. The soundness of Rule 6 follows from Lemma 1. For proving Rule 7 we suppose there is an embedding e from S in $\mathcal{G}$. So $e(t_1) = e(t_2)$ and e can be considered as an embedding from $\phi_{t_1 \hookrightarrow t_2}(S)$ in $\mathcal{G}$. Hence $e(t_3) = e(t_4)$ for each $(t_3 = t_4) \in E$. For proving Rule 8, let $\mathcal{G}$ satisfies $(S, \{(a = b)\})$ for $a, b \in \mathcal{U}_S$ and $a \neq b$. This means that there is no embedding of S in $\mathcal{G}$, so for all embeddings e of S in $\mathcal{G}$ all possible equalities hold.
Independence:
We need Rule 0 to derive $(\{(\$x, \$y, \$z)\}, \{(\$x = \$y)\}) \vdash (\{(\$x, \$y, \$z)\}, \{(\$x = \$y)\})$.
We need Rule 1 to derive $\emptyset \vdash (\{(\$x, \$y, \$z)\}, \{(\$x = \$x)\})$.
We need Rule 2 to derive $(\{(\$x, \$y, \$z)\}, \{(\$x = \$y)\}) \vdash (\{(\$x, \$y, \$z)\}, \{(\$y = \$x)\})$.
We need Rule 3 to derive $(\{(\$x, \$y, \$z)\}, \{(\$x = \$y), (\$y = \$z)\}) \vdash (\{(\$x, \$y, \$z)\}, \{(\$x = \$z)\})$.

We need Rule 4 to derive $(\{(\$x, \$y, \$z)\}, \{(\$x = \$y), (\$x = \$z)\}) \vdash (\{(\$x, \$y, \$z)\}, \{(\$x = \$y)\})$.

We need Rule 5 to derive $\{((\{(\$x, \$y, \$z)\}, \{(\$x = \$y)\}), (\{(\$x, \$y, \$z)\}, \{(\$x = \$z)\}))\} \vdash (\{(\$x, \$y, \$z)\}, \{(\$x = \$y), (\$x = \$z)\})$.

We need Rule 6 to derive $(\{(\$x, \$y, \$z)\}, \{(\$x = \$y)\}) \vdash (\{(\$x', \$y', \$z')\}, \{(\$x' = \$y')\})$.

We need Rule 7 to derive $(\{(\$x, \$y, \$z)\}, \{(\$x = \$y)\}), (\{(\$x, \$x, \$z)\}, \{(\$x = \$z)\})) \vdash (\{(\$x, \$y, \$z)\}, \{(\$x = \$z)\})$.

We need Rule 8 to derive $(\{(\$x, \$y, \$z)\}, \{(a = b)\}) \vdash (\{(\$x, \$y, \$z)\}, \{(\$x = \$y)\})$ with $a, b \in \mathcal{U}_S$ and $a \neq b$.

Completeness:

We have to prove that $\mathcal{EC} \models (S, E) \Rightarrow \mathcal{EC} \vdash (S, E)$. Without loss of generality we can suppose by Rules 4 and 5 that $\mathcal{EC} = \{(S_i, \{(t_i = t_i')\}) \mid 1 \leq i \leq n\}$ and $E = \{(t = t')\}$ respectively. Let $\{(S_i, \{(t_i = t_i')\}) \mid 1 \leq i \leq n\} \not\vdash (S, \{(t = t')\})$. We will prove that $\{(S_i, \{(t_i = t_i')\}) \mid 1 \leq i \leq n\} \not\models (S, \{(t = t')\})$.

The following proof of completeness resembles and simulates the chasing algorithm introduced in Section 3.1. Indeed:

1. First we construct a sequence of sets of triples of terms $(\mathcal{K}_j)_{j \geq 0}$. $\mathcal{K}_0 = S$. We construct the sequence progressively, by induction : suppose we have already constructed $(\mathcal{K}_0, \ldots, \mathcal{K}_j)$. If there is a $i_j, 1 \leq i_j \leq n$ and a homomorphism $e_{i_j} : V_{S_{i_j}} \cup \mathcal{U}_{S_{i_j}} \to V_{\mathcal{K}_j} \cup \mathcal{U}_{\mathcal{K}_j}$ with $e_{i_j}(t_{i_j}) \neq e_{i_j}(t_{i_j}')$ and $e_{i_j}(t_{i_j}) = a$, $e_{i_j}(t_{i_j}') = b$ and $a, b \in \mathcal{U}_{\mathcal{K}_j}$. In 3 we prove that $\mathcal{EC} \vdash (S, \{(e_{i_j}(t_{i_j}) = e_{i_j}(t_{i_j}'))\})$, so $\mathcal{EC} \vdash (S, \{(a = b)\})$ implying by Rule 8 that $\mathcal{EC} \not\vdash (S, \{(t = t')\})$, which results in a contradiction. Otherwise we distinguish two possibilities:

   - for all $i_j, 1 \leq i_j \leq n$ and all homomorphisms $e_{i_j} : V_{S_{i_j}} \cup \mathcal{U}_{S_{i_j}} \to V_{\mathcal{K}_j} \cup \mathcal{U}_{\mathcal{K}_j}$ holds $e_{i_j}(t_{i_j}) = e_{i_j}(t_{i_j}')$. Then the sequence ends with $\mathcal{K}_j$.
   - otherwise there is a $i_j, 1 \leq i_j \leq n$ and a homomorphism $e_{i_j} : V_{S_{i_j}} \cup \mathcal{U}_{S_{i_j}} \to V_{\mathcal{K}_j} \cup \mathcal{U}_{\mathcal{K}_j}$ with $e_{i_j}(t_{i_j}) \neq e_{i_j}(t_{i_j}')$ and not $e_{i_j}(t_{i_j}), e_{i_j}(t_{i_j}') \in \mathcal{U}_{\mathcal{K}_j}$. Then $\mathcal{K}_{j+1} = \phi_{e_{i_j}(t_{i_j}) \hookleftarrow e_{i_j}(t_{i_j}')}(\mathcal{K}_j)$.

   Clearly we see that:

   (a) this is a finite sequence $\mathcal{K}_0, \ldots, \mathcal{K}_m$.

   (b) for all $j, 0 \leq j \leq m$ it holds that:

   $$\mathcal{K}_j = \phi_{e_{i_{j-1}}(t_{i_{j-1}}) \hookleftarrow e_{i_{j-1}}(t_{i_{j-1}}'), \ldots, e_{i_0}(t_{i_0}) \hookleftarrow e_{i_0}(t_{i_0}')}(S).$$

   (c) $g(\mathcal{K}_m)$ satisfies all $(S_i, \{(t_i = t_i')\})$, where g maps every URI to itself and every variable to a new and distinct URI.

2. We also define a sequence of homomorphisms $(h_j)_{0 \leq j \leq m}$, $h_j : V_S \cup \mathcal{U}_S \to V_{\mathcal{K}_j} \cup \mathcal{U}_{\mathcal{K}_j}$ with $h_0(t) = t$, for all $t \in V_S \cup \mathcal{U}_S$ and $h_{j+1} = \phi_{e_{i_j}(t_{i_j}) \hookleftarrow e_{i_j}(t_{i_j}')} \circ h_j$.

   Clearly we see that:

   (a) $h_j = \phi_{e_{i_{j-1}}(t_{i_{j-1}}) \hookleftarrow e_{i_{j-1}}(t_{i_{j-1}}'), \ldots, e_{i_0}(t_{i_0}) \hookleftarrow e_{i_0}(t_{i_0}')}$.

   (b) $g \circ h_m$ is an embedding of S in $g(\mathcal{K}_m)$.

3. We will prove by induction that $\mathcal{EC} \vdash (S, \{(e_{i_j}(t_{i_j}) = e_{i_j}(t'_{i_j}))\})$ for $0 \leq j < m$.

   For $j = 0$, $e_{i_0} : V_{S_{i_0}} \cup \mathcal{U}_{S_{i_0}} \to V_S \cup \mathcal{U}_S$ and $\mathcal{EC} \vdash (S_{i_0}, \{(t_{i_0} = t'_{i_0})\})$ by Rule 0, so $\mathcal{EC} \vdash (S, \{(e_{i_0}(t_{i_0}) = e_{i_0}(t'_{i_0}))\})$ by Rule 7.

   For $0 < j < m$, we know by induction $\mathcal{EC} \vdash (S, \{(e_{i_k}(t_{i_k}) = e_{i_k}(t'_{i_k}))\})$ for $0 \leq k < j$ (*). Furthermore we have 1.b (**) and $e_{i_j} : V_{S_{i_j}} \cup \mathcal{U}_{S_{i_j}} \to V_{\mathcal{K}_j} \cup \mathcal{U}_{\mathcal{K}_j}$ and $\mathcal{EC} \vdash (S_{i_j}, \{(t_{i_j} = t'_{i_j})\})$ so by Rule 6 we have $\mathcal{EC} \vdash (\mathcal{K}_j, \{(e_{i_j}(t_{i_j}) = e_{i_j}(t'_{i_j}))\})$ (***).

   Applying Lemma 2 on (*,**,***) we conclude $\mathcal{EC} \vdash (S, \{(e_{i_j}(t_{i_j}) = e_{i_j}(t'_{i_j}))\})$.

4. We prove by induction that $h_j(u) = h_j(u')$ implies $\mathcal{EC} \vdash (S, \{(u = u')\})$, for all $0 \leq j \leq m$, where u and u' are terms. Clearly, for $j = 0$ it holds that $h_0(u) = h_0(u')$ implies that u and u' are the same term and by Rule 1 $\mathcal{EC} \vdash (S, \{(u = u')\})$. Lét now $0 < j \leq m$ and $h_j(u) = h_j(u')$. If $h_{j-1}(u) = h_{j-1}(u')$ then by induction $\mathcal{EC} \vdash (S, \{(u = u')\})$. If, otherwise, $h_{j-1}(u) \neq h_{j-1}(u')$ then we have:

   (a) $h_{j-1}(u) = h_{j-1}(e_{i_{j-1}}(t_{i_{j-1}}))$, so by induction we have that $\mathcal{EC} \vdash (S, \{(u = e_{i_{j-1}}(t_{i_{j-1}}))\})$.

   (b) $h_{j-1}(u') = h_{j-1}(e_{i_{j-1}}(t'_{i_{j-1}}))$, so by induction we have that $\mathcal{EC} \vdash (S, \{(u' = e_{i_{j-1}}(t'_{i_{j-1}}))\})$.

   (c) By 3. we have $\mathcal{EC} \vdash (S, \{(e_{i_{j-1}}(t_{i_{j-1}}) = e_{i_{j-1}}(t'_{i_{j-1}}))\})$.

   (d) By Rules 2 and 3 and (a), (b) and (c) we have that $\mathcal{EC} \vdash (S, \{(u = u')\})$.

5. Suppose now that $\mathcal{EC} \nvdash (S, \{(t = t')\})$. So by 4. we know that $h_m(t) \neq h_m(t')$ and $g \circ h_m(t) \neq g \circ h_m(t')$. From 1.c we know that $g(\mathcal{K})$ satisfies $\mathcal{EC}$, but does not satisfy (S, E) by 2.b and $g \circ h_m(t) \neq g \circ h_m(t')$. Hence the existence of $g(\mathcal{K})$ proves that $\mathcal{EC} \nvDash (S, E)$.

3.3 Chasing Algorithm for FCs Using EGCs

As a corollary of the correspondence between FCs and EGCs, we can effectively re-use the chasing algorithm of EGCs for checking implication of FCs. This is done in the algorithm below by translating the input FCs into EGCs and then executing the chasing algorithm of Section 3.1.

Input:

A set of FCs $\{(S_i, L_i \to R_i) \mid 1 \leq i \leq n\}$ and an FC $(S, L \to R)$.

Output:

Does it hold that

$$\{(S_i, L_i \to R_i) \mid 1 \leq i \leq n\} \models (S, L \to R)$$

Algorithm:

1. Rewrite the $(S_i, L_i \to R_i), 1 \leq i \leq n$ as EGCs (S'_i, E'_i) and $(S, L \to R)$ as EGCs (S', E') according to Theorem 1.

2. Apply the chasing algorithm for EGCs to $(S'_i, E'_i), 1 \leq i \leq n$ and (S', E')

Since the FCs are considered as EGCs, the proof of the following corollary directly follows from Theorems 1 and 2.

Corollary 1. *The algorithm above is correct.*

Example 5. Let
$(S_1, L_1 \to R_1) = (\{(\$p, \$q, \$r), (\$s, \$t, \$u)\}, \{\$p\} \to \{\$t\})$ and
$(S, L \to R) = (\{(\$x, a, \$y), (\$y, \$z, b)\}, \{\$y\} \to \{\$z\})$.
Does it hold that $(S_1, L_1 \to R_1)) \models (S, L \to R)$?

1. $(S_1', E_1') = (\{(\$p_1, \$q_1, \$r_1), (\$s_1, \$t_1, \$u_1), (\$p_1, \$q_2, \$r_2), (\$s_2, \$t_2, \$u_2)\},$
   $\{(\$t_1 = \$t_2)\})$
   $(S', E') = (\{(\$x_1, a, \$y_1), (\$y_1, \$z_1, b), (\$x_2, a, \$y_1), (\$y_1, \$z_2, b)\},$
   $\{(\$z_1 = \$z_2)\})$
2. • $\overline{\mathcal{G}} = \{(x_1, a, y_1), (y_1, z_1, b), (x_2, a, y_1), (y_1, z_2, b)\}$.
   • Consider the embedding e of $\{(\$p_1, \$q_1, \$r_1), (\$s_1, \$t_1, \$u_1), (\$p_1, \$q_2, \$r_2),$
     $(\$s_2, \$t_2, \$u_2)\}$ in $\overline{\mathcal{G}}$ with $e(\$p_1) = x_1$, $e(\$q_1) = a$, $e(\$r_1) = y_1$, $e(\$s_1) =$
     y_1, $e(\$t_1) = z_1$, $e(\$u_1) = b$, $e(\$q_2) = a$, $e(\$r_2) = y_1$, $e(\$s_2) = y_1$, $e(\$t_2) =$
     z_2, $e(\$u_2) = b$. $z_1 = e(\$t_1) \neq e(\$t_2) = z_2$, so all occurrences of z_2 are re-
     placed by z_1 in $\overline{\mathcal{G}}$. Hence $\overline{\mathcal{G}} = \{(x_1, a, y_1), (y_1, z_1, b), (x_2, a, y_1), (y_1, z_1, b)\}$.
   • There is no embedding e of S_1' in $\overline{\mathcal{G}}$ with $e(\$t_1) \neq e(\$t_2)$. Hence step 2
     of the chasing algorithm for EGCs stops and since $\overline{\mathcal{G}}$ satisfies (S', E') we
     conclude that $(S_1, L_1 \to R_1)) \models (S, L \to R)$.

Example 6. Let
$(S_1, L_1 \to R_1) = (\{(\$u, \$v, \$w)\}, \{\$v\} \to \{\$w\})$ and
$(S, L \to R) = (\{(\$x, a, \$y), (\$z, b, c), (\$t, b, d)\}, \{\$x\} \to \{\$y\})$.
Does it hold that $(S_1, L_1 \to R_1)) \models (S, L \to R)$?

1. $(S_1', E_1') = (\{(\$u_1, \$v_1, \$w_1), (\$u_2, \$v_1, \$w_2)\}, \{(\$w_1 = \$w_2)\})$
   $(S', E') = (\{(\$x_1, a, \$y_1), (\$z_1, b, c), (\$t_1, b, d), (\$x_1, a, \$y_2), (\$z_2, b, c),$
   $(\$t_2, b, d)\}, \{(\$y_1 = \$y_2)\})$
2. • $\overline{\mathcal{G}} = \{(x_1, a, y_1), (z_1, b, c), (t_1, b, d), (x_1, a, y_2), (z_2, b, c), (t_2, b, d)\}$.
   • Consider the embedding e of $(\$u_1, \$v_1, \$w_1), (\$u_2, \$v_1, \$w_2)$ in $\overline{\mathcal{G}}$ with
     $e(\$u_1) = z_1$, $e(\$v_1) = b$, $e(\$w_1) = c$, $e(\$u_2) = t_1$, $e(\$w_2) = d$. $c =$
     $e(\$w_1) \neq e(\$w_2) = b$. Since we cannot equalize c and b we conclude that
     $(S_1, L_1 \to R_1)) \models (S, L \to X)$ for all $X \subseteq V_{S_1}$, and so $(S_1, L_1 \to R_1)) \models$
     $(S, L \to R)$.

The existence of a complete axiomatization for FCs is still an open problem.
Given the semantic similarities between EGCs and FCs, we conjecture that such
axiomatization exists. For the time being, we can indirectly generate FCs by
using the rules for the equality generating constraints of Section 3.2. Indeed,
Theorem 1 says that FCs can be expressed as EGCs. Since the Rules 1-8 are
sound and complete for EGCs, they are also sound and complete for FCs represented as EGCs.

4 Related Work

RDF is a W3C recommendation and the reader interested in a thorough treatment of the language may find useful the official W3C documents available at [24]

and [26]. In [15], Gutierrez et al. provide formal foundations for RDF databases and propose an early query language coupled with a study of its computational properties. Theoretical aspects of SPARQL, the query language for RDF, are investigated in [21,1] and [20]. The problem of schema evolution and RDF database updates is studied in [10]. From a practical stand, RDF is the backbone of Tim Berners-Lee's vision on linked data [17]. Other applications of RDF databases include social networks representation [19], bioinformatics [23] and data integration [22].

The amount of literature on relational constraints in general and on dependencies in particular is immense. We mention here only the research which is close to our work. Functional dependencies were first discussed by Codd in [11], who observed that relations in which certain patterns of functional dependencies occur do not behave as expected. Chasing algorithm for relational databases are discussed by Sadri et al. in [28] and the first axiomatization of functional dependencies was proposed by Armstrong in [2].

Integrity constraints have also been extensively studied in the context of XML databases. In [14], the authors incorporate simple key, foreign and inverse constraints to XML databases with DTDs. This work is refined and extended with additional complexity bound results in [13]. XML path constraints are studied in [7], where the authors show that the implication problem is recursively enumerable (r.e.) complete and finite implication problem is co-r.e. complete. In [6], the authors study absolute and relative key constraints and show that reasoning with these type of constraints can be done in a tractable way. The specific case of functional dependencies in XML is studied in [32].

Constraints are an important component of the semantic web vision. In [8], the complexity of the description logics $\mathcal{DLR}$ with identification constraints and functional dependencies is studied. Lutz et al. [18] study a similar problem but in the presence of a concrete domain. Unfortunately, their complexity results cannot be extrapolated directly to our setting of RDF with EGCs and FCs, as the data models of [8] and [18] are radically different from ours.

Constraints were first introduced into an RDF framework by Lausen at al. [16]. The main motivation for adding constraints in [16] was the need to migrate a relational data base with primary and foreign keys into an RDF graph without loosing semantic information. The authors show how constraints such as keys and foreign keys can be encoded into the original RDF graph by means of introducing additional nodes in an extended RDF vocabulary. Functional constraints are defined in terms of properties of RDF interpretations over objects of the same type (or class). Our formulation of functional constraints is different from that of [16], as in our case they can not only be defined for properties (predicates in the terminology of this paper) but also between objects, subjects, or any combination of them (as it is done in several instances of Example 2). Equality generating constraints are not considered in [16]. In [29], Smith et al. exploit the knowledge encoded in integrity constraints (tuple-generating and equality generating dependencies) in order to speed up the processing time for solving SPARQL queries. To the best of our knowledge, deductive systems for the type of constraints presented in the current paper have not been studied in the literature before.

5 Conclusion

Integrity constraints have been recognized as an important tool in modern database systems. They have been applied with success in contexts as diverse as data integrity enforcement, semantic query optimization and data integration and exchange. In this paper we introduced two kinds of constraints into the RDF data model. Our motivation stems from the relevance of similar constraints in the relational model. The two types of constraints we study are functional and equality generating constraints. For both types we introduce an Armstrong-like scheme of rules and show how to translate functional dependencies into equality generating constraints; and we show that the converse is not possible. We also presented algorithms to generate all the logical consequences of an initial set of either functional or equality generating constraints.

This paper is an effort towards a general theory of reasoning with integrity constraints in RDF. Our next goal is to incorporate in our framework so-called tuple-generating dependencies (TGDs). TGDs in the relational model play an important role in mediator-based systems and data exchange. Together with this extension, we plan to implement these three types of constraints into an SPARQL engine. Incorporating these constraints in semantically enriched models such RDFS [24] is another interesting line of future research.

A relevant open problem is complexity checking. At least two important questions still need to be addressed. How difficult is to check whether an integrity constraint is satisfied by a database, or satisfiable at all, and what is the complexity of answering SPARQL queries in the presence of integrity constraints.

With the notion of constraints in place, it immediately arises the issue of RDF databases consistency. It would be interesting to study how to handle RDF databases that are inconsistent with a given set of RDF constraints. The development of this line of research will probably borrow concepts and techniques from its relational counter part [5].

Acknowledgments. We would like to thank the anonymous reviewers for carefully reading this paper and for many helpful comments.

References

1. Angles, R., Gutierrez, C.: The Expressive Power of SPARQL. In: Sheth, A.P., Staab, S., Dean, M., Paolucci, M., Maynard, D., Finin, T., Thirunarayan, K. (eds.) ISWC 2008. LNCS, vol. 5318, pp. 114–129. Springer, Heidelberg (2008)
2. Armstrong, W.W.: Dependency structures of data base relationships. In: IFIP Congress, pp. 580–583 (1974)

3. Beeri, C., Fagin, R., Howard, J.H.: A complete axiomatization for functional and multivalued dependencies in database relations. In: Proceedings of the 1977 ACM SIGMOD International Conference on Management of Data, Toronto, Canada, August 3-5, pp. 47–61 (1977)
4. Beeri, C., Vardi, M.Y.: The implication problem for data dependencies. In: Even, S., Kariv, O. (eds.) ICALP 1981. LNCS, vol. 115, pp. 73–85. Springer, Heidelberg (1981)
5. Bertossi, L.E.: Consistent query answering in databases. SIGMOD Record 35(2), 68–76 (2006)
6. Buneman, P., Davidson, S.B., Fan, W., Hara, C.S., Tan, W.C.: Reasoning about keys for XML. Inf. Syst. 28(8), 1037–1063 (2003)
7. Buneman, P., Fan, W., Weinstein, S.: Path constraints in semistructured and structured databases. In: Proceedings of the Seventeenth ACM SIGACT-SIGMOD-SIGART Symposium on Principles of Database Systems (PODS), Seattle, Washington, June 1-3, pp. 129–138 (1998)
8. Calvanese, D., De Giacomo, G., Lenzerini, M.: Identification constraints and functional dependencies in description logics. In: Nebel, B. (ed.) IJCAI, pp. 155–160. Morgan Kaufmann, San Francisco (2001)
9. Chakravarthy, U.S., Grant, J., Minker, J.: Logic-based approach to semantic query optimization. ACM Transactions on Database Systems 15(2), 162–207 (1990)
10. Chirkova, R., Fletcher, G.H.L.: Towards well-behaved schema evolution. In: 12th International Workshop on the Web and Databases, WebDB 2009, Providence, Rhode Island, USA, (June 28, 2009)
11. Codd, E.F.: A relational model of data for large shared data banks. Commun. ACM 13(6), 377–387 (1970)
12. Denecker, M., Cortés-Calabuig, A., Bruynooghe, M., Arieli, O.: Towards a logical reconstruction of a theory for locally closed databases. ACM Trans. Database Syst. 35(3) (2010)
13. Fan, W., Libkin, L.: On XML integrity constraints in the presence of DTDs. Journal of the ACM 49(3), 368–406 (2002)
14. Fan, W., Siméon, J.: Integrity constraints for XML. In: Proceedings of the Nineteenth ACM SIGMOD-SIGACT-SIGART Symposium on Principles of Database Systems (PODS), Dallas, Texas, USA, May 15-17, pp. 23–34 (2000)
15. Gutierrez, C., Hurtado, C.A., Mendelzon, A.O.: Foundations of semantic web databases. In: Proceedings of the Twenty-third ACM SIGACT-SIGMOD-SIGART Symposium on Principles of Database Systems (PODS 2004), Paris, France, June 14-16, pp. 95–106 (2004)
16. Lausen, G., Meier, M., Schmidt, M.: Schmidt Sparqling constraints for RDF. In: Proceedings 11th International Conference on Extending Database Technology (EDBT 2008), Nantes, France, March 25-29, pp. 499–509 (2008)
17. Linked data. Obtainable via (2006), http://www.w3.org/DesignIssues/LinkedData.html
18. Lutz, C., Milicic, M.: Milicic Description logics with concrete domains and functional dependencies. In: de Mántaras, R.L., Saitta, L. (eds.) ECAI, pp. 378–382. IOS Press, Amsterdam (2004)
19. San Martín, M., Gutierrez, C.: Representing, Querying and Transforming Social Networks with RDF/SPARQL. In: Aroyo, L., Traverso, P., Ciravegna, F., Cimiano, P., Heath, T., Hyvönen, E., Mizoguchi, R., Oren, E., Sabou, M., Simperl, E. (eds.) ESWC 2009. LNCS, vol. 5554, pp. 293–307. Springer, Heidelberg (2009)
20. Muñoz, S., Pérez, J., Gutierrez, C.: Simple and efficient minimal rdfs. J. Web Sem. 7(3), 220–234 (2009)

21. Pérez, J., Arenas, M., Gutierrez, C.: Semantics and complexity of SPARQL. ACM Trans. Database Syst. 34(3) (2009)
22. Quilitz, B., Leser, U.: Querying Distributed RDF Data Sources with SPARQL. In: Bechhofer, S., Hauswirth, M., Hoffmann, J., Koubarakis, M. (eds.) ESWC 2008. LNCS, vol. 5021, pp. 524–538. Springer, Heidelberg (2008)
23. Semantic bioinformatics (2006), http://esw.w3.org/Semantic_Bioinformatics
24. RDF schema (2004), http://www.w3.org/TR/rdf-schema/
25. RDF primer (2004), http://www.w3.org/TR/rdf-primer/
26. RDF semantics (2004), http://www.w3.org/TR/rdf-mt/
27. Reiter, R.: On integrity constraints. In: Vardi, M. (ed.) Proceedings of Conference on Theoretical Aspects o Reasoning about Knowledge, pp. 97–111 (1988)
28. Sadri, F., Ullman, J.D.: The interaction between functional dependencies and template dependencies. In: Proceedings of the 1980 ACM SIGMOD International Conference on Management of Data, Santa Monica, California, May 14-16, pp. 45–51 (1980)
29. Schmidt, M., Meier, M., Lausen, G.: Foundations of SPARQL query optimization. In: Proceedings 13th International Conference Database Theory, ICDT 2010 (2010)
30. SPARQL protocol and RDF query language (SPARQL). Obtainable via (2008), http://www.w3.org/TR/rdf-sparql-query/
31. Thalheim, B.: Integrity constraints in (Conceptual) database models. In: Kaschek, R., Delcambre, L. (eds.) The Evolution of Conceptual Modeling. LNCS, vol. 6520, pp. 42–67. Springer, Heidelberg (2011)
32. Vincent, M.W., Liu, J.: Functional dependencies for XML. In: Zhou, X., Zhang, Y., Orlowska, M.E. (eds.) APWeb 2003. LNCS, vol. 2642, pp. 22–34. Springer, Heidelberg (2003)
33. Winslett, M.: A model-based approach to updating databases with incomplete information. ACM Trans. Database Syst. 13(2), 167–196 (1988)

Types and Constraints: From Relational to XML Data

Nicole L. Bidoit-Tollu

Univ. Paris-Sud - UMR CNRS 8623 - INRIA Saclay
LRI Database Group & INRIA Leo Team
nicole.bidoit@lri.fr

Abstract. The goal of this article is to show that, in the context of XML data processing, information conveyed by schema or XML types is a powerful component to deploy optimization methods. We focus on the one hand on recent work developed for optimizing query and update evaluation for main-memory engines and on the other hand on techniques for checking XML query-update independence. These methods are all based on static type analysis. The aim of the article is to show how types rank before constraints for XML data processing and the presentation of each method is kept informal.

Keywords: XML, Schema, Type, Query, Update, Optimization.

1   Introduction

Integrity constraints have been considered from the beginning as a key component of information systems and databases. They are fundamental not to say mandatory for specifying the semantic of data. Integrity constraints provide a way to fill the gap between information and data. Integrity constraints also raise many problems and beginning with efficient constraint checking and enforcing integrity constraints, repairing inconsistent database states, etc. They play a major role in the process of query optimization, called semantic query optimization, where the constrains known to hold on the database are used to rewrite queries into equivalent and more efficient ones. Integrity constraints and rewriting techniques based on constraints have also been successful for developing query rewriting using views, for data exchange, peer data exchange, data integration, etc.

Types can also be viewed as constraints, but in a different fashion. Intuitively, in the database world, integrity constraints are content-based properties whereas types are structural properties. A type consists of a possibly infinite set of values and also, in programming languages, of a set of operations on those values. A type may be atomic or structured. Roughly, a composite/structured type is build using existing types and type constructors like record, set, list, etc. In the context of databases, types have been essentially investigated in the context of the object-oriented database model where typing [28,29] shares features of conventional object-oriented programming languages and of taxonomy systems where data is organized in hierarchy of classes and subclasses. Typing helps to detect programming errors which is of major importance for developing database applications and managing huge amount of data.

K.-D. Schewe, and B. Thalheim (Eds.): SDKB 2010, LNCS 6834, pp. 40–53, 2011.

There is a very large body of research on using constraints for query optimization. However, contrary to programming languages, typing in database has been rarely investigated for optimization purpose. The aim of the article is to give some evidence that, in the context of XML data processing, types are becoming as important as constraints[1], and provide ways to optimize XML queries and updates as well as it provides ways to develop static analysis for checking other critical properties such as query update independence.

The article is organized as follows. The next section is an introductory discussion on constraints and types and covers the relational model and XML data. The rest of the article is dedicated to present some ongoing work investigating optimization techniques for XML document processing based on static analysis, making an extensive use of the information given by types or schemas. The presentation is devoted to pieces of work that have been conducted in the Leo team [4]. It certainly does not aim at covering all issues and existing studies. The style of the presentation remains informal and mainly relies on examples. Section 3 addresses query optimization and Section 4 update optimization for main-memory engines. Section 5 focuses on update query independence.

2 Preliminaries

Let us start by revisiting the relational model. Types in the relational model are tremendously simple. Given a set of attributes U, a set of atomic values, called domain, is assigned to each attribute. A relational database schema over U is given by a set of relation names $\mathscr{R}$ and a mapping (a type assignment) τ assigning to each relation name r a finite subset of U^2. Thus, a relational type is a finite set of attributes. For instance, the relational schema defined by $\mathscr{R}=\{R, S\}$ with $\tau(R)=\{A, B, C\}$ and $\tau(S)=\{A, D\}$ is usually denoted $\mathscr{R}=\{R(A, B, C), S(A, D)\}$. Relational types are of course useful for writing queries either using the algebra or SQL as well as for writing updates. They are also useful for checking well-typedness of queries and infer their output type. For instance, the expression $\pi_{AC}(\sigma_{D='foo'}([R] \bowtie [S]))$ is well typed wrt to the schema $\mathscr{R}$ above. The output type for this expression is $\{A, C\}$. For instance, [37] investigates how the principal type of a relational expression can be computed, giving all possible assignments of types to relation names under which the expression is well-typed. This study is extended to the nested relational calculus in [36]. However, relational types are quite "poor". They are equivalent to record types in programming languages. More sophisticated types are associated to the non first normal form model and to the complex object model model [11]. Integrity constraints have been introduced in order to increase the semantic contents of relational databases. Amon integrity constraints, the following are the most studied classes: functional dependencies [34,51], equality generating dependencies and tuple generating dependencies [15]. Integrity constraints, as opposed to relational types, can be used for query optimization. The chase [13,45] is probably one of the most known example of a technique based on dependencies and allowing for minimizing the number of joins of an algebraic query expression, and

---

[1] The frontier between types and constraints may is also not as clear-cut as for relational databases.

[2] For now, we leave integrity constraints out of the specification of a database schema.

recent investigation has proved its efficiency in practice [48]. Integrity constraints, especially functional dependencies, are also very useful for optimizing updates: schema normalization [33], avoiding update anomalies, can be viewed as some kind of update optimization.

In the relational world, types are almost totally useless for optimization purpose. Constraints have a better place whereas physical data structures and access methods provide the real solutions to optimization problems in practice [50].

Semi-structured data [25,12] and XML data [2] are classically introduced as self-describing and schema-less: in its general setting, semi-structured data are abstracted by labelled graphs; well-formed XML documents are ordered labelled trees as described for instance by the *Document Object Model* [41]. Simple tree representations of XML documents are given in Fig. 1. Interestingly enough, almost every published article whose scope is XML management with a database perspective, makes the assumption of a schema or type constraining the structure of XML documents when they do not investigate schemas and types for XML themselves. XML schemas aim at defining the set of allowable labels and also the way they can be structured. In the first place, XML schemas are meant to distinguish meaningful documents from those that are not and provides the user with a concrete semantic of the documents. The document on the left hand side of Fig. 1 is well-formed: it is a labelled tree. However, this document is not valid wrt the DTD described by the following rules: $doc \rightarrow a*, a \rightarrow bc*d, b \rightarrow String$, $d \rightarrow e$. These rules specify that the root of the document should be labelled by doc, that the children of the root should be labelled by a (it is not the case for the document considered here because the root node has its last child labelled by e) and the children of a nodes should be first a node labelled by b followed by possibly several nodes labelled c, and finally a node labelled d, etc. Figure proposes another example of a DTD and a document valid wrt that DTD.

XML schemas turn out to bring many advantages for validation, data integration, translation, etc They are very useful for the specification of meaningful queries over XML data and can be used for query optimization. The main practical languages for describing XML types are *Document Type Definition (DTD)* which is indeed part of the original definition of XML [2] and is probably the most widely used, and *XML Schema* [52,24] which is a more elaborate, not to say overly complex, schema notation based on XML itself. Many other proposals for schema languages have flourished: DSD [43], RelaxNG [32], Shematron [42], Assertion Grammars [49]. See for instance [47,44] for a formal classification and a comparison of these languages.

What about XML integrity constraints? It is often claimed that schemas and constraints are both properties that restrict the allowed documents and thus that the frontier between schemas or types and constraints is not as clear-cut as for relational databases. Although ID attributes in a DTD can be used to uniquely identify an element within an XML document, these attributes can not be used to express constraints such as keys. Although XML schemas allow to specify keys or references in terms of Xpath [18], such style of specification is rather intricate especially when it comes to reasoning about constraints. Indeed, constraints for semi-structured data and XML [38,39], keys and foreign keys for XML [26,27] have received a lot of attention from the database community. Update anomalies and normal forms for XML documents have been investigated in

[14]. Unified formalisms for capturing schema and integrity constraints for XML have also been studied in order to reason about types and constraints [19].

As opposed to relational databases, optimization techniques based on integrity constraints have not yet been investigated whereas schema or type-based optimization techniques are already used [46] in query engines.

To conclude this preliminary section, we briefly proceed to a short discussion on *element type*, a notion that will be used in the next sections. Each optimization techniques discussed next uses the information provided by a schema, namely a DTD, in order to assign types to the elements of a document valid wrt to the schema. Considering a document t and an element or node n in t, the type of n is, in its simplest form, its label. An alternative to this very simple notion of element type is to consider the chain of labels that match the path from the document root node of t to n. The former notion is that used in Sections 3 and 4, resp. for query and update optimization. The latter is central to Section 5 for dealing with query-update independence. Obviously, the notion of element type based on labels is less precise than the notion of element type based on chains although this last one is still not fully precise. Let us illustrate this with the example of Fig. 1: on the left side, the circled nodes of the document are typed by the label e; on the right side, the circled nodes of the (same) document are typed by the chain $doc.a.d.e$; the chain type is more precise as it allows to distinguish e nodes that can be reached by navigating along $doc.a.d.e$ paths from those that cannot be reached that way; however, it is not precise enough to make the distinction between e nodes whose parent has at least one sibling labelled by c from those whose parent has no such sibling. Thus, in some sense, both notions of element type, label and chain, are approximations.

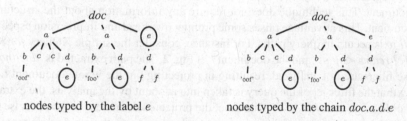

nodes typed by the label e nodes typed by the chain $doc.a.d.e$

Fig. 1. Labels and chains as type approximation for XML element

3   Type-Based Optimization for XML Queries

XQuery [9] is now well-recognized as a flexible and powerful language allowing to query collections of XML documents. As such, it is used not only for querying XML databases but also for instance to process XML files. In the latter context, main-memory XQuery engines like Galax [3], Saxon [8], QizX [6,5], and eXist [1] are used to query files as they avoid building secondary storage structures. The price to pay or more exactly the problem to face is main-memory limitations of these systems (see [46]) because, in such configuration, the whole document is required to be loaded in main-memory before query processing. Main-memory XQuery engines are unable to process very large documents. Projecting XML document is an optimization technique introduced by [46] to address such limitation. The simplicity of the method is one of the key of its efficiency. Given a query Q over an XML document t, the idea is to determine, in a static manner, that is by analyzing the query expression and, if available, the type or schema of the queried documents, which part t' of the document t is needed in order to evaluate Q, and then, at loading time, to prune the document t; finally the query Q is evaluated in main-memory against the pruned document t'. This technique is quite powerful because in general, queries are very selective and only a small part of the initial document is relevant to the evaluation of the query. The core of the method, which determines its efficiency, resides in the static analysis of the query Q: how precise is it?

All the examples developed next are build using the DTD D and the XML document t depicted in Figure 2.

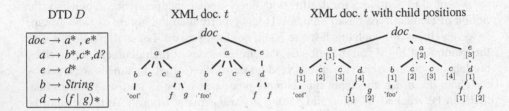

Fig. 2. Running example : a DTD D and a document t

The initial proposal of [46] determines the data needs of the query Q by extracting all path expressions in Q. These paths are evaluated at loading time to prune the initial document. This technique does not require any information about the structure of the document. This advantage raises some pruning overhead and imprecision especially when // axis occurs in query paths. For instance, consider the simple XQuery *for $x in /doc//[c] return ⊲/yes>* and the document t of Fig. 2. The path extracted is */doc//node()* because filters are not analyzed, resulting in projecting out the whole document t. Assuming that the filter [c] of the query is taken into account by the analysis, the extracted path would be given by */doc//c*. This time, the projected document will be precise (and indeed is the result of the query Q) however, at loading time, the whole document will be explored by the query path, thus causing some pruning execution overhead. It is clear that, in this case, the knowledge of the DTD D for the document t, gives the opportunity to refine the extracted path */doc//c* to */doc/a/c* which avoids during projection for visiting and checking e elements for instance. This is what typed-based projection is about [17]. The type-based query scenario is as follows:

1. from the query Q and DTD D, a type projector π is inferred,
2. the document t, valid wrt D, is projected following π in a streaming manner, at loading time,
3. and finally, the query Q is evaluated over $\pi(t)$.

The main result [17] is that $Q(t)=Q(\pi(t))$.

The type projector is specified by a set of node types given by labels. Execution of a type projector at loading time is straightforward. It consists of projecting nodes whose labels (types) belong to the type projector. Extracting a type projector π for a query Q given a DTD D is a two phase process whose first step extracts the paths of the query Q and the second step strongly relies on the type information given by D to generate the expected set of node types.

Example 1. For the query Q specified below, the paths extracted are /doc/a, /doc/a//d and /doc/a//text(). The type extraction based on the DTD of Fig. 2 allows one to generate the type projector $\pi = \{doc, a, b, d, String\}$ because nodes of type d that are descendants of nodes of type a are indeed children of nodes of type a and nodes of type $String$ that are descendants of nodes of type a are children of nodes of type b.

Query Q	Projected document $\pi(t)$

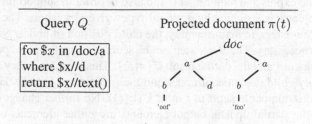

```
for $x in /doc/a
where $x//d
return $x//text()
```

One can notice here that the evaluation of the projector avoids exploring the right most subtree of the document (Fig. 2) whose root is labelled by e even though this subtree contains nodes of type d.

Experiments have been done showing the benefits of the type-based projection optimization for queries. The method provides significant improvement of performance both in terms of memory consumption and time.

4   Type-Based Optimization for XML Updates

In this section, we show that, type-based projection can also be used to optimize main-memory XML update processing. The update language considered is XQuery Update Facility (XUF) [10] with its two phase semantics: given a complex update expression U and a document t, the first phase generates a so-called update pending list, a list of elementary updates, and the second phase evaluates the update pending list over the document t. We focus on main-memory XUF processing which of course suffers of the same limitation as main-memory XQuery evaluation: XUF main-memory engines fails to process very large documents. For instance, eXist [1], QizX/open [6] and Saxon [7] are unable to update documents whose size is greater than 150 MB (no matter the update query at hand).

The scenario and type-based projection described for XML queries, cannot be applied directly for updates. Indeed, it is rather obvious to see that updating the projection of a document t will not produce the expected result unless the projection equals the whole document which is, of course, not very promising from an optimization point of view. We have developed in [20,21] a type-based optimization method for update.

The update scenario is different from that for query optimization and is now composed of four steps:

1. from the update U and the DTD D, a type projector π is inferred,
2. the document t, valid wrt D, is projected following π in a streaming manner, at loading time,
3. the update U is evaluated over the projection $\pi(t)$ and produces a partial result $U(\pi(t))$,
4. finally, in order to produce the final result $U(t)$, the initial document t is merged with $U(\pi(t))$, in a streaming manner, at writing-serializing time.

The projector extracted for updates, a 3-level type projector, has been designed in order to capture update expression requirements and also in order to support the *Merge* phase. The 3-level projector is specified by 3 sets of types given by labels. The projection of the document t registers, in main-memory, the child position of nodes. No rewriting of the update U is necessary. The *Merge* step can be seen as a synchronized parsing of both the initial document t and the partial result $U(\pi(t))$. This requires a very small amount of memory. Only child positions of nodes and the projector π are checked in order to decide whether to output elements of t or of $U(\pi(t))$. No further changes are made on elements after the partial update: output elements are either elements of the original document t or elements of $U(\pi(t))$.

We start by explaining the last step of the update scenario (*Merge*) and then we outline the main ideas behind the 3-level type projector specification. The presentation remains informal, it does not cover all aspects of the method, even important ones, and relies on examples.

Example 2. Let us consider the simple update U whose expression is given in the left part of the next figure. This update intends to delete b children of a nodes having at least one d child. Here, the projector is meant to extract from the document the part which is used either to prepare the update or which is the target of the changes made by the update. For this example and for sake of simplicity, we use a (1-level) projector $\pi=\{doc, a, b, d\}$.

The *Merge* step parses in a synchronized manner both the input document t and the partial result $U(\pi(t))$. The rightmost part of Figure 2 shows the document t with child positions marked in square brackets under node labels. Wrt our example, executing *Merge* over t and $U(\pi(t))$ is quite obvious until after processing the node $a[1]$ of t together with the node $a[1]$ of $U(\pi(t))$. The two next nodes parsed by *Merge* are: the node $b[1]$, child of $a[1]$ in t and the node $d[4]$, child of $a[1]$ in $U(\pi(t))$. The child positions of these nodes and the information that the label a belongs to the type projector π allows one to identify that the node $b[1]$ should not be output: the initial document t is further parsed without producing any element in the output. Then, the two next nodes examined by *Merge* are: the node $c[2]$, child of $a[1]$ in t and the node $d[4]$, child of $a[1]$ in $U(\pi(t))$. This time, the child positions of these nodes and the information that the label c does not belong to the type projector π are used to output the node $c[2]$ and further parse the initial document t.

Update U	Projected doc. $\pi(t)$	Partial update of $U(\pi(t))$
for \$x in /doc/a where \$x/d return delete \$x/b	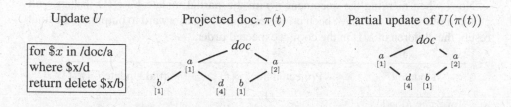	

The main issues that motivated the specification of the new type projector are: dealing with update expressions and ensuring correctness and efficiency of the *Merge* step. The type projector is specified by a tuple $\pi=(\pi_{no},\pi_{olb},\pi_{eb})$ where each set π_x is a set of labels. Thus here, as for query optimization, element types are approximated by labels. The behavior of the 3-level projector is as follows:

A node of the document t whose label belongs to π_{no} is projected. The children of such nodes will be candidate for projection depending on their label and π.

A node of the document t whose label belongs to π_{olb} is projected together with all its children even though their labels do not belong to π. This π_{olb} component of the projector is introduced in order to correctly handle insertion at *Merge* time as well as mixed-content. This is illustrated by the next example.

A node of the document t whose label belongs to π_{eb} is projected together with all its descendants, even though their labels do not belong in π. Introducing this π_{eb} component of the projector is required for dealing with element extraction for instance in the context of moving some elements.

Indeed, the two components π_{olb} and π_{eb} bring more precision and efficiency. They minimize the projection size and speed up the type projector execution by avoiding to put in the projector the labels of some of the nodes that need to be projected. Interestingly enough, the 3-level projector designed for updates provides significant improvements for pure queries.

The extraction of the 3-level projector from the update is based on a sophisticated extraction of paths from the update expression which is followed by a type derivation relying on the DTD D.

Example 3. Let us consider the update U below which intends to insert an h element as first child of any node labelled by a. The 3-level projector extracted from this update is given by: $\pi_{no}=\{doc\}$, $\pi_{olb}=\{a\}$ and $\pi_{eb}=\{\}$. Thus, while projecting the document t given in Fig. 2 wrt π all children of the nodes labelled a are projected. Note that neither the type c nor the type d occur in π. Note also that the right most subtree of the tree whose root is labelled by e is not projected because e does not belong to the projector. When updating the projection $\pi(t)$, the new elements are inserted without child position. It should be understood that the positions in $\pi(t)$ correspond to child position of the nodes in the input document t.

Now, when merging the document t with the partial update $U(\pi(t))$, because all children of the node $a[1]$ have been projected, it is straightforward to output, in the final result, the children of $a[1]$ in the correct expected order.

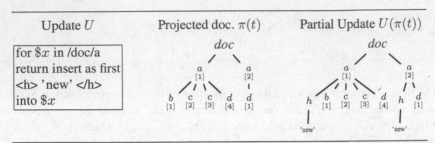

Update U	Projected doc. $\pi(t)$	Partial Update $U(\pi(t))$

Extensive experiments of the type-based optimization method for updates have been conducted and their results validate the effectiveness of the approach. They show that the technique succeeds in its primarily purpose: making possible to update very large documents with main-memory systems. Interestingly enough, the tests show that even when projection is not necessary because of memory limitation, using projection can reduce execution time as well. See [21] for a report on these experiments.

5   Type-Based Method for Testing XML Query-Update Independence

The aim of the last section is to illustrate another use of static type analysis for XML which targets, once again, optimization but in a rather different manner. Here, the issue is to statically detect query-update independence. A query and an update are independent when the update execution does not require refreshing the query result and this for any possible input document. Detecting query-update independence is of crucial importance in many contexts: to avoid view re-materialization after update; to ensure isolation, when queries and updates are executed concurrently; to enforce access control policies. In the general case, that is for the full XQuery and XUF languages, static independence detection is undecidable [16]. This means that static analysis methods for detecting query-update independence are expected to be sound approximation as completeness is unreachable.

Recently, [16] has introduced a technique for statically detecting query-update independence: a schema is assumed available; a set of types (approximated by labels) is inferred from the query which captures the nodes accessed by the query; similarly, a set of types is inferred from the update which captures the set of nodes impacted by the update; an empty intersection of these two sets entails independence.

A path-based approach has been proposed in [40] in order to check commutativity of update expressions which is of crucial importance for optimization and view maintenance. This technique, which does not use schema information, can be adapted to deal with queries: two sets of paths are extracted resp. from the query and from the update in the style of [46]; no overlapping of the paths in these two sets entails independence. Both techniques are effective for a wide class of XQueries and XUF and have negligible time performance.

Example 4. Let us assume that the available schema information is given by the following DTD: $doc \rightarrow a^*, b$ $a \rightarrow (b?, c)^*$ $c \rightarrow d$.

Let us first consider the query Q_1 specified by the path doc/b together with the update U_1 given by *for $x in doc/a/c return delete $x/d*. For this simple case, both methods detect independence. The schema-based method infers the sets of types $\{b\}$ and $\{a, c, d\}$ resp. for Q_1 and U_1 whereas the path-based method infers the sets of paths $\{doc/b\}$ and $\{doc/a/c, doc/d\}$.

For the second example, let us consider the query Q_1 together with the update U_2 given by *for each $x in doc return delete $x//d*. The schema-based method returns the set of types $\{a, c, d\}$ for U_2 and thus is able to detect independence. However, the path-based (schema-less) method infers, for U_2, the set of paths $\{doc//d\}$ which overlaps $\{doc/b\}$ and is unable to detect independence.

Finally, the last example considers the query Q_2 given by *for $x in doc/a/b return <g> $x </g>* and the update U_1. The types associated to Q_2 by the schema-based method are $\{a, b\}$ and as it intersects $\{a, c, d\}$, independence is not spotted. However, the path associated with Q_2 by the path-based method is $doc/a/b$ and does not overlap paths associated with U_1, thus independence can be recognized.

The previous examples show that the two methods are not comparable, none of them subsume the other, and both suffer from a lack of precision for different reasons. The schema-based approach fails because the label approximation of element type is far too imprecise or not good enough. The path-based approach fails because it is too imprecise for complex axes (descendant, ancestor, horizontal axes). The approach developed in [22,23] aims at improving precision of static analysis for query-update independence. Because using schema information is often decisive (see case Q_1-U_2) as well as keeping path information (see case Q_2-U_1), this new approach consists in some hybridization of types (approximated by labels) and paths. The key idea is to use a more precise approximation (abstraction) of types for document elements. In [22,23], the notion of element type considered is that of a chain, a sequence of labels describing the path that should be navigated on to reach an element. The static analysis developed in [22,23] relies on a schema analysis radically different from that of [16,31,30,35]. The scenario of the chain-based query-update independence detection is as follows (it assumes available a schema given by a DTD or EDTD):

A set of chains is inferred from the query Q. These chains are divided into 3 kinds:
  (a) used chains, intuitively pointing to document nodes used to evaluate the query Q but not involved directly in constructing the result of Q.
  (b) return chains, intuitively pointing to document nodes potentially useful for constructing the elements in the result of Q.
  (c) element chains, typing new elements constructed by a query (as a matter of fact, this kind of chains is important for the inference of update chains).

A set of chains is inferred from the update U which are called update chain and characterize nodes whose subtree is updated.

Checking query-update independence of Q and U relies on
  (i) checking (no overlapping of) update chains against return chains, and
  (ii) checking (no overlapping of) update chains against used chains

Example 5. Here, the DTD is not explicitly specified: it is the well-known bibliography schema. Let us consider the query Q given by the Xpath *//book[editor]/title* and the update U specified by *for $x in //book insert <author/> into $x*.

For the query Q, *bib.book.editor* is a used chain: elements pointed by this path need to exist although they do not enter in the result of the query. The chain *bib.book.title#* is a return chain because it points to possible result elements.

For the update U, the update chain *bib.book : author* is inferred: it is build using the used chain *bib.book* and the element chain *author*; it is meant to capture that an update (here an insertion) may be executed below elements pointed by the chain *bib.book* and that the new elements inserted have type *author*. Inferring the type of inserted elements is very important to increase the precision of detecting query-update independence. Checking independence for Q and U proceeds to the following tests:

(i) is the return chain *bib.book.title#* a prefix of the update chain *bib.book : author* ? and is the update chain *bib.book : author* a prefix of the return chain *bib.book.title#* ? The answer to both questions here is no.
(ii) is the update chain *bib.book : author* a prefix of the used chain *bib.book.editor* ? Once again the answer to this question is no.
Therefore, independence of Q and U is inferred. Note here that both methods introduced by [16] and [40] fail to detect independence for this example.

The static analysis underlying the query-update independence presented in [22,23] is quite sophisticated. As a matter of fact, in the presence of recursive schemas, avoiding inference of infinite set of chains is a critical and rather intricate problem. An upper bound to the number of chains to be inferred has been determined, in terms of some structural properties of the query and of the update. Extensive tests of the chain-based analysis are conducted in order to validate its precision and also its time consumption.

6   Conclusion

The query optimization method, the update optimization method and the query update independence test that have been introduced in the article are all based on the static analysis of the query or/and update expression(s) and make use of the type information given by the schema of the documents. These methods show that, in the context of XML data management, schemas play an important role. For the projection-based optimization methods, type information is used for filtering fragments of the processed documents that are relevant to the queries or updates. These methods are not based on rewriting as optimization methods based on integrity constraints but still should be considered as semantic optimization. We are currently working on several directions in order to further reduce the size of projected documents mainly by further refining the query or update expression analysis. One direction relies on making use of the kind of elementary updates occurring in a complex update expression to generate a sophisticated projector. Another direction relies on using chain rather than label for specifying the update projector, chain being a better approximation of element type than label. We are also investigating how our projection-based update optimization method can be applied to temporal XML documents in order to ensure both a compact storage of such documents and their efficient management.

Acknowledgement. It is a great pleasure for the author to thank Klaus-Dieter Schewe and Bernhard Thalheim for inviting me to present this work to the Semantics in Data and Knowledge Bases Workshop as a satellite event of ICALP 2010 in Bordeaux. I would like also to express my sincere and warm gratitude to Dario Colazzo for his leading collaboration and friendly support.

This work has been partially supported by the Codex ANR-08-DEFIS-004 project.

References

1. eXist, http://exist.sourceforge.net/
2. Extensible Markup Language (XML) 1.0, 5th Edn., http://www.w3.org/TR/REC-xml/
3. Galax, http://www.galaxquery.org
4. Leo, http://leo.saclay.inria.fr/
5. QizX Free-Engine-3, http://www.xmlmind.com/qizx/free_engine.html
6. QizX/open, http://www.xmlmind.com/qizx/qizxopen.shtml
7. SAX, http://www.saxproject.org/
8. Saxon-ee, http://www.saxonica.com/
9. XQuery 1.0: An XML Query Language, http://www.w3.org/xquery
10. Xquery update facility 1.0, http://www.w3.org/TR/2008/CR-xquery-update-10-20080801
11. Abiteboul, S., Beeri, C.: The power of languages for the manipulation of complex values. VLDB J. 4(4), 727–794 (1995)
12. Abiteboul, S., Buneman, P., Suciu, D.: Data on the Web: From Relations to Semistructured Data and XML. Morgan Kaufmann, San Francisco (1999)
13. Aho, A.V., Sagiv, Y., Ullman, J.D.: Efficient optimization of a class of relational expressions. ACM Trans. Database Syst. 4(4), 435–454 (1979)
14. Arenas, M., Libkin, L.: A normal form for xml documents. ACM Trans. Database Syst. 29, 195–232 (2004)
15. Beeri, C., Vardi, M.Y.: The implication problem for data dependencies. In: Even, S., Kariv, O. (eds.) ICALP 1981. LNCS, vol. 115, Springer, Heidelberg (1981)
16. Benedikt, M., Cheney, J.: Schema-based independence analysis for xml updates. In: VLDB (2009)
17. Benzaken, V., Castagna, G., Colazzo, D., Nguyen, K.: Type-based XML projection. In: VLDB (2006)
18. Berglund, A., Boag, S., Chamberlin, D., Fernández, M., Robie, J., Siméon, J.: XML Path Language (XPath) 2.0 (2005), http://www.w3.org/TR/xpath20
19. Bidoit, N., Colazzo, D.: Testing xml constraint satisfiability. Electr. Notes Theor. Comput. Sci. 174(6), 45–61 (2007)
20. Bidoit, N., Colazzo, D., Malla, N., Sahakyan, M.: Projection based optimization for xml updates. In: 1st International Workshop on Schema Languages for XML, X-Schemas 2009 (2009)
21. Bidoit, N., Colazzo, D., Malla, N., Sahakyan, M.: Projection based optimization for xml updates. In: EDBT (to appear, 2011)
22. Bidoit, N., Colazzo, D., Ulliana, F.: Detecting xml query-update independence. In: Méry, D., Merz, S. (eds.) IFM 2010. LNCS, vol. 6396, Springer, Heidelberg (2010)

23. Bidoit, N., Colazzo, D., Ulliana, F.: Detecting xml query-update independence. In: BDA (2010)
24. Biron, P.V., Malhotra, A.: XML Schema Part 2: Datatypes Second Edition. Technical report, World Wide Web Consortium, W3C Recommendation (October 2004)
25. Buneman, P.: Semistructured data. In: PODS, pp. 117–121 (1997)
26. Buneman, P., Davidson, S.B., Fan, W., Hara, C., Tan, W.-C.: Reasoning about keys for XML. In: Ghelli, G., Grahne, G. (eds.) DBPL 2001. LNCS, vol. 2397, p. 133. Springer, Heidelberg (2002)
27. Buneman, P., Davidson, S.B., Fan, W., Hara, C.S., Tan, W.C.: Keys for xml. Computer Networks 39(5), 473–487 (2002)
28. Buneman, P., Ohori, A.: Polymorphism and type inference in database programming. ACM Trans. Database Syst. 21(1), 30–76 (1996)
29. Cardelli, L.: A semantics of multiple inheritance. Inf. Comput. 76(2/3), 138–164 (1988)
30. Cheney, J.: Flux: functional updates for xml. In: ICFP (2008)
31. Cheney, J.: Regular expression subtyping for XML query and update languages. In: Gairing, M. (ed.) ESOP 2008. LNCS, vol. 4960, pp. 32–47. Springer, Heidelberg (2008)
32. Clark, J., Makoto, M.: Relax NG specification, http://www.oasis-open.org/committees/relax-ng
33. Codd, E.F.: Further normalization of the data base relational model. IBM Research Report, San Jose, California, RJ909 (1971)
34. Codd, E.F.: Relational completeness of data base sublanguages. In: Rustin, R. (ed.) Database Systems, pp. 65–98. Prentice Hall and IBM Research Report RJ 987, San Jose (1972)
35. Colazzo, D., Ghelli, G., Manghi, P., Sartiani, C.: Static analysis for path correctness of XML queries. J. Funct. Program. 16(4-5) (2006)
36. den Bussche, J.V., Gucht, D.V., Vansummeren, S.: A crash course on database queries. In: PODS, pp. 143–154 (2007)
37. den Bussche, J.V., Waller, E.: Polymorphic type inference for the relational algebra. J. Comput. Syst. Sci. 64(3), 694–718 (2002)
38. Fan, W., Libkin, L.: On xml integrity constraints in the presence of dtds. J. ACM 49(3), 368–406 (2002)
39. Fan, W., Siméon, J.: Integrity constraints for xml. J. Comput. Syst. Sci. 66(1), 254–291 (2003)
40. Ghelli, G., Rose, K.H., Siméon, J.: Commutativity analysis for XML updates. ACM Trans. Database Syst. 33(4) (2008)
41. Hors, A.L., Hégaret, P.L., Wood, L., Nicol, G., Robie, J., Champion, M., Byrne, S.: Document object model (dom). Technical report, World Wide Web Consortium, W3C Working Draft (2003)
42. Jelliffe, R.: The Schematron: An XML structure validation language using patterns in trees, http://xml.coverpages.org/schematron.html
43. Klarlund, N., Møller, A., Schwartzbach, M.I.: The dsd schema language. Autom. Softw. Eng. 9(3) (2002)
44. Klarlund, N., Schwentick, T., Suciu, D.: Xml: Model, schemas, types, logics, and queries. In: Logics for Emerging Applications of Databases, pp. 1–41 (2003)
45. Maier, D., Mendelzon, A.O., Sagiv, Y.: Testing implications of data dependencies (abstract). In: SIGMOD Conference, p. 152 (1979)
46. Marian, A., Siméon, J.: Projecting XML documents. In: VLDB 2003(2003)
47. Murata, M., Lee, D., Mani, M.: Taxonomy of xml schema languages using formal language theory. In: Extreme Markup Languages (2001)

48. Popa, L., Deutsch, A., Sahuguet, A., Tannen, V.: A chase too far? In: SIGMOD Conference, pp. 273–284 (2000)
49. Raggett, D.: Assertion Grammar, http://www.w3.org/People/Raggett/dtdgen/Docs/
50. Ramakrishnan, R., Gehrke, J.: Database Management Systems. McGraw-Hill Science/Engineering/Math (2002)
51. Thalheim, B.: Dependencies in Relational Databases. Teubner Verlagsgesellschaft, Stuttgart and Leipnitz (1991)
52. Thompson, H.S., Beech, D., Maloney, M., Mendelsohn, N.: XML Schema Part 1: Structures Second Edition. Technical report, World Wide Web Consortium, W3C Recommendation (October 2004)

Answers that Have Integrity

Hendrik Decker*

Instituto Tecnológico de Informática, Universidad Politécnica de Valencia, Spain

Abstract. Answers to queries in possibly inconsistent databases may not have integrity. We formalize 'has integrity' on the basis of a definition of 'causes'. A cause of an answer is a minimal excerpt of the database that explains why the answer has been given. An answer has integrity if one of its causes does not overlap with any cause of integrity violation.

1 Introduction

We continue the development of 'answers that have integrity' (in short, *AHI*) in databases that may suffer from extant violations of integrity. It has begun in [6], for databases, queries, constraints and answers without negation. In this paper, definitions and results are generalized to be applicable also if there is negation.

Consistent query answering (CQA) [1] is a popular approach to provide useful answers in inconsistent databases. Roughly, CQA defines an answer to be consistent if the answer is true in each minimal repair. Unfortunately, the consistency of answers is not invariant under different notions of minimality.

We elaborate the alternative idea of answers that 'have integrity', i.e, answers that are reasonably correct in the presence of integrity violation. This idea is based on 'causes', i.e., certain extracts of the database that explain why an answer is given, or why a constraint is violated. Intuitively, an answer has integrity if one of its causes does not overlap with any cause of integrity violation.

Arguably, AHI does not suffer from any ambivalence of minimality, nor from several other shortcomings associated to CQA. However, while computing AHI for definite databases and queries is very simple, it seems to be as complex as computing CQA in general.

Apart from some background of database logic, we broach, in Section 2, the only-if halves of predicate completions as a basis for defining causes of negative answers. Section 3 contains the main definitions for characterizing causes. In Section 4, we define and discuss how to compute AHI. In Section 5, we compare AHI to related work. In Section 6, we conclude with an outlook to further work.

2 Preliminaries

In 2.1, we address the foundations of the database logic upon which the remainder of the paper is built. In 2.2, we make explicit an implicit part of the database, viz. ground instances of the only-if halves of predicate definitions, since they may contribute to causes for explaining negative answers.

---

* Supported by FEDER and the Spanish grants TIN2009-14460-C03, TIN2010-17139.

2.1   Background

As a formal framework, we opt for *datalog*. We denote logical consequence by $\models$. We use the abbreviation *iff* for 'if and only if'.

We assume a universal language denoted by $\mathcal{L}$ that contains a finite universal domain $\mathcal{L}^c$ of constant terms over which each attribute variable in each database ranges. W.l.o.g., we represent the elements in $\mathcal{L}^c$ by natural numbers. By overloading, we use $=$ as the identity predicate in $\mathcal{L}$, as the assignment symbol in substitutions of variables with terms, and as meta-level equality. Since ',' is used as the conjunction operator between literals in the body of clauses, we use ';' as the delimiter between elements of sets of clauses.

As in [21], we call each database without any occurrence of negative literals in the body of its clauses a *definite* database, and each database without self-recursive definitions of predicates a *hierarchical* database. As opposed to definite databases, which may contain self-recursive definitions of predicates, hierarchical database clauses may contain negative literals in their body. Unless mentioned otherwise, each database considered in this paper is assumed to be hierarchical. Answers that have integrity in definite databases are studied in [6].

We say that a formula F is a *conjunctive sentence* if F is a universally closed non-empty conjunction of literals. If all literals in F are positive, we also say that F is a *definite sentence*.

For each database D and each conjunctive sentence F, we write $D(F) = true$ and say 'F is *true* in D' if F is a logical consequence of the theory associated to D (e.g., the completion of D, or some standard model theory such as the set of stable models of D). Otherwise, we write $D(F) = false$ and say 'F is *false* in D'.

Let D be a database and L a ground literal such that $D(L) = true$. We say that L is *terminal* in D if the atom of L does not match the head of any clause with non-empty body in D. For instance, $\sim p(1, 2)$ is terminal in $\{p(x, 1) \leftarrow q(x); q(1)\}$. If the predicates in $\mathcal{L}$ are partitioned, as usual, into extensional and intensional ones, then each extensional fact is terminal.

We assume, w.l.o.g., that each query is a conjunctive query, possibly with negative literals, where the predicates in the query are defined by clauses in the database. Similarly, we assume that each integrity constraint (shortly, constraint) is a *denial*, i.e., a clause with empty head and a conjunction of (possibly negative) literals as its body. Each finite set of constraints is called an *integrity theory*.

We assume each clause C to be *range-restricted*, i.e., each variable in C occurs is a positive literal in the body of C.

We do not flatten databases by materializing the definition of predicates or by representing the database by some standard model, since such an unfolding of database clauses with non-empty body may lead to a loss of causal information.

Example 1. The two databases $D_1 = \{p \leftarrow r;\ r;\ s\}$ and $D_2 = \{p \leftarrow s;\ r;\ s\}$ have the same flattened version: $\{p;\ r;\ s\}$. That version, however, does not provide to identify that r is part of the cause of the truth of p in D_1 and s is not, nor that s is part of the cause of the truth of p in D_2 and r is not.

Definition 1. For each database D, let D^+ denote the set of ground instances of clauses in D.

2.2   Only-if Halves

In [6], we have defined causes for positive answers in definite databases. For that, it was sufficient to define a cause very simply as a minimal subset of D^+ of which the answer is a consequence. Now, we are going to deal also with negation.

Since causes are meant to be some sort of explanation, causes of negative answers and positive consequences thereof need to recur on the negative information that is conveyed by the database. Negative consequences of databases usually are justified by some closure axioms. For negative consequences of definite databases, the closed world assumption *CWA* [23] usually is the closure axiom of choice. For each hierarchical database D, the completion $comp(D)$ (which coincides with CWA for definite databases without recursion) is the standard axiomatization for inferring negative consequences from D.

For each predicate p in $\mathcal{L}$, the well-known *iff-completion* (also called *predicate completion* or, in short, *completion*) of p is defined in [5,21].

Example 2. Let $D = \{p(x,1) \leftarrow r(x); \; p(1,y) \leftarrow s(y,z); \; s(1,2); \; s(2,3)\}$. Further, let us assume that p, r and s are the only predicate symbols in $\mathcal{L}$. Then, $comp(D)$ consists of the following iff-completions, each of which is a universally closed sentence with existentially quantified 'local' variables that do not occur in the head of any clause. We omit the universal quantifier prenex for all non-local variables in the completions below, and also the equality theory associated to $comp(D)$ that interprets $=$ as identity.

$$p(x,y) \;\leftrightarrow\; (y=1 \wedge r(x) \;\vee\; x=1 \wedge \exists z(s(y,z)))$$
$$\sim r(x)$$
$$s(x,y) \;\leftrightarrow\; (x=1 \wedge y=2 \;\vee\; x=2 \wedge y=3)$$

Definition 2. Let D be a database, $p(x_1, \ldots, x_n)$ an atom in $\mathcal{L}$, $\underline{p}$ the iff-completion of p in $comp(D)$, n $(n \geq 0)$ the arity of p, θ a (not necessarily ground) substitution of the variables $x_1, \ldots, x_n$ and $A = p(x_1, \ldots, x_n)\theta$.

a) The *iff-completion* $\underline{A}$ of A is obtained by applying θ to the $\forall$-quantified variables in $\underline{p}$.

b) The sentence obtained by replacing $\leftrightarrow$ in $\underline{A}$ with $\rightarrow$ is called the *only-if half* of $\underline{A}$, and A is called the *head* of that sentence.

c) Let D^- denote the set of only-if halves of all ground atoms in $\mathcal{L}$. Assume that D^- is factorized modulo renamings of variables.

For easy reading, we are going to represent elements of D^- in a simplified form, if possible. It is obtained by replacing equations with their truth value and applying common equivalence-preserving laws for the composition of subformulas with *true* or *false*. Elements of D^- the simplification of which is *true* are omitted.

Example 3. For D as in Example 2, the only-if half of $\underline{p}$ is
$$p(x, y) \rightarrow (y = 1 \wedge r(x) \vee x = 1 \wedge \exists z(s(y, z))).$$
Its instance
$$p(1, 1) \rightarrow (1 = 1 \wedge r(1) \vee 1 = 1 \wedge \exists z(s(1, z))),$$
obtained by the substitution $\{x = 1, y = 1\}$, is obviously equivalent to
$$p(1, 1) \rightarrow (true \wedge r(1) \vee true \wedge \exists z(s(1, z)))$$
which can be further simplified to
$$p(1, 1) \rightarrow (r(1) \vee \exists z(s(1, z))).$$
Similarly, the instance
$$p(2, 3) \rightarrow (3 = 1 \wedge r(2) \vee 2 = 1 \wedge \exists z(s(3, z)))$$
obtained by the substitution $\{x = 2, y = 3\}$ of x and y is equivalent to
$$p(2, 3) \rightarrow (false \wedge r(2) \vee false \wedge \exists z(s(3, z)))$$
which simplifies to
$$p(2, 3) \rightarrow false$$
which finally is equivalent to
$$\sim p(2, 3).$$
Similarly, the instance $s(2, 3) \rightarrow (2 = 1 \wedge 3 = 2 \vee 2 = 2 \wedge 3 = 3)$ of the only-if half
of the completion of s first simplifies to $s(2, 3) \rightarrow (false \wedge false \vee true \wedge true)$,
which is equivalent to $s(2, 3) \rightarrow true$, which is equivalent to *true*.

3   Excerpts, Explanation Bases, Causes

We develop a formal notion of our intuition of 'cause' in three steps.

First, we define an 'excerpt' of a database D to consist of a 'positive' and a
'negative excerpt', i.e., a subset of D^+ (Definition 1) and, resp., a subset of D^-
(Definition 2c).

Second, we define, for each database D and each sentence F that is *true* in
D, an 'explanation base' of F in D to be an excerpt E of D such that F is a
logical consequence of E.

Third, we define a 'cause' of F in D to be a minimal explanation base of F
in D. Thus, a cause is an explanation base that is free of superfluous elements.

Similarly, we define the causes of an answer substitution θ of the variables
in a query $\leftarrow B$ in D to be the causes of $\forall(B\theta)$, i.e., the universal closure of
$B\theta$, in D, and the causes of the violation of a denial constraint $\leftarrow B$ as the
causes of the answer *yes* (i.e., the identity substitution) to the query $\leftarrow$ *violated*
in $D \cup \{violated \leftarrow B\}$, where *violated* is a distinguished 0-ary predicate that does
not occur in D.

In section 4, we will then define that an answer to a query in a database
D 'has integrity' if it has a cause that does not overlap with any cause of the
violation of any constraint in D.

3.1   Excerpts

Definition 3.   Let D be a database and P a set of ground sentences. P is called a *positive excerpt* of D if $P \subseteq D^+$.

The following result entails that the truth of a definite sentence in a positive excerpt P of a definite database cannot be non-monotonically changed by adding possibly non-definite clauses to P.

Theorem 1.   For each positive excerpt P of some database and each conjunctive sentence F such that $P \models F$, F is *true* in each database of which P is a positive excerpt.

To prove Theorem 1, it is useful to observe that the premise $P \models F$ entails that F necessarily is a definite sentence and that there is a definite database P' such that $P' \subseteq P$ and $P'(F) = true$. Then, Theorem 1 is a direct consequence of Definition 3 and the monotonicity of definite databases.

As soon as an excerpt is supposed to capture not only positive, but also negative consequences of some database D, the latter need to be made explicit. That motivates Definition 4, below, which recurs on ground only-if halves in D^-.

Definition 4.   Let D be a database and N a set of ground sentences. N is called a *negative excerpt* of D if $N \subseteq D^-$.

As in Example 2, we assume that the usual equality theory of $comp(D)$ is associated by default to each negative excerpt.

Now, we are in the position to formalize our intuition of 'excerpt'.

Definition 5.   Let D be a database, P a positive excerpt of D and N a negative excerpt of D. Then, the tuple $E = (P, N)$ is called an *excerpt* of D. P is called the *positive part*, and N the *negative part* of E. For each excerpt E, we denote its positive part by E^+, its negative part by E^-, and the union of E^+ and E^- by $\hat{E}$. We say that two excerpts E, E' *overlap* if $\hat{E} \cap \hat{E}' \neq \emptyset$.

The generalization of Theorem 1 below follows from Definitions 3 and 5.

Theorem 2.   For each excerpt E of some database and each conjunctive sentence F such that $\hat{E} \models F$, F is *true* in each database of which E is an excerpt.

A partial order $\leq$ is defined in a natural way for excerpts, as follows.

Definition 6.   Let D be a database and $E = (P, N)$, $E' = (P', N')$ be two excerpts of D. We define that $E \leq E'$ if $\hat{E} \subseteq \hat{E}'$, i.e., if $P \subseteq P'$ and $N \subseteq N'$. We write $E < E'$ and say E *is smaller than* E' if $E \leq E'$ and not $E' \leq E$ holds.

3.2   Explanation Bases

An 'explanation base' E of the truth of a conjunctive sentence F (shortly, an 'explanation base' of F) in a database D is going to be defined as an excerpt E of D such that F is a logical consequence of $\hat{E}$. For definite databases and definite conjunctive sentences, a similar but simpler definition has been presented in [6].

Example 4. Let $D = \{p \leftarrow q; \, p \leftarrow r; \, q; \, r; \, s\}$. Clearly, $P_1 = \{p \leftarrow q; \, q\}$ is a positive excerpt of D that serves to explain why p is *true* in D. Also $P_2 = \{p \leftarrow r; \, r\}$ is a positive excerpt of D that explains why p is *true* in D.

It is easy to see that no negative excerpts are needed in order to explain positive consequences of any definite database D; positive excerpts of D are sufficient, as illustrated in Example 4. However, for causally explaining negative consequences or, more generally, consequences of databases with negation in the body of clauses, positive excerpts are not sufficient.

Indeed, it is not possible to infer any negative logical consequence, such as sentences represented by negative literals or denials, from any positive excerpt. Of course, negative consequences can be inferred from the completion of each positive excerpt, but not each such consequence is necessarily *true* in the given database. For instance, all ground negative literals are *true* in the empty database, which, by Definition 8, is a positive excerpt of each database D. Moreover, Example 5 below shows that the invariance results expressed in Theorems 1 and 2 cease to hold if negation is allowed in D or F.

Example 5. Consider again $D = \{p \leftarrow q; \, p \leftarrow r; \, q; \, r; \, s\}$ and P_i $(i = 1, 2)$ as in example 4. While each definite sentence that is *true* in P_i is also *true* in each database D' of which P_i is a positive excerpt, negative consequences of P_i do not necessarily hold in each such D'. For instance, the conjunctive sentence $s \wedge \sim t$ is *true* in D and each P_i, but is *false* in $D' = D \cup \{t\}$, although each P_i is a positive excerpt also of D'. Hence, P_i is not sufficient for explaining p.

The circumstance that positive excerpts are insufficient in general for explaining negative consequences of hierarchical databases can be seen by an even simpler example.

Example 6. It is not possible to characterize a cause of $\sim q$ in $D = \{p\}$ by any subset of D. In particular, none of the positive excerpts $\emptyset$ and $\{p\}$ of D may explain $\sim q$ in D since each of them is also a positive excerpt of $D' = D \cup \{q\}$, while the truth value of $\sim q$ is not the same in D and D'.

In the preceding example, the absence of q in D must be captured explicitly for explaining why $\sim q$ is *true* in D. Thus, each explanation base is going to consist of a positive and a negative excerpt, as defined subsequently.

Definition 7. Let D be a database, E an excerpt of D, and F a conjunctive sentence such that $D(F) = true$. E is called an *explanation base* of F in D if $\hat{E} \models F$.

Example 7

a) Let $D = \{p \leftarrow q, s; \, q; \, r\}$ and $F = \sim p$. Clearly, $(\emptyset, \{p \rightarrow q, s; \, \sim s\})$ is an explanation base of F in D. However, neither $E_1 = (\{p \leftarrow q, s\}, \{\sim s\})$ nor $E_2 = (\{p \leftarrow q, s; \, q\}, \{\sim s\})$ is an explanation base of F in D, since F is not a logical consequence of $\hat{E}_i$ $(i = 1, 2)$. Note that both excerpts E_i of D are also excerpts of $D' = D \cup \{p \leftarrow r\}$, but $D'(F) = false$.

b) Let $D = \{p(x) \leftarrow q(x), \sim r(x);\ q(1);\ q(2);\ r(3)\}$. Then, $D(p(1)) = true$, but $p(1)$ is not explainable by any positive excerpt of D alone, since each subset of D^+ is also a positive excerpt of $D' = \{p(x) \leftarrow q(x), \sim r(x);\ q(1);\ q(2);\ r(1)\}$, but $D'(p(1)) = false$. However, $p(1)$ can be explained by the excerpt $E = (\{p(1) \leftarrow q(1), \sim r(1);\ q(1)\}, \{\sim r(1)\})$ of D, since $\hat{E} \models p(1)$, and $p(1)$ is indeed $true$ in each database D' of which E is an excerpt.

The result below is an immediate consequence of Definition 7 and Theorem 2.

Theorem 3. For each database D, each conjunctive sentence F, each explanation base E of F in D, and each database D' of which E is an excerpt, it follows that $D'(F) = true$.

Theorem 3 expresses that the truth of each conjunctive sentence F in D that is explained by some explanation base of F in D is independent of any clause that is present or absent in D but not captured by E. Note that this result holds although database negation is non-monotonic. Also the consequences of Definition 7 in Proposition 1, below, hold in spite of non-monotonicity.

Proposition 1. Let D be a database, F a conjunctive sentence such that $D(F) = true$, and E an explanation base of F in D. Then, the following holds.
a) $E^+(F) = true$.
b) For each literal L that is terminal in D, $(\{L\}, \emptyset)$ is the only explanation base of L in D if L is positive, and $(\emptyset, \{L\})$ is the only explanation base of L in D if L is negative.
c) For each excerpt E' of D such that $E \leq E'$, E' is an explanation base of F in D.

Part a of Proposition 1 says that F is $true$ in the positive part of each explanation base E of F in D. However, as we have seen in examples 6 and 7b, F is not necessarily $true$ of each database of which E^+ is a positive excerpt. Yet, F is $true$ of each database of which E is an excerpt, according to Theorem 3. Part b says that each ground literal with extensional predicate explains itself. Part c says that each excerpt which contains an explanation base of F in D also is an explanation base of F in D. Thus, each explanation base is sufficient for inferring the explained sentence from it, but its truth does not necessarily depend on each element in a given explanation base, in general. Such a condition of necessity is going to be added in the definition of causes, in 3.3.

3.3 Causes

As shown by Proposition 1c, there may be superfluous literals in an explanation base, i.e., the presence or absence of such literals in an explanation base of some formula F in some database D is irrelevant for explaining the truth of F in D.

Example 8. Clearly, $(\{p(1) \leftarrow r(1, 2);\ r(1, 2);\ s(3)\}, \emptyset)$ is an explanation base of $p(1)$ in $D = \{p(x) \leftarrow r(x, y);\ r(1, 1);\ r(1, 2);\ r(2, 2);\ s(3)\}$, but $s(3)$ is superfluous for explaining $p(1)$ in D.

Thus, a cause of F in D is going to be defined as a minimal explanation base, without irrelevant elements, as follows.

Definition 8. For each database D, each conjunctive sentence F and each explanation base E of F in D, E is called a *cause* of F in D if there is no explanation base of F in D that is smaller than E.

Thus, a cause of a sentence F in a database D is an explanation base E of F in D without superfluous clauses, i.e., it is not possible to explain F with any extract obtained by dropping any element from E.

In Definitions 9–11, Definition 8 is extended to positive and negative answers, constraint violation and satisfaction, and to integrity violation and satisfaction.

Definition 9. Let D be a database, B a conjunction of literals, θ a substitution of the variables in B such that $\forall (B\theta) = true$, and E a cause of $\forall (B\theta)$ in D.

a) If $\leftarrow B$ is a query, we say: E is a *cause of the answer θ to $\leftarrow B$ in D.*

b) If $\leftarrow B$ is a constraint, we say: E is a *cause of the violation* of $\leftarrow B$ in D.

Definition 10. Let D be a database, B a conjunction of literals, and E a cause of the answer *yes* (i.e., the identity substitution) to the query $\leftarrow \sim answer$ in $D \cup \{answer \leftarrow B\}$, where *answer* be a 0-ary predicate not occurring in D.

a) If $\leftarrow B$ is a query, we say: E is a *cause of the answer no* to $\leftarrow B$ in D.

b) If $\leftarrow B$ is a constraint, we say: E is a *cause of the satisfaction* of $\leftarrow B$ in D.

The following results are immediate consequences of Definitions 9 and 10.

Proposition 2. Let D be a database, E an excerpt of D, A a ground atom, B a conjunction of literals, θ a substitution, and *answer* a predicate that does not occur in D.

a) E is a cause of the answer *yes* (resp., *no*) to $\leftarrow A$ in D iff E is a cause of the answer *no* (resp., *yes*) to $\leftarrow \sim A$ in D.

b) E is a cause of the answer θ to $\leftarrow B$ in D iff $(E^+ \cup \{answer \leftarrow B\theta\gamma \mid \gamma$ is a substitution, $B\theta\gamma$ is ground$\}, E^-)$ is a cause of the answer *yes* to $\leftarrow answer$ in $D \cup \{answer \leftarrow B\}$.

c) If $\leftarrow B$ is a query, then E is a cause of the answer *no* to $\leftarrow B$ in D iff $(E^+, E^- \cup \{answer \rightarrow \exists B\})$ is a cause of $\sim answer$ in $D \cup \{answer \leftarrow B\}$.

d) If $\leftarrow B$ is a constraint, then E is a cause of the satisfaction of $\leftarrow B$ in D iff $(E^+, E^- \cup \{answer \rightarrow \exists B\})$ is a cause of $\sim answer$ in $D \cup \{answer \leftarrow B\}$.

Definition 11. Let D be a database, $IC = \{I_1, \ldots, I_n\}$ an integrity theory containing n constraints of the form $I_i = \leftarrow B_i$ ($1 \leq i \leq n$, $n > 0$), and E a cause of the answer *no* (resp., *yes*) to $\leftarrow \sim answer$ in $D \cup \{answer \leftarrow B_i \mid 1 \leq i \leq n\}$, where *answer* be a 0-ary predicate not occurring in D. Then, we say that E is a *cause of the violation of integrity* (resp., a *cause of the satisfaction of integrity*) in (D, IC), or simply, a *cause of the violation* (resp., *satisfaction*) of IC in D.

Below, Examples $9a, b$ illustrate Definitions 8 and $9a$. Examples $9c, d$ illustrate Definition $9b$. Examples $9e, f$ illustrate Definition $10a$. Examples $9g–i$ illustrate Definition $10b$; $9i$ also is an example for Definition 11. Finally, Example $9j$ shows that causes of the violation of integrity (Definition 11) may not be composed of the causes of the violation of constraints in that theory (Definition $9b$).

Example 9

a) Let $D = \{p \leftarrow q(1, 2); \ q(2, y) \leftarrow r(y); \ r(1)\}$. The only cause of $\sim p$ in D, as well as of the answer *yes* to $\leftarrow \sim p$ in D, is $(\emptyset, \ \{p \rightarrow q(1, 2); \ \sim q(1, 2)\})$.

b) Let $D = \{p \leftarrow \sim q; \ q \leftarrow \sim r; \ q \leftarrow \sim s\}$. The two causes of $\sim p$ and of the answer *yes* to $\leftarrow \sim p$ in D are $(\{q \leftarrow \sim r\}, \{p \rightarrow \sim q; \ \sim r\})$ and $(\{q \leftarrow \sim s\}, \{p \rightarrow \sim q; \ \sim s\})$.

c) Let $D = \{p \leftarrow q; \ p \leftarrow \sim q\}$ and $I = \ \leftarrow p$. The two causes of the violation of I in D are $(\{p \leftarrow \sim q\}, \{\sim q\})$ and $(D, \emptyset)$.

d) Let $D = \{p(x) \leftarrow r(x); r(1)\}$ and $I = \exists x (r(x) \wedge \sim p(x))$ be a constraint. Clearly, $D(I) = false$ (in fact, I is violated in each database that contains $p(x) \leftarrow r(x)$). A denial form of I is $\leftarrow violated$, where *violated* is defined by $\{violated \leftarrow \sim q; \ q \leftarrow r(x), \sim p(x)\}$ (q is a fresh 0-ary predicate). Thus, the causes of the violation of I in D are the causes of *violated* in $D' = D \cup \{violated \leftarrow \sim q; \ q \leftarrow r(x), \sim p(x)\}$. Thus, for each $\mathcal{K} \subseteq \mathcal{L}^c$ such that $1 \in \mathcal{K}$, a cause of *violated* in D' is given by $(\{violated \leftarrow \sim q\} \cup \{p(i) \leftarrow r(i) \mid i \in \mathcal{K}\}, \{q \rightarrow \exists x (r(x) \wedge \sim p(x))\} \cup \{\sim r(i) \mid i \notin \mathcal{K}\})$. There are no other causes of *violated* in D'.

e) Let $D = \{p \leftarrow q(1, x); \ q(2, y) \leftarrow r(y); \ r(1)\}$. The only cause of the answer *no* to the query $\leftarrow p$ in D is $(\emptyset, \ \{p \rightarrow q(1, i) \mid i \in \mathcal{L}^c\} \cup \{\sim q(1, i) \mid i \in \mathcal{L}^c\})$.

f) Let $D = \{p \leftarrow r(x), s(x); r(1); s(2)\}$. Each cause E of the answer *no* to $\leftarrow p$ in D contains the excerpt $E_0 = (\emptyset, \{p \rightarrow \exists x (r(x), s(x)); \sim s(1); \sim r(2)\})$ of D. Each E also contains, for each $i \in \mathcal{L}^c$, $i > 2$, either $\sim r(i)$ or $\sim s(i)$, and nothing else.

g) Let $D = \{p \leftarrow q; \ p \leftarrow \sim q; \ q\}$ and $I = \ \leftarrow \sim p$. The two causes of the satisfaction of I in D (i.e., of p in D) are $(\{p \leftarrow q; \ q\}, \emptyset)$ and $(\{p \leftarrow q; \ p \leftarrow \sim q\}, \emptyset)$.

h) Let $D = \{r(1), \ r(3), \ s(2), \ s(4)\}$ and $I = \ \leftarrow r(x), s(x)$ a constraint. Depending on the extent of $\mathcal{L}^c$, there may be many causes of the satisfaction of I in D. The positive part of each such cause is empty, and each contains the excerpt $(\emptyset, \{violated \rightarrow \exists x (r(x), s(x))\} \cup \{\sim s(1), \sim s(3), \sim r(2), \sim r(4)\})$ of $D \cup \{violated \leftarrow r(x), s(x)\}$. (Recall that the cause of the satisfaction of I in D is the cause of $\sim violated$ in $D \cup \{violated \leftarrow r(x), s(x)\}$.) Moreover, the negative part of each cause of the satisfaction of I in D contains, for each $i > 4$ in $\mathcal{L}^c$, either $\sim r(i)$ or $\sim s(i)$, and no other element.

i) Let $D = \{p \leftarrow q, \sim q\}$, $I_1 = \ \leftarrow p$ and $I_2 = \ \leftarrow \sim p$. The only cause of the satisfaction of I_1 as well as of the violation of I_2 in D is $(\emptyset, \{p \rightarrow q, \sim q\})$, which also is the only cause of the violation of $IC = \{I_1, I_2\}$ in D.

j) Let $D = \{r(1, 1); \ s(1)\}$, $I_1 = \ \leftarrow r(x, x)$, $I_2 = \ \leftarrow r(x, y), s(y)$ and $IC = \{I_1; I_2\}$. The only cause of the violation of IC in D is $(\{r(1, 1)\}, \emptyset)$, which is smaller than the single cause $(D, \emptyset)$ of the violation of I_2 in D.

Note that examples $9\,c, g,\ i$ feature constraints and an integrity theory that, together with the rules in the database, are either tautological (i.e., always satisfied) or contradictory (i.e., always violated), no matter which facts are in the database. Interestingly, some of the causes in the mentioned examples are not devoid of database facts, as one could suspect, since the truth of tautological satisfaction and the falsity of contradictory violation is independent of the presence or absence of facts in the database. The use of facts for explaining the violation of contradictory constraints also means that our concept of causes is applicable even in databases with unsatisfiable integrity theories, as opposed to CQA.

4   Defining and Computing AHI

In 4.1, we define that an answer to a query in a database D 'has integrity' if one of its causes does not overlap with any cause of the violation of integrity in D. In 4.2, we show how to compute explanation bases and causes. In 4.3, we address the problem of computing sufficiently many causes for checking if answers have integrity.

4.1   Defining AHI

Definition 12. Let D be a database, IC an integrity theory, $\leftarrow B$ a query and α an answer to $\leftarrow B$ in D. (i.e., α is either a substitution or the answer no).

a) We say that α *has weak integrity* in (D, IC) if there is a cause of the answer in D that does not overlap with any cause of the violation of IC in D.

b) We say that α *has strong integrity* if there is a cause of the answer in D that does not overlap with any cause of the violation of any constraint in IC in D.

Example 10. Consider D as in Example $9f$ and let $\leftarrow \sim p$ be a constraint. According to Proposition 2, the causes of its violation in D are the same as the causes of the answer no to the query $\leftarrow p$. From Definition 12, it follows that the answers $x = 1$ and $x = 2$ to the queries $\leftarrow r(x)$ and, resp., $\leftarrow s(x)$ both have strong integrity, while the answer no to $\leftarrow p$ does not even have weak integrity.

It is easy to see that an answer has weak integrity if it has strong integrity. Thus, we may say that an answer *does not have integrity* if it does not have weak integrity. However, weak and strong integrity of answers according to Definition 12 are not equivalent, as shown by the following example.

Example 11. Let $D = \{r(1,1);\ s(1)\}$, $IC = \{\leftarrow r(x,x);\ \leftarrow r(x,y), s(y)\}$. The answer $x = 1$ to the query $\leftarrow s(x)$ in D has weak integrity, since its only cause $(\{s(1)\}, \emptyset)$ does not overlap with the only cause $(\{r(1,1)\}, \emptyset)$ of the violation of IC in D. However, it does not have strong integrity, since $(\{s(1)\}, \emptyset)$ overlaps with the cause $(\{r(1,1);\ s(1)\}, \emptyset)$ of the violation of the constraint $\leftarrow r(x,y), s(y)$. The answer $\{x=1, y=1\}$ to $\leftarrow r(x,y)$ in D does not have integrity, since its only cause $(\{r(1,1)\}, \emptyset)$ overlaps with some cause of the violation of IC in D (in fact, it is identical with the only cause of the violation of IC in D).

Example 11 illustrates the differentiation of weak and strong integrity in Definition 12. In fact, a distinction between different grades of integrity is desirable, since, for instance, the violation of $\leftarrow r(x, y), s(y)$, which is caused, among others, by the presence of $s(1)$ in D, may cast some doubt on the integrity of the answer $x = 1$ to the query $\leftarrow s(x)$ in D. Even more refined differentiations of the integrity of answers are possible, as shown in [6] for definite databases and conjunctive queries without negative literals.

4.2   Computing Explanations and Causes

As seen in [6], SLD resolution [18,21] provides an easy way to compute causes of positive answers and integrity violation of definite queries and denials in definite databases. Each cause of each answer corresponds to a refutation R that computes the answer: input clauses of R, instantiated with the substitution computed by R, are the elements of the cause. Hence, AHI can be computed by comparing causes drawn from refutations with causes of integrity violation. If the latter have been computed ahead of query time, then checking for overlaps can already be done while the answer is computed.

Similarly, for each SLDNF refutation R and each finitely failed SLDNF tree T of some query in a database, an explanation for the answer computed by R or, resp., T can be obtained as described below in Definition 14. To prepare this definition, we first recall some basic SLDNF issues from [21] and ask the reader to agree on some denotations.

Let D be a database and $\leftarrow B$ a query. An *SLDNF computation* of $D \cup \{\leftarrow B\}$ is either an SLDNF refutation or a finitely failed tree of $D \cup \{\leftarrow B\}$. Each SLDNF computation involves one top-rank computation and possibly several subsidiary computations of lower rank, spawned by the selection of ground negative literals in goals of derivations.

It is easy to see that no finitely failed tree of rank n-1 that is subsidiary to some finitely failed tree T of rank n could contribute anything to explain the answer no computed by T. Thus, such subsidiary trees are ignored in Definition 13. It characterizes the set of computations involved in an SLDNF computation S that contribute to an explanation of the answer to the root of S.

Definition 13.   Let S be an SLDNF computation of rank n $(n \geq 0)$.

a) The set S_r of *explanatory refutations* of S consists of each refutation R of rank k involved in S such that either $k = n$ and $R = S$, or $k < n$ and R is subsidiary to a tree in S_t of rank $k + 1$.

b)   The set S_t of *explanatory trees* of S consists of each finitely failed tree T of rank k involved in S such that either $k = n$ and $T = S$, or $k < n$ and T is subsidiary to a refutation in S_r of rank $k + 1$.

Note that the mutual recursion of parts a and b in Definition 13 does not pose any problem since D is hierarchical, i.e., the rank of each computation is bounded by the rank of the top-rank computation, and the rank of each subsidiary computation decreases iteratively until the lowest rank without subsidiary inferences is reached.

An SLDNF computation S is called *fair* if, in each tree $T \in S_t$ and each goal G in T, one of the most recently introduced literals is selected in G.

For each refutation R, let θ_R denote the substitution computed by R. The projection of θ_R to the variables in the root of R is the *computed answer* of R. For each database D, each query $\leftarrow B$ and each finitely failed tree T of $D \cup \{\leftarrow B\}$, the *computed answer* of T is *no*.

For each clause C, each only-if half H and each substitution θ, let $C\theta$, resp., $H\theta$ denote the formula obtained by applying θ to the $\forall$-quantified variables in C or, resp., H. For each only-if half H, let $h(H)$ denote the head of H.

Now, we are in the position to define computed explanations.

Definition 14. For each SLDNF computation S, the *computed explanation* E_S of S consists of

$$E_S^+ = \{C\theta_R \mid C \in D,\ R \in S_r,\ C \text{ is input clause in } R\}$$

and

$$E_S^- = \{H\gamma \mid H\gamma \in D^-,\ \gamma \text{ is a ground substitution,}$$
$$h(H) \text{ is selected in some node of some tree in } S_t\}.$$

Thus, E_S^+ is obtained by instantiating the positive input clauses of each refutation $R \in S_r$ with θ_R. E_S^- is obtained by collecting the only-if-halves of all ground instances of each positive literal selected in any node of any tree in S_t.

Example 12. Let $D = \{p(x) \leftarrow q(x,x);\ q(1,2);\ q(2,3)\}$. The answer *no* to the query $\leftarrow p(x)$ is computed by a finitely failed tree consisting of a single branch rooted at $\leftarrow p(x)$, which is reduced to the goal $\leftarrow q(x,x)$, which fails. The only-if halves of the two selected positive literals in the tree are $p(x) \rightarrow q(x,x)$ and $q(x,x) \rightarrow (x{=}1 \wedge x{=}2 \vee x{=}2 \wedge x{=}3)$. The latter obviously is equivalent to $\sim q(x,x)$. Thus, $(\emptyset,\ \{p(i) \rightarrow q(i,i) \mid i \in \mathcal{L}^c\} \cup \{\sim q(i,i) \mid i \in \mathcal{L}^c\})$ is the computed explanation of the tree, which in fact is also a cause of $\sim p(x)$ in D.

Theorem 4 is easily inferred from Definition 14.

Theorem 4. For each database D, each query $\leftarrow B$ and each SLDNF computation S of $D \cup \{\leftarrow B\}$, the computed explanation of S is an explanation base of the answer computed by S. If $S_t = \emptyset$, then the computed explanation of S is a cause of the answer computed by S.

The following example illustrates that explanations computed by finitely failed SLDNF trees are not necessarily causes, since they may not be minimal explanation bases.

Example 13. Let $D = \{p \leftarrow q, r;\ r \leftarrow s\}$. Depending on the selection function, there are three SLDNF trees of $D \cup \{\leftarrow p\}$. In each, the goal $\leftarrow q, r$ is derived from the root. Then, if q is selected, the computation terminates with failure. If, instead, r is selected, the derived goal $\leftarrow q, s$ may fail in two ways, after selecting either q or s. Hence, depending on the selection, precisely one of the following three explanation bases $(\emptyset,\ \{p \rightarrow q \wedge r;\ \sim q\})$, $(\emptyset,\ \{p \rightarrow q \wedge r;\ r \rightarrow s;\ \sim q\})$, $(\emptyset,\ \{p \rightarrow q \wedge r;\ r \rightarrow s;\ \sim s\})$ can be drawn from the respective SLDNF tree. Only the first and the last of these explanation bases are causes of the answer *no* to the query $\leftarrow p$ in D, while the middle one is not because it properly contains the first one and thus is not minimal.

If, in Example 13, a fair selection policy is employed, the computation of a non-minimal explanation is avoided. However, fair selection alone is not enough, in general.

Example 14. Let $D = \{p \leftarrow q(x), r;\ q(1)\}$. Fair left-to-right selection computes the explanation $(\emptyset,\ \{p \to q(i) \wedge r \mid i \in \mathcal{L}^c\} \cup \{\sim q(i) \mid i \neq 1\} \cup \{\sim r\})$ of the answer *no* to $\leftarrow p$ in D, in which each $\sim q(i)$ is superfluous.

Thus, each explanation E computed by a SLDNF computation must eventually be minimized, by checking if any proper subset of E satisfies Definition 8. Also, selection strategies such as those proposed in [9] can be used to obtain finitely failed trees with minimal explanations.

4.3   Computing Causes for AHI

As stated by Theorem 4, each finitely failed SLDNF tree computes a single explanation base, from which a cause for explaining its root can be drawn. However, Definition 12 entails that *all* causes of violations may be needed for deciding if the answer *no* to a given query has integrity or not. Thus, SLDNF computations may be incomplete for computing AHI. That is illustrated in the following continuation of Example 13.

Example 15. Depending on whether q or r is selected in the goal $\leftarrow q, r$, the cause drawn from a fair finitely failed SLDNF tree of $D \cup \{\leftarrow p\}$ is either $E_1 = (\emptyset, \{p \to q \wedge r;\ \sim q\}$ or $E_2 = (\emptyset, \{p \to q \wedge r;\ r \to s;\ \sim s\}$. Now, let $\leftarrow \sim q$ be a constraint. Clearly, the cause $(\emptyset, \{\sim q\})$ of its violation in D overlaps with E_1 but not with E_2. Hence, each SLDNF computation of $D \cup \{\leftarrow p\}$ that selects literals from left to right fails to detect that the answer *no* to $\leftarrow p$ in D has integrity.

The incompleteness of SLDNF for computing all minimal explanations of answers had already been identified in [9]. A solution similar to that in [9] can be applied for attaining completeness. Essentially, it consists in fairly selecting and trying to resolve not just one, but several literals in each goal derived from the root, such that several finitely failed trees are obtained. In Example 15, for instance, both q and r have to be selected and processed for obtaining two finitely failed SLDNF trees, from which the two causes E_1 and E_2 can be drawn.

At worst, each fairly selectable literal in each goal of an explanatory finitely failed SLDNF tree may have to be selected and attempted to be resolved, when aiming to draw sufficiently many causes from SLDNF computations, for computing AHI. Thus, the number of explanatory finitely failed trees to be built may grow linearly with the number of selectable literals, polynomially with the rank of computations and exponentially with the depth of explanatory finitely failed trees. This indicates a worst case complexity of computing AHI like that of CQA.

Example 16, a continuation of Example $9f$, shows that not each cause can be drawn from the set of explanatory SLDNF computations obtained by selecting and resolving (if possible) each literal in the goals of explanatory finitely failed trees.

Example 16. Clearly, two SLDNF trees are built when selecting and resolving both $r(x)$ and $s(x)$ in the goal $\leftarrow r(x), s(x)$ derived from $\leftarrow p$. Using input clauses $r(1)$ or, resp., $s(2)$, the respective resolvents $\leftarrow s(1)$ and $\leftarrow r(2)$ are derived. Each of them fails when selected and processed, and so does the respective tree. From the two trees, $E_1 = (\emptyset, \{p \rightarrow \exists x(r(x), s(x))\} \cup \{\sim r(i) \mid i \in \mathcal{L}^c, i \neq 1\} \cup \{\sim s(1)\})$ and, resp., $E_2 = (\emptyset, \{p \rightarrow \exists x(r(x), s(x))\} \cup \{\sim s(i) \mid i \in \mathcal{L}^c, i \neq 2\} \cup \{\sim r(2)\})$ can be drawn as a cause of the answer *no* of $D \cup \{\leftarrow p\}$.

Depending on $\mathcal{L}^c$, many more causes of that answer may exist. For instance, $E = (\emptyset, \{p \rightarrow \exists x(r(x), s(x))\} \cup \{\sim r(i) \mid i \in \mathcal{L}^c, i \notin \{1; 3\}\} \cup \{\sim s(1); \sim s(3)\})$ cannot be drawn from any of the two trees above, according to Definition 13. However, E_1 and E_2 are sufficient for determining if the computed answer has integrity or not, since each possible overlap with any cause of the answer *no* to $\leftarrow p$ in D contains at least one of the elements in $\hat{E}_1 \cup \hat{E}_2$.

For instance, consider the constraint $I = \leftarrow \sim r(3)$. The cause of its violation in D is $(\emptyset, \{\sim r(3)\})$. That overlaps with E_1, but not with E_2. Hence, the two trees of $D \cup \{\leftarrow p\}$ obtained as described above yield that the answer *no* to $\leftarrow p$ has integrity in $(D, \{I\})$.

The preceding example illustrates that the number of causes for explaining an answer may far exceed the number of causes that can be drawn from SLDNF computations, even if not just one, but several finitely failed trees are built for obtaining sufficiently many causes of negative answers. Nevertheless, the following lemma can be shown, by induction on the rank of computations. The symbol α below may either stand for some answer substitution or the answer *no*. In words, the lemma states that each element in each cause is contained in some cause drawn from a computed explanation.

Lemma. For each database D, each query $\leftarrow B$, each answer α to $\leftarrow B$ in D, each cause E of α and each $e \in \hat{E}$, there is an SLDNF computation S of $D \cup \{\leftarrow B\}$ with computed answer α such that $e \in \hat{E}'$, where $\hat{E}'$ is a cause drawn from $\hat{E}_S$.

From that, the subsequent result about the soundness and completeness of computing AHI with SLDNF can be inferred.

Theorem 5. Let D be a database, IC an integrity theory, $\leftarrow B$ a query, and α an answer to $\leftarrow B$ in D.

a) α has weak integrity iff there is an SLDNF computation S of $D \cup \{\leftarrow B\}$ with computed answer α and a cause E of α drawn from S that does not overlap with any cause drawn from any SLDNF computation of the violation of IC in D.

b) α has strong integrity iff there is an SLDNF computation S of $D \cup \{\leftarrow B\}$ with computed answer α and a cause E of α drawn from S that does not overlap with any cause drawn from any SLDNF computation of the violation of any constraint $I \in IC$ in D.

5 Related Work

In 5.1, we take first steps of comparing AHI with CQA. In 5.2, we relate belief revision, knowledge assimilation and abduction to AHI. In 5.3, we address other related work.

5.1 AHI vs. CQA

There is yet no comprehensive analysis of commonalities and differences between AHI and CQA. However, each of the following paragraphs identifies a point in favour of answers that have integrity.

The simplicity of the basic definitions of AHI appears to be on a par with the simplicity of the basic definitions of CQA. However, the minimality of explanation bases required in Definition 8 does not suffer from the ambivalence of the minimality of repairs in CQA.

As seen in 4.1, Definition 12 provides for a differentiation of various degrees of consistency. Such a differentiation is not provided by CQA. For instance, recall that, in Example 11, the answer $x = 1$ to the query $\leftarrow s(x)$ in D has weak but not strong integrity. According to CQA, the same answer also is a consistent answer to the same query, since the only minimal repair of the violation of IC is $D' = \{s(1)\}$, obtained by deleting $r(1,1)$ from D. However, CQA does not distinguish different grades of the consistency of answers, such as the distinction of weak and strong integrity in Definition 12. In fact, some doubts may be raised on the consistency of the answer $y = 1$ to the query $\leftarrow s(y)$ in D, as claimed by CQA, since the violation of the constraint $\leftarrow r(x,y), s(y)$ is caused, among others, by the presence of $s(1)$ in D.

Inconsistency can be measured in accordance with AHI, simply by counting causes, or by comparing sets of causes of the violation of constraints. A similar way to measure inconsistency in accordance with CQA could be to quantify the minimality of repairs, but that appears to be less simple, again due to the multiplicity of notions of minimality.

By definition, an answer has integrity only if it is *true* in the given database. More precisely, if, for an answer substitution θ of a query $\leftarrow B$ in a database D, $\forall(B\theta)$ has integrity in D, then $D(\forall(B\theta)) = true$. Similarly, if the answer *no* to $\leftarrow B$ in D has integrity, then $D(\forall(\sim B)) = true$. As opposed to that, consistent answers according to CQA may be *false* in the given database. For instance, let $D = \{p\}$ be a database and $IC = \{\leftarrow p\}$ an integrity theory. Clearly, the answer *yes* to the query $\leftarrow p$ does not have integrity and is not consistent. However, this answer as well as the information about its lack of integrity is given only by AHI, not by CQA. In fact, the answer to $\leftarrow p$ in D given by CQA is *no*, since the only minimal repair is the empty database. Arguably, the information conveyed by the answer according to AHI (that p is *true* in D but does not have integrity) is more useful than the answer *no* according to CQA.

Answers may or may not have integrity in databases with unsatisfiable integrity theories. As opposed to that, each answer is consistent by definition of CQA if integrity is unsatisfiable. That is because each answer is vacuously *true* in each repair if there is no repair. For instance, let $D = \{r(a), s(b, b)\}$ and $IC = \{\exists s(x, x); \leftarrow s(x, y)\}$, which is clearly unsatisfiable. Rewriting $\exists s(x, x)$ in denial form yields $IC' = \{\leftarrow \sim q; \leftarrow s(x, y)\}$ and $D' = D \cup \{q \leftarrow s(x, x)\}$. The answer $\{x=a\}$ to the query $\leftarrow r(x)$ in D' has integrity, while the answer $\{x=b\}$ to $\leftarrow s(x, x)$ does not. Yet, both answers are consistent by the definition of CQA.

CQA does not consider that the integrity theory, rather than the database could be in need of a repair, while AHI is impartial wrt both possibilities. For example, let $D = \{q(1, 2, 3, 1), q(2, 3, 2, 4), q(2, 1, 2, 3)\}$, $IC = \{\leftarrow q(x, y, x, z)\}$ and $\leftarrow q(2, x, y, z)$ be a query. Clearly, none of the two answers given to the query has integrity in (D, IC), since their respective cause coincides with one of the two causes $(\{q(2, 3, 2, 4)\}, \emptyset)$, $(\{q(2, 1, 2, 3)\}, \emptyset)$ of the violation of IC in D. The answer to the same query according to CQA is *no*, since the only minimal repair of D is to delete the two tuples given as answers according to AHI. However, it might well be that IC, rather than D is in need of a repair (which can of course only be determined if the particular 'real-world' meanings of q and IC are taken into account). For instance, a reasonable repair of IC could be $IC' = \{\leftarrow q(x, y, z, y)\}$. For any change of IC, all answers given to queries in D according to AHI remain the same, while answers given by CQA may change completely, such as they do in the preceding example.

Causes for AHI in definite and in hierarchical databases can be computed by SLD, resp., SLDNF derivations and only-if halves of predicate completions, i.e., by conventional query answering procedures and, for hierarchical databases, a well-known logic programming concept. As opposed to that, each of the four known approaches to compute CQA [4] appears to be more complicated or more unusual: One uses techniques from semantic query optimization [3]. Two others compute CQA from compact representations of repairs, either by conflict graphs or by extended disjunctive logic programs. Finally, repairs can be computed explicitly in order to decide whether an answer is *true* in each repair.

5.2   Repairing, Belief Revision, Knowledge Assimilation, Abduction

AHI and CQA tolerate inconsistency, since extant integrity violations may persist after the query has been answered. A less tolerant way to query a database D that is inconsistent with its integrity theory IC is to actually repair D, i.e., to minimally update D such that the resulting database satisfies IC, and then query that database. In the context of knowledge bases, repairing is often called 'belief revision' [25]. However, the minimality of repairs suffers from the ambivalence already mentioned for CQA. Moreover, repairs usually are not unique, i.e. an answer given with regard to a particular repair may not be a correct answer with regard to some other repair. AHI does not suffer from such ambiguities.

A field closely related to repairing and belief revision is knowledge assimilation (abbr. KA) [8]. For a database D, a query R (sometimes called 'update request') and an integrity theory IC that is satisfied in D, KA is asked to compute minimal updates such that the updated database satisfies IC and R is *true* in it. View updating is a well-known special case of KA. Again, such updates are not unique in general, and their minimality is ambivalent.

Abduction is a technique to compute KA [16]. Several abductive resolution procedures, e.g., as described in [17,24,14,13,22], are able to compute answers in a given database D, together with a set H of hypothesized facts, such that $D \cup H$ is consistent with regard to a given integrity theory. The hypothesized facts of abductively computed answers can also be interpreted as partial repairs of extant integrity violations. (For a definition and discussion of partial repairs, see [10].) We conjecture that the answers computed by the cited procedures in the partially repaired databases have integrity. Moreover, a striking similarity of AHI and the abductive (C)IFF procedures in [14,22] is that each of them makes explicit use of only-if halves of predicate completions.

5.3   Other Related Work

In [15], negative database consequences such as those that can be inferred from iff-completions are made explicit for inconsistency-tolerant reasoning (and, in particular, query answering) with explicit representations of the database theory, including its integrity constraints. The formalizations in [15] have to sacrifice several classical inference rules that are cornerstones of the logic framework assumed in this paper, such as modus ponens and reductio ad absurdum.

Lots of other work is going on in terms of inconsistency-tolerant and paraconsistent reasoning, which all is somehow related to CQA, AHI or avoiding the inference of arbitrary answers according to the *ex contradictione quodlibet* principle. For instance, inconsistency tolerance is discussed broadly in [2]. Another example is inconsistency-tolerant integrity checking (abbr. ITIC), which has been related to procuring the improvement of answer consistency in databases with extant integrity violations in [10]. As outlined in [7,6], a new approach to inconsistency-tolerant integrity checking is possible, based on the concept of causes as described in 3.3. As already indicted in 5.1, causes can also be used to measure inconsistency, similar to quantifying inconsistency by counting the number of violated instances of constraints, as done in [11].

There is a millenia-old tradition of philosophical treatment of causality. More recently, it has come to bear on informatics and AI, mostly in the form of probabilistic or counterfactual reasoning, as witnessed by a growing number of congresses about computing and philosophy. Those treatments of causality mostly go beyond the framework of causes as in this paper, which is confined by the comparatively simple theory of databases, the semantics of which is given by nothing but the completions of predicates.

6   Conclusion

This paper generalizes the concept of answers that have integrity (AHI) as presented in [6]. AHI distinguishes useful from doubtful answers: an answer is doubtful, i.e., does not have integrity, iff its causes overlap with the causes of integrity violation in the given state.

The contribution of this paper is twofold. Firstly, the definition of causes in [6] has been extended to negative answers, by taking the only-if halves of completed predicate definitions into account. That extension permits to apply the simple conceptual idea of answers that have integrity also to queries, constraints and databases involving datalog negation. Secondly, the computation of positive answers that have integrity by SLD, for definite queries in definite databases, has been generalized by suitable extensions of SLDNF to positive and negative answers for first-order queries in hierarchical databases.

In upcoming work, we intend to investigate the conjecture that it may suffice to check overlaps of terminal literals in causes for deciding if an answer has integrity or not. In [7], we have shown that this conjecture holds for positive answers to queries and constraints in definite databases.

Also, ways to avoid redundant multiple selection of literals in goal nodes is an important issue to be explored, in order to limit the cost of cause-of-failure computations. For instance, consider $D = \{q(1), r(1), s(2)\}$. Four of the six finitely failed SLDNF trees in the cause computation of $D \cup \{\leftarrow q(x), r(x), s(x)\}$ yield the same cause of the answer *no* to the given query, i.e., three of them are redundant. This redundancy can be avoided without sacrificing completeness by, e.g., never selecting any ground literal that is *true* in D, in any cause-of-failure computation.

Moreover, we intend to look into possibilities of computing AHI by other procedures for query evaluation, such as abductive logic programming [12,22] or answer set computing [20].

Moreover, it should be interesting to look into explanation bases and causes for a fresh take on explanations in expert systems [19].

References

1. Arenas, M., Bertossi, L., Chomicki, J.: Consistent query answers in inconsistent databases. In: Proc. 18th PODS, pp. 68–79. ACM Press, New York (1999)
2. Bertossi, L., Hunter, A., Schaub, T.: Introduction to inconsistency tolerance. In: Bertossi, L., Hunter, A., Schaub, T. (eds.) Inconsistency Tolerance. LNCS, vol. 3300, pp. 1–14. Springer, Heidelberg (2005)
3. Chakravarthy, S., Grant, J., Minker, J.: Logic-based approach to semantic query optimization. ACM TODS 15(2), 162–207 (1990)
4. Chomicki, J.: Consistent Query Answering: Five Easy Pieces. In: Schwentick, T., Suciu, D. (eds.) ICDT 2007. LNCS, vol. 4353, pp. 1–17. Springer, Heidelberg (2006)
5. Clark, K.: Negation as Failure. In: Gallaire, H., Minker, J. (eds.) Logic and Data Bases, pp. 293–322. Plenum Press, New York (1978)
6. Decker, H.: Toward a Uniform Cause-Based Approach to Inconsistency-Tolerant Database Semantics. In: Meersman, R., Dillon, T., Herrero, P. (eds.) OTM 2010. LNCS, vol. 6427, pp. 983–998. Springer, Heidelberg (2010)
7. Decker, H.: Basic causes for the Inconsistency Tolerance of Query Answering and Integrity Checking. In: Proc. 21st DEXA Workshop, pp. 318–322. IEEE CPS, Los Alamitos (2010)
8. Decker, H.: Some Notes on Knowledge Assimilation in Deductive Databases. In: Kifer, M., Voronkov, A., Freitag, B., Decker, H. (eds.) Dagstuhl Seminar 1997, DYNAMICS 1997, and ILPS-WS 1997. LNCS, vol. 1472, pp. 249–286. Springer, Heidelberg (1998)

9. Decker, H.: On Explanations in Deductive Databases. In: Proc. 3rd Workshop on Foundations of Models and Languages for Data and Objects, vol. 91/3, pp. 173–185. Inst.f.Informatik, Tech.Univ.Clausthal, Informatik-Bericht (1991)
10. Decker, H., Martinenghi, D.: Inconsistency-tolerant Integrity Checking. Transactions of Knowledge and Data Engineering 23(2), 218–234 (2011)
11. Decker, H., Martinenghi, D.: Modeling, Measuring and Monitoring the Quality of Information. In: Heuser, C.A., Pernul, G. (eds.) ER 2009. LNCS, vol. 5833, pp. 212–221. Springer, Heidelberg (2009)
12. Denecker, M., Kakas, A.: Abduction in Logic Programming. In: Kakas, A.C., Sadri, F. (eds.) Computational Logic: Logic Programming and Beyond. LNCS (LNAI), vol. 2407, pp. 402–436. Springer, Heidelberg (2002)
13. Dung, P., Kowalski, R., Toni, F.: Dialectic proof procedures for assumption-based admissible argumentation. Artif. Intell. 170(2), 114–159 (2006)
14. Fung, T., Kowalski, R.: The IFF proof procedure for abductive logic programming. J. Logic Programming 33(2), 151–165 (1997)
15. Hinrichs, T., Kao, J., Genesereth, M.: Inconsistency-Tolerant Reasoning with Classical Logic and Large Databases. In: Proc. 8th SARA, pp. 105–112. AAAI Press, Menlo Park (2009)
16. Kakas, A., Kowalski, R., Toni, F.: The role of abduction in logic programming. In: Handbook of Logic in Artificial Intelligence and Logic Programming, vol. 5, pp. 235–324. Oxford University Press, Oxford (1998)
17. Kakas, A., Mancarella, P.: Database Updates through Abduction. In: Proc. 16th VLDB, pp. 650–661. Morgan Kaufmann, San Francisco (1990)
18. Kowalski, R.: Predicate Logic as a Programming Language. In: Proc. 6th IFIP, pp. 569–574. North-Holland, Amsterdam (1974)
19. Liebowitz, J.: Handbook of Applied Expert Systems. CRC Press, Boca Raton (1998)
20. Lifschitz, V.: What is Answer Set Computing? In: Proc. 23rd AAAI, pp. 1594–1597 (2008)
21. Lloyd, J.: Foundations of Logic Programming, 2nd edn. Springer, Heidelberg (1987)
22. Mancarella, P., Terreni, G., Sadri, F., Toni, F., Endriss, U.: The CIFF proof procedure for abductive logic programming with constraints: Theory, implementation and experiments. TPLP 9(6), 691–750 (2009)
23. Reiter, R.: On closed world data bases. In: Gallaire, H., Minker, J. (eds.) Logic and Data Bases, pp. 119–140. Plenum Press, New York (1978)
24. Toni, F., Kowalski, R.: Reduction of abductive logic programs to normal logic programs. In: Proc. 12th ICLP, pp. 367–381. MIT Press, Cambridge (1995)
25. Williams, M.-A.: Applications of Belief Revision. In: Kifer, M., Voronkov, A., Freitag, B., Decker, H. (eds.) Dagstuhl Seminar 1997, DYNAMICS 1997, and ILPS-WS 1997. LNCS, vol. 1472, pp. 287–316. Springer, Heidelberg (1998)

Characterization of Optimal Complements of Database Views Defined by Projection

Stephen J. Hegner

Umeå University, Department of Computing Science
SE-901 87 Umeå, Sweden
hegner@cs.umu.se
http://www.cs.umu.se/~hegner

Abstract. A complement to a database view Γ is a second view Γ' which provides the information necessary to reconstruct the entire state of the main schema. View complementation is central in situations in which a view is to be updated, since the complement Γ' embodies the information not contained in Γ. In general, Γ may have many complements. In this work, an approach to identifying and constructing optimal relational complements for relational views defined by projections, including not only single projections but also sets of projections, is initiated. The approach is based upon the idea of identifying when the main schema has a governing join dependency; that is, a join dependency which implies all others. Four distinct classes of such governing dependencies are identified, corresponding to ordinary complements as well as three distinct types of dependency-preserving complements.

1 Introduction

A view of a database schema embodies partial, but in general not total, information about the state of the schema. To recover the remaining information, a second view, called a complement, may be used. To illustrate the surrounding ideas, a set of four closely related schemata and some of their views will be considered. Table 1 provides a summary of the associated notation and of their properties. Each of the four schemata has the same, single relation symbol $R[ABCD]$; they differ only in the set of constraints which govern them, which in each case consists of a set of functional dependencies (FDs). Sets of attributes are represented in the conventional relational format; $ABCD$ denotes $\{A, B, C, D\}$. The view $\Pi_{\mathbf{W}}^{\mathbf{E}_i}$ recaptures the projection of the relation $R[ABCD]$ of $\mathbf{E}_i$ onto the subset $\mathbf{W}$ of $ABCD$. The relation symbol of the view schema $\mathbf{E}_i^{\mathbf{W}}$ is denoted $R_{\mathbf{W}}[\mathbf{W}]$. The symbol $\pi_{ABC}^{\mathbf{E}_i}$ denotes the associated view morphism (i.e., the projection mapping itself). For example, $\Pi_{ABC}^{\mathbf{E}_0} = (\mathbf{E}_0^{ABC}, \pi_{ABC}^{\mathbf{E}_0})$ is the projection of $R[ABCD]$ of $\mathbf{E}_0$ onto ABC; the relation symbol of this view is $R_{ABC}[ABC]$, and the view morphism is $\pi_{ABC}^{\mathbf{E}_0}$ projects $R[ABCD]$ onto $R_{ABC}[ABC]$.

In this simple context, for $\Pi_{\mathbf{W}_2}^{\mathbf{E}_i}$ to be a complement of $\Pi_{\mathbf{W}_1}^{\mathbf{E}_i}$, it is necessary and sufficient that the join dependency (JD) $\bowtie[\mathbf{W}_1, \mathbf{W}_2]$ hold. This follows immediately from the classical result [24, Thm. 1], which establishes further that,

K.-D. Schewe, and B. Thalheim (Eds.): SDKB 2010, LNCS 6834, pp. 73–95, 2011.
© Springer-Verlag Berlin Heidelberg 2011

Table 1. Example schemata and their views

Schema	Relation	Constraints	Views for $\mathbf{W} \subseteq ABCD$
$\mathbf{E}_0$	$R[ABCD]$	$\mathcal{F}_0 = \{C \to D\}$	$\Pi_{\mathbf{W}}^{\mathbf{E}_0} = (\mathbf{E}_0^{\mathbf{W}}, \pi_{\mathbf{W}}^{\mathbf{E}_0})$
$\mathbf{E}_1$	$R[ABCD]$	$\mathcal{F}_1 = \{B \to D, C \to D\}$	$\Pi_{\mathbf{W}}^{\mathbf{E}_1} = (\mathbf{E}_1^{\mathbf{W}}, \pi_{\mathbf{W}}^{\mathbf{E}_1})$
$\mathbf{E}_2$	$R[ABCD]$	$\mathcal{F}_2 = \{B \to C, C \to D\}$	$\Pi_{\mathbf{W}}^{\mathbf{E}_2} = (\mathbf{E}_2^{\mathbf{W}}, \pi_{\mathbf{W}}^{\mathbf{E}_2})$
$\mathbf{E}_3$	$R[ABCD]$	$\mathcal{F}_3 = \{B \to C, C \to D, D \to B\}$	$\Pi_{\mathbf{W}}^{\mathbf{E}_3} = (\mathbf{E}_3^{\mathbf{W}}, \pi_{\mathbf{W}}^{\mathbf{E}_3})$

in the context of FDs, this JD holds iff at least one of the FDs $\mathbf{W}_1 \cap \mathbf{W}_2 \to \mathbf{W}_1$, $\mathbf{W}_1 \cap \mathbf{W}_2 \to \mathbf{W}_2$ holds; i.e., iff $\mathbf{W}_1 \cap \mathbf{W}_2$ is a key for at least one of the projections.

In the setting of $\mathbf{E}_0$, it is thus the case that $\Pi_{CD}^{\mathbf{E}_0}$ is a complement of $\Pi_{ABC}^{\mathbf{E}_0}$. Furthermore, amongst projections, it is a minimal complement, in the sense that no projection whose attribute set is a proper subset of CD is also a complement. Of course, there are other complements; indeed $\Pi_{BCD}^{\mathbf{E}_0}$, $\Pi_{ACD}^{\mathbf{E}_0}$, and even $\Pi_{ABCD}^{\mathbf{E}_0}$ are each complements of $\Pi_{ABC}^{\mathbf{E}_0}$ as well. However, these are all larger than $\Pi_{CD}^{\mathbf{E}_0}$ in that they recapture more attributes and hence more information about the state of $\mathbf{E}_0$.

To see why this minimality is important, suppose that it is desired to update the state of $\Pi_{ABC}^{\mathbf{E}_0}$. In general, there are many ways to reflect such an update back to $\mathbf{E}_0$. For example, let the state of $\mathbf{E}_0$ be $M_{00} = \{R(a_1, b_1, c_1, d_1), R(a_2, b_2, c_2, d_2)\}$, so that the state of $\mathbf{E}_0^{ABC}$ is $N_{00} = \{R(a_1, b_1, c_1), R(a_2, b_2, c_2)\}$. Suppose further that the desired new state of $\mathbf{E}_0^{ABC}$ is $N_{01} = \{R(a_3, b_1, c_1), R(a_2, b_2, c_2)\}$. Two possibilities for translation of this view update to the main schema $\mathbf{E}_0$ include $M_{01} = \{R(a_3, b_1, c_1, d_1), R(a_2, b_2, c_2, d_2)\}$ and $M_{01'} = \{R(a_3, b_1, c_1, d_3), R(a_2, b_2, c_2, d_2)\}$. Of these two, M_{01} seems the more natural, in that it does not alter the CD projections of the tuples. $M_{01'}$ makes the additional and rather arbitrary change of d_1 to d_3. This preference is formalized by the classical constant-complement strategy [3]. The update (M_{00}, M_{01}) on the main schema is the only one which is a reflection of the update (N_{00}, N_{01}) on $\Pi_{ABC}^{\mathbf{E}_0}$ and which holds the state of the complement $\Pi_{CD}^{\mathbf{E}_0}$ constant. Indeed, since the states of $\Pi_{ABC}^{\mathbf{E}_0}$ and the complement $\Pi_{CD}^{\mathbf{E}_0}$ together determine the state of $\mathbf{E}_0$, there can be only one such reflection. The appeal of the constant-complement strategy is that the reflection is limited to that part of the state of the main schema which is determined by the view to be updated. The rest of the state of the main schema, as captured by the complement, is left unchanged. Although a classical approach, the constant-complement strategy has seen renewed interest in recent years [20] [21] [14], and is also related to other modern approaches to view updates, such as those based upon lenses [7] [12].

It was noted already in the initial seminal paper on the subject that a view almost always has many complements [3, Thm. 4.4]. A question which arises immediately is whether by choosing a complement other than $\Pi_{CD}^{\mathbf{E}_0}$, a reflection other than (M_{00}, M_{01}), such as (M_{00}, M_{01}'), is possible for the view update (N_{00}, N_{01}) on $\Pi_{ABC}^{\mathbf{E}_0}$. The answer is a qualified yes, but a rather "unnatural" complement is required. An example of such an unnatural complement for a similar schema and view may be found in [14, Sec. 1.3]. However, it has been shown that for a very wide range of schemata and views which occur in practice, in which the schemata have a natural order structure and the morphisms are order preserving, the reflection of the view update is in fact independent of the choice of complement [14, Thm. 4.4], [17, Thm. 53]. Under these conditions, (M_{00}, M_{01}) is the only reasonable translation of (N_{00}, N_{01}) from initial state M_{00}. Nevertheless, the set of view updates which are allowed under the constant-complement strategy does in fact depend upon the choice of complement. As noted above, $\Pi_{BCD}^{\mathbf{E_0}}$, the projection onto $R[BCD]$, is also a complement of $\Pi_{ABC}^{\mathbf{E_0}}$, as is $\Pi_{ACD}^{\mathbf{E_0}}$. The view update (N_{00}, N_{01}) is also supported via constant complement $\Pi_{BCD}^{\mathbf{E_0}}$, with the same reflection, but not with constant complement $\Pi_{ACD}^{\mathbf{E_0}}$. On the other hand, with $N_{01'} = \{R(\mathsf{a}_1, \mathsf{b}_3, \mathsf{c}_1), R(\mathsf{a}_2, \mathsf{b}_2, \mathsf{c}_2)\}$, the view update $(N_{00}, N_{01'})$ is supported with constant complement $\Pi_{CD}^{\mathbf{E_0}}$, as well as with constant complement $\Pi_{ACD}^{\mathbf{E_0}}$, via the reflection (M_{00}, M_{01}'') with $M_{01}'' = \{R(\mathsf{a}_3, \mathsf{b}_3, \mathsf{c}_1, \mathsf{d}_1), R(\mathsf{a}_2, \mathsf{b}_2, \mathsf{c}_2, \mathsf{d}_2)\}$, but not with constant complement $\Pi_{BCD}^{\mathbf{E_0}}$. The reason is clear. $\Pi_{CD}^{\mathbf{E_0}}$ is a smaller complement than either $\Pi_{BCD}^{\mathbf{E_0}}$ or $\Pi_{ACD}^{\mathbf{E_0}}$, and the smaller the complement, the less that must be held constant, and so the larger the set of possible view updates. Thus, in order to maximize the set of view updates which are supported, the complement must be minimized.

It is easy to see that $\Pi_{CD}^{\mathbf{E_0}}$ is the unique minimal complement to $\Pi_{ABC}^{\mathbf{E_0}}$ amongst projections; it is thus called an *optimal* projective complement. Unfortunately, there are simple examples for which there are incomparable minimal complements, so no such optimal complement exists. The schema $\mathbf{E_1}$ provides one such setting, in which both $\Pi_{CD}^{\mathbf{E_1}}$ and $\Pi_{BD}^{\mathbf{E_1}}$ are minimal complements to $\Pi_{ABC}^{\mathbf{E_1}}$ within the family of projections. That both $\Pi_{CD}^{\mathbf{E_1}}$ and $\Pi_{BD}^{\mathbf{E_1}}$ are complements of $\Pi_{ABC}^{\mathbf{E_1}}$ follows from the classical result [24, Thm. 1] noted above. Furthermore, since the setting is completely symmetric with respect to attributes B and C, there is no way to prefer one over the other. Thus, it is not possible, in general, to expect an optimal projective complement, even in the basic setting of FDs and views which are projections. Consequently, there is no complement which supports all updates which any other complement does. For example, if the state of $\mathbf{E_1}$ is M_{00} as given above, then the update on $\Pi_{ABC}^{\mathbf{E_1}}$ from $N_{10} = \{R(\mathsf{a}_1, \mathsf{b}_1, \mathsf{c}_1), R(\mathsf{a}_2, \mathsf{b}_2, \mathsf{c}_2)\}$, to $N_{11} = \{R(\mathsf{a}_1, \mathsf{b}_3, \mathsf{c}_1), R(\mathsf{a}_2, \mathsf{b}_2, \mathsf{c}_2)\}$ is supported with constant complement $\Pi_{CD}^{\mathbf{E_1}}$ but not with constant complement $\Pi_{BD}^{\mathbf{E_1}}$, while the update from $N_{10'} = \{R(\mathsf{a}_1, \mathsf{b}_1, \mathsf{c}_1), R(\mathsf{a}_2, \mathsf{b}_2, \mathsf{c}_2)\}$, to $N_{11'} = \{R(\mathsf{a}_1, \mathsf{b}_1, \mathsf{c}_3), R(\mathsf{a}_2, \mathsf{b}_2, \mathsf{c}_2)\}$ is supported with constant complement $\Pi_{BD}^{\mathbf{E_1}}$ but not with constant complement $\Pi_{CD}^{\mathbf{E_1}}$.

There is a further, central issue. A cover (i.e., a logical representation) of the constraints $\mathcal{F}_0 = \{C \rightarrow D\}$ of $\mathbf{E_0}$ embeds into the pair $\{\Pi_{ABC}^{\mathbf{E_0}}, \Pi_{CD}^{\mathbf{E_0}}\}$; indeed; $C \rightarrow D$ itself embeds into $\Pi_{CD}^{\mathbf{E_0}}$. This implies that whether an update to $\Pi_{ABC}^{\mathbf{E_0}}$ is supported by constant complement $\Pi_{CD}^{\mathbf{E_0}}$ is determined by the state of $\mathbf{E_0}^{ABC}$ alone; it is not necessary to know the state of $\mathbf{E_0}^{CD}$. In the classical setting, it is said that $\Pi_{ABC}^{\mathbf{E_0}}$ and $\Pi_{CD}^{\mathbf{E_0}}$ are *independent* [24, Thm. 2]. The updates to $\Pi_{ABC}^{\mathbf{E_0}}$ which are allowed with constant complement $\Pi_{CD}^{\mathbf{E_0}}$ are exactly those which keep the view $\Pi_C^{\mathbf{E}_0}$ defined by the common column of $\Pi_{ABC}^{\mathbf{E}_0}$ and $\Pi_{CD}^{\mathbf{E}_0}$ constant. In this case, $\{\Pi_{ABC}^{\mathbf{E}_0}, \Pi_{CD}^{\mathbf{E}_0}\}$ is said to form a *meet-complementary pair* [14, Def. 2.12], with $\Pi_C^{\mathbf{E}_0}$ their *meet*.

On the other hand, in the context of $\mathbf{E}_1$, neither $\{\Pi_{ABC}^{\mathbf{E}_1}, \Pi_{CD}^{\mathbf{E}_1}\}$ nor $\{\Pi_{ABC}^{\mathbf{E}_1}, \Pi_{BD}^{\mathbf{E}_1}\}$ forms a meet-complementary pair. Indeed, $B \to D$ cannot be embedded into the first pair while $C \to D$ cannot be embedded into the second. Consequently, it cannot be determined in general whether a given update to $\Pi_{ABC}^{\mathbf{E}_1}$ is supported via constant complement without knowing the state of the complementary view. For example, the update on $\Pi_{ABC}^{\mathbf{E}_1}$ from N_{10} to $N_{12} = \{R(a_1, b_2, c_1), R(a_2, b_2, c_2)\}$ is supported with constant complement $\Pi_{CD}^{\mathbf{E}_1}$ if the state of $\mathbf{E}_1$ is $M_{11} = \{R(a_1, b_1, c_1, d_1), R(a_2, b_2, c_2, d_1)\}$, but not if it is M_{00}. Thus, requiring a meet complement for the constant-complement strategy is critical. Interestingly, $\Pi_{ABC}^{\mathbf{E}_1}$ does have an optimal projective meet complement, namely, $\Pi_{BCD}^{\mathbf{E}_1}$, which is obtained by combining $\Pi_{BD}^{\mathbf{E}_1}$ and $\Pi_{CD}^{\mathbf{E}_1}$.

The schema $\mathbf{E}_2$ illustrates yet another possibility, in which both $\Pi_{BD}^{\mathbf{E}_2}$ and $\Pi_{CD}^{\mathbf{E}_2}$ are minimal projective complements of $\Pi_{ABC}^{\mathbf{E}_2}$, yet only $\{\Pi_{ABC}^{\mathbf{E}_2}, \Pi_{CD}^{\mathbf{E}_2}\}$ forms a meet-complementary pair. Thus, it is possible for a schema to have several minimal projective complements, of which only one is a meet complement.

In view of these three examples, it might be conjectured that an optimal meet complement always exists, at least in the context of projections of a universal schema which is constrained by FDs. That this is not the case is illustrated by the situation surrounding the schema $\mathbf{E}_3$. In that context, both $\Pi_{CD}^{\mathbf{E}_3}$ and $\Pi_{BD}^{\mathbf{E}_3}$ are minimal meet complements of $\Pi_{ABC}^{\mathbf{E}_3}$. Indeed, $\mathcal{F}_3$ is equivalent to $\mathcal{F}_3' = \{B \to C, C \to B, C \to D, D \to C\}$, which embeds into $\{\Pi_{ABC}^{\mathbf{E}_3}, \Pi_{CD}^{\mathbf{E}_3}\}$, as well as equivalent to $\mathcal{F}_3'' = \{B \to C, C \to B, B \to D, D \to B\}$, which embeds into $\{\Pi_{ABC}^{\mathbf{E}_3}, \Pi_{BD}^{\mathbf{E}_3}\}$. Consequently, in this case, there is no optimal meet complement.

In summary, it the case that, even in the context of simple universal relational schemata constrained only by FDs, there are many possibilities regarding the existence of optimal complements and optimal meet complements. The goal of this paper is to address the issues surrounding such optimal complements in a systematic fashion.

The organization of the paper is as follows. Section 2 provides an overview of the basic terminology and notation required for the following sections, Section 3 comprises the main part of the paper. Four fundamental notions of optimal complement are developed, first for the case of views on a universal relational schema defined by single projections, and then for the more general context of views defined by sets of projections. Finally, Sec. 4 provides conclusions and sketches some further directions.

2   Database Schemata, Views, and Complements

Although the main focus in this paper is upon views defined by projection on the classical relational model, the underlying theory is not based upon any particular data model. Rather, the set-based model described in [14] and [15] is more than adequate. It is in fact simpler to present the underlying theory in a general context, and only afterwards to specialize it to the relational context. In this section, the key ideas of the underlying theoretical model are outlined. Much of the material is based upon earlier papers, such as [14], although the classification scheme of Definition 2.5 is new.

Summary 2.1 (Database schemata and views). In the underlying theory of this work, a database schema $\mathbf{D}$ is just a set. This set, denoted $\mathsf{LDB}(\mathbf{D})$, consists of the *legal databases* of $\mathbf{D}$. Thus, a database schema is modelled by its instances alone; constraints, schema structure, and the like are not represented explicitly.

A *morphism* $f : \mathbf{D}_1 \to \mathbf{D}_2$ of database schemata is a function $f : \mathsf{LDB}(\mathbf{D}_1) \to \mathsf{LDB}(\mathbf{D}_2)$. A *view* of the schema $\mathbf{D}$ is a pair $\Gamma = (\mathbf{V}, \gamma)$ in which $\mathbf{V}$ is a schema and $\gamma : \mathbf{D} \to \mathbf{V}$ is a surjective database morphism. In the relational context, a morphism is usually defined using the relational algebra or calculus, but the abstraction to a function on states is adequate for the framework developed here.

The *congruence* of Γ is the equivalence relation on $\mathsf{LDB}(\mathbf{D})$ defined by $(M_1, M_2) \in \mathsf{Congr}(\Gamma)$ iff $\gamma(M_1) = \gamma(M_2)$. Views with identical congruences are considered "abstractly the same" for the purposes of this work. The views $\Gamma_1 = (\mathbf{V}_1, \gamma_1)$ and $\Gamma_2 = (\mathbf{V}_2, \gamma_2)$ of $\mathbf{D}$ are *equivalent* or *(congruence) isomorphic* iff $\mathsf{Congr}(\Gamma_1) = \mathsf{Congr}(\Gamma_2)$. In general, views with vastly different representations may have the same congruence. However, in the context of the examples of this paper, which are all relational and defined by projections, unless two views are "obviously" equivalent, they will generally have distinct congruences. Such equivalences occur in particular in the context of views defined by sets of projections, where a view with a single relation is equivalent to one with two relations connected by a join dependency. See Definition 3.22 and Example 3.24 for examples. The bottom line is that in this paper $\mathsf{Congr}(\Gamma)$ may be regarded as identifying the view Γ up to an obvious relational equivalence.

A congruence on $\mathsf{LDB}(\mathbf{D})$ may be represented by the partition which it induces [22, Sec. 1]. The partition of $\mathsf{LDB}(\mathbf{D})$ induced by $\mathsf{Congr}(\Gamma)$ is denoted $\mathsf{Partition}(\mathsf{Congr}(\Gamma))$.

There is a natural partial order on the equivalence classes of the views of $\mathbf{D}$, given by $\Gamma_2 \preceq_{\mathbf{D}} \Gamma_1$ iff $\mathsf{Congr}(\Gamma_1) \subseteq \mathsf{Congr}(\Gamma_2)$. If $\Gamma_2 \preceq_{\mathbf{D}} \Gamma_1$, then every pair $\{M_1, M_2\} \subseteq \mathsf{LDB}(\mathbf{D})$ which is distinguished by Γ_2 (in the precise sense that $\gamma_2(M_1) \neq \gamma_2(M_2)$) is also distinguished by Γ_1. Less formally, Γ_1 preserves at least as much information about the state of $\mathbf{D}$ as does Γ_2. The notation $\Gamma_2 \prec_{\mathbf{D}} \Gamma_1$ means that $\Gamma_2 \preceq_{\mathbf{D}} \Gamma_1$ holds but $\Gamma_1 \preceq_{\mathbf{D}} \Gamma_2$ does not.

It is easy to see that $\Gamma_2 \preceq_{\mathbf{D}} \Gamma_1$ iff every block of $\mathsf{Partition}(\mathsf{Congr}(\Gamma_2))$ is the union of blocks of $\mathsf{Partition}(\mathsf{Congr}(\Gamma_1))$. If $\Gamma_2 \preceq_{\mathbf{D}} \Gamma_1$, there is thus a unique view morphism $\lambda\langle \Gamma_1, \Gamma_2 \rangle : \Gamma_1 \to \Gamma_2$, called the *relativization morphism* from Γ_1 to Γ_2, which sends a block of $\mathsf{Partition}(\mathsf{Congr}(\Gamma_1))$ to the block which contains it in $\mathsf{Partition}(\mathsf{Congr}(\Gamma_2))$.

Summary 2.2 (Complements and Optimality). The pair $\{\Gamma_1 = (\mathbf{V}_1, \gamma_1), \Gamma_2 = (\mathbf{V}_2, \gamma_2)\}$ of views of the database schema $\mathbf{D}$ is said to be *complementary* if the *decomposition mapping* $\gamma_1 \times \gamma_2 : \mathsf{LDB}(\mathbf{D}) \to \mathsf{LDB}(\mathbf{V}_1) \times \mathsf{LDB}(\mathbf{V}_2)$ given on elements by $M \mapsto (\gamma_1(M), \gamma_2(M))$ is injective. This is nothing more than a repackaging of the classical idea of a lossless decomposition. Γ_2 is said to be a *complement* of Γ_1, and vice versa. The inverse $(\gamma_1 \times \gamma_2)^{-1} : (\gamma_1 \times \gamma_2)(\mathsf{LDB}(\mathbf{D})) \to \mathsf{LDB}(\mathbf{D})$ of the decomposition mapping is called the *reconstruction mapping*.

Given a set $\mathcal{V}$ of views of $\mathbf{D}$, call a complement $\Gamma_2 \in \mathcal{V}$ of Γ_1 *minimal* relative to $\mathcal{V}$ if there is no complement $\Gamma_2' \in \mathcal{V}$ with the property that $\Gamma_2' \prec_{\mathbf{D}} \Gamma_2$. Call Γ_2 *optimal* relative to $\mathcal{V}$ if for every other complement $\Gamma_2' \in \mathcal{V}$, it must be the case that $\Gamma_2 \preceq_{\mathbf{D}} \Gamma_2'$. Less formally, a complement is minimal relative to $\mathcal{V}$ if no other complement in $\mathcal{V}$ is smaller, and it is optimal relative to $\mathcal{V}$ if every other complement in $\mathcal{V}$ is at least as large. Thus, there may be many incomparable minimal complements, but there is at most one optimal complement, or, better put, all optimal complements must have the same congruence.

If each member of $\{\Gamma_1, \Gamma_2\}$ is a minimal (resp. optimal) complement of the other relative to $\mathcal{V}$, then it is called a *minimal complementary pair* (resp. *optimal complementary pair*) relative to $\mathcal{V}$.

Summary 2.3 (Fully commuting pairs and meet complements). The pair $\{\Gamma_1 = (\mathbf{V}_1, \gamma_1), \Gamma_2 = (\mathbf{V}_2, \gamma_2)\}$ of views of $\mathbf{D}$ is said to be *fully commuting* [14, Def. 2.12] if $\mathsf{Congr}(\Gamma_1) \circ \mathsf{Congr}(\Gamma_2) = \mathsf{Congr}(\Gamma_2) \circ \mathsf{Congr}(\Gamma_1)$, with "$\circ$" denoting the ordinary composition of relations. If $\{\Gamma_1, \Gamma_2\}$ furthermore forms a complementary pair, then it is called *meet-complementary pair*, and Γ_1 and Γ_2 are called *meet complements* of one another. In the case that $\{\Gamma_1, \Gamma_2\}$ forms a fully commuting pair, the view whose congruence is $\mathsf{Congr}(\Gamma_1) \circ \mathsf{Congr}(\Gamma_2)$ is called the *meet* of Γ_1 and Γ_2, and is denoted $\Gamma_1 \wedge \Gamma_2$.

The importance of full commutativity is that is recaptures dependency preservation in an abstract fashion. Specifically, if $\{\Gamma_1, \Gamma_2\}$ forms a fully commuting pair, with $N_1 \in \mathsf{LDB}(\mathbf{V}_i)$ for $i \in \{1, 2\}$, then there is an $M \in \mathsf{LDB}(\mathbf{D})$ with $\gamma_i(M) = N_i$ for $i \in \{1, 2\}$ iff $\lambda\langle \Gamma_1, \Gamma_1 \wedge \Gamma_2\rangle(N_1) = \lambda\langle \Gamma_2, \Gamma_1 \wedge \Gamma_2\rangle(N_2)$. If $\{\Gamma_1, \Gamma_2\}$ is furthermore a complementary pair, then this M is necessarily unique [14, Thm. 2.14].

In the context of projections on universal schemata constrained by full dependencies (including FDs in particular), the meet, when it exists, is always the projection on the columns common to the two views [14, Prop. 2.17]. For example, in the context of $\mathbf{E}_0$ of Sec. 1, $\Pi_{ABC}^{\mathbf{E}_0} \wedge \Pi_{CD}^{\mathbf{E}_0} = \Pi_C^{\mathbf{E}_0}$.

Minimal and optimal meet complements are defined in the natural way. Let Γ be a view of the $\mathbf{D}$, and let $\mathcal{V}$ be any set of views of $\mathbf{D}$. Define $\mathsf{MeetSet}\langle \mathcal{V}; \Gamma\rangle$ to be the subset of $\mathcal{V}$ which identifies just those views which are meet complements of Γ. A *minimal* (resp. *optimal*) meet complement of the view Γ relative to the set $\mathcal{V}$ of views is a minimal (resp. optimal) complement relative to $\mathsf{MeetSet}\langle \mathcal{V}; \Gamma\rangle$.

Summary 2.4 (The constant-complement approach to view update). While the results of this paper are presented and may be understood without any reference to the constant-complement view-update strategy, the latter forms the motivation for exploring the notion of optimal complement in the first place. Therefore, a brief sketch of this approach is presented. For details, consult [3] and [14].

An *update* on the database schema $\mathbf{D}$ is a pair $(M_1, M_2) \in \mathsf{LDB}(\mathbf{D}) \times \mathsf{LDB}(\mathbf{D})$. M_1 is the current state, and M_2 the new state. To describe the situation surrounding an update request on the view $\Gamma = (\mathbf{V}, \gamma)$, it is sufficient to specify the current state M_1 of the main schema and the desired new state N_2 of the view schema $\mathbf{V}$. The current state of the view can be computed as $\gamma(M_1)$; it is only the new state M_2 of the main schema (subject to $N_2 = \gamma(M_2)$) which must be obtained from an update strategy. Formally, an *update request* from Γ to $\mathbf{D}$ is a pair (M_1, N_2) in which $M_1 \in \mathsf{LDB}(\mathbf{D})$ (the old state of the main schema) and $N_2 \in \mathsf{LDB}(\mathbf{V})$ (the new state of the view schema). A *realization* of (M_1, N_2) along Γ is an update (M_1, M_2) on $\mathbf{D}$ with the property that $\gamma(M_2) = N_2$. The update (M_1, M_2) is called a *reflection* (or *translation*) of the view update $(\gamma(M_1), N_2)$. Thus, the realization (M_1, M_2) tells how to reflect the view update $(\gamma(M_1), N_2)$ to the main schema $\mathbf{D}$ when the state of $\mathbf{D}$ is M_1.

Given a second view $\Gamma' = (\mathbf{V}', \gamma')$ of $\mathbf{D}$ which is a complement of Γ, the realization (M_1, M_2) of (M_1, N_2) is *defined by constant complement* Γ' if $\gamma'(M_1) = \gamma'(M_2)$. It is easy to see that there can be only one realization of (M_1, N_2) which is defined by constant complement Γ', given explicitly by $(M_1, (\gamma \times \gamma')^{-1}(N_2, \gamma'(M_1)))$ if and only if the latter exists, so the translation truly is defined by Γ'. The family $S \subseteq \mathsf{LDB}(\mathbf{D}) \times \mathsf{LDB}(\mathbf{V})$ of update requests on Γ is *defined by constant complement* Γ' if for every $(M_1, N_2) \in S$, $(M_1, (\gamma \times \gamma')^{-1}(N_2, \gamma'(M_1)))$ exists and is a realization of (M_1, N_2). Update reflections which are defined by constant complement have many desirable properties; see in particular [14, Sec. 1] for an overview with examples.

If the pair $\{\Gamma, \Gamma'\}$ is meet complementary, an important additional property is guaranteed; namely, that whether an update to the state of Γ is allowed with constant complement Γ' is independent of the state of Γ'. Specifically, the view update (N, N') to Γ is allowed iff $\lambda \langle \Gamma, \Gamma \wedge \Gamma' \rangle (N) = \lambda \langle \Gamma, \Gamma \wedge \Gamma' \rangle (N')$; that is, iff the update keeps the meet view constant. Examples have already been given in introduction. This property is crucial because it provides a form of closure to Γ; all allowable update operations may be identified locally.

Definition 2.5 (Types of complements and complementary pairs). As observed in the discussion surrounding the examples of Sec. 1, there are several distinct levels of optimality of a complementary view which arise when combining notions of ordinary and meet complements. Because it is precisely such notions of optimality which will be addressed in Sec. 3, it is important to identify and label these systematically. Relative to a base set $\mathcal{V}$ of views of the schema $\mathbf{D}$, there are four principal types of complements of a given view Γ, defined as follows.

Type 0: An optimal complement of Γ *of type 0* relative to $\mathcal{V}$ is an ordinary optimal complement of Γ relative to $\mathcal{V}$, as described in Summary 2.2 above.

Type 1: An optimal complement of Γ *of type 1* relative to $\mathcal{V}$ is an optimal meet complement of Γ relative to $\mathcal{V}$, as described in Summary 2.3 above.

Type 2: An optimal complement of Γ *of type 2* relative to $\mathcal{V}$ is is simultaneously an optimal meet complement of Γ (and hence of type 1) and a minimal complement relative to $\mathcal{V}$.

Type 3: An optimal complement of Γ *of type 3* relative to $\mathcal{V}$ is is simultaneously an optimal meet complement of Γ (and hence of type 1) and an optimal complement of Γ relative to $\mathcal{V}$ (and hence of type 0).

For $i \in \{0, 1, 2, 3\}$, if each member of $\{\Gamma_1, \Gamma_2\}$ is an optimal complement of the other of type i, then $\{\Gamma_1, \Gamma_2\}$ is called an *optimal complementary pair of type i* relative to $\mathcal{V}$.

These four types are summarized in Table 2.

Table 2. Types of optimal complements for the view Γ

Type of complement	Set of possible complements	
	$\mathcal{V}$	MeetSet$\langle \mathcal{V}; \Gamma \rangle$
0	optimal	—
1	—	optimal
2	minimal	optimal
3	optimal	optimal

Note that this is not a linear hierarchy. While type $3 \Rightarrow$ type 0 and type $3 \Rightarrow$ type $2 \Rightarrow$ type 1, no other subsumptions hold.

To illustrate these classifications in the context of the examples of Sec. 1, let Π-Views$\langle \mathbf{E}_i \rangle$ denote the set of all views of the schema $\mathbf{E}_i$ (for $i \in \{0, 2, 2, 3\}$) which are defined by projections. This notion is formalized more carefully in Definition 3.2, but the main idea should already be clear. In this context, the following hold.

($\mathbf{E}_0$:). The set $\{\Pi_{ABC}^{\mathbf{E}_0}, \Pi_{CD}^{\mathbf{E}_0}\}$ is an optimal complementary pair for all four types relative to Π-Views$\langle \mathbf{E}_0 \rangle$.

($\mathbf{E}_1$:). The set $\{\Pi_{ABC}^{\mathbf{E}_1}, \Pi_{BCD}^{\mathbf{E}_1}\}$ is an optimal complementary pair of type 1 relative to Π-Views$\langle \mathbf{E}_1 \rangle$. It is not an optimal complementary pair for any of the other three types. Neither $\{\Pi_{ABC}^{\mathbf{E}_1}, \Pi_{CD}^{\mathbf{E}_1}\}$ nor $\{\Pi_{ABC}^{\mathbf{E}_1}, \Pi_{BD}^{\mathbf{E}_1}\}$ is an optimal complementary pair for any of the four types, although in both cases each element of the pair is a minimal complement of the other relative to Π-Views$\langle \mathbf{E}_1 \rangle$.

($\mathbf{E}_2$:). The set $\{\Pi_{ABC}^{\mathbf{E}_2}, \Pi_{CD}^{\mathbf{E}_2}\}$ is an optimal complementary pair of types 1 and 2 relative to Π-Views$\langle \mathbf{E}_2 \rangle$. It is not an optimal complementary pair for types 0 or 3; indeed, there is no view which is an optimal complement of $\Pi_{ABC}^{\mathbf{E}_2}$ of type 0 relative to Π-Views$\langle \mathbf{E}_2 \rangle$.

($\mathbf{E}_3$:). The pair $\{\Pi_{ABC}^{\mathbf{E}_3}, \Pi_{CD}^{\mathbf{E}_3}\}$ is not an optimal complementary pair relative to Π-Views$\langle \mathbf{E}_3 \rangle$ for any of the four types.

Although the above examples illustrate situations in which the optimality properties are symmetric between the two views, this need not be the case. For example, $\Pi_{ABC}^{\mathbf{E}_0}$ is an optimal complement of $\Pi_{BCD}^{\mathbf{E}_0}$ of all four types relative to Π-Views$\langle \mathbf{E}_0 \rangle$, while $\Pi_{BCD}^{\mathbf{E}_0}$ is not an optimal complement of $\Pi_{ABC}^{\mathbf{E}_0}$ for any of the four types.

The type classification described in Definition 2.5 has important interpretations within the context of constant-complement update. If Γ' forms a type-3 complement to Γ within the context $\mathcal{V}$ of views under consideration, then every update to Γ which is supported by any complement in $\mathcal{V}$ is supported by Γ', and whether the update is supported or not may be determined from the state of Γ alone. If Γ' forms a type-1 or type-2 complement, every update to Γ which is supported in an independent fashion, that is, without further knowledge of the state of the main schema, is supported by constant complement Γ'. Other constant complement updates to Γ may be possible, but whether or not they are realizable may depend upon the state of that complement. Type 2 provides the further strength that no other complement supports a superset of those view updates supported by constant-complement Γ'. Type 0 provides no support at all for independence.

From the discussions of Summary 2.4 and Definition 2.5, it is apparent that the smaller the complement Γ' (in the sense of the ordering $\preceq_{\mathbf{D}}$), the larger the set of of update requests which are supported. In particular, if there is an optimal complement, then it must support all update requests which are supported by any constant complement. This is made more precise in the following.

Proposition 2.6 (Optimal complements and constant-complement updates). *Let $\mathbf{D}$ be a database schema, $\mathcal{V}$ a set of views of $\mathbf{D}$, Γ a view of $\mathbf{D}$, $i \in \{0, 1, 2, 3\}$, and Γ' an optimal complement of Γ of type i relative to $\mathcal{V}$.*

(a) *If $i \in \{0, 3\}$, then every view update which is defined by constant complement for some complement $\Gamma'' \in \mathcal{V}$ of Γ is defined by constant complement Γ' as well.*

(b) *If $i \in \{1, 2, 3\}$, then every view update which is defined by constant complement for some meet complement $\Gamma'' \in \mathcal{V}$ of Γ is defined by constant complement Γ' as well.* □

In that which follows, in particular for Theorem 3.15 and Theorem 3.23, both of which identify optimal complements in a given setting, there is a natural corollary concerning constant-complement updates which follows from the given theorem and the above proposition. These corollaries will not be stated explicitly, but they should be kept in mind as a fundamental application of these theorems.

3 Optimal Complements in the Context of Projections of a Universal Relation

In the classical relational decomposition theory, the standard setting is that defined by projections on a universal schema which is constrained by a join - dependency [4] [10], often derived from functional dependencies [2]. Although the motivation for studying such decompositions has been largely based upon schema normalization, the ideas apply equally well to the problem of characterizing complements. In this section, a theory of optimal complements is developed within the familiar framework of projections on a universal schema.

In that which follows, it is assumed that the reader is familiar with the standard relational model and its notation, as may be found in [23] and [1].

Notation 3.1 (Universal Relation Schema). Throughout the rest of this section, unless specifically stated to the contrary, take $\mathbf{U}$ to be a finite nonempty set of attributes and $\mathbf{E_U}$ the *universal relation schema* with $R[\mathbf{U}]$ its sole relation symbol. With $\mathcal{F}$ a set of constraints, $\mathbf{E_U^{\mathcal{F}}}$ denotes this same schema constrained by $\mathcal{F}$; i.e., $\mathsf{Constr}(\mathbf{E_U^{\mathcal{F}}}) = \mathcal{F}$. Unless stated to the contrary, $\mathcal{F}$ will be taken to be an arbitrary set of first-order constraints (without non-nullary function symbols).

The symbol $\models$ will be used to denote semantic entailment of constraints.

Definition 3.2 (Projective views). A *projective view* or (Π-*view*) on $\mathbf{E_U^{\mathcal{F}}}$ is a projection on some of the attributes of $\mathbf{U}$. More precisely, for $\mathbf{U}' \subseteq \mathbf{U}$, $\Pi_{\mathbf{U}'}^{\mathbf{E_U^{\mathcal{F}}}}$ is the view which is defined on tuples by $t \mapsto t[\mathbf{U}']$ and which is extended to relations in a tuple-by-tuple fashion. The morphism of this view is denoted $\pi_{\mathbf{U}'}^{\mathbf{E_U^{\mathcal{F}}}}$, and the view schema is $\mathbf{E_{U'}}^{\pi_{\mathbf{U}'}(\mathcal{F})}$. As this notation quickly becomes quite cumbersome, the superscripts will be dropped when the context is clear. The view which is the projection of $\mathbf{E_U^{\mathcal{F}}}$ onto attributes $\mathbf{U}'$ is then denoted by simply $\Pi_{\mathbf{U}'} = (\mathbf{E_{U'}}, \pi_{\mathbf{U}'})$. The set of all Π-views on $\mathbf{E_U^{\mathcal{F}}}$ is denoted $\Pi\text{-Views}\langle \mathbf{E_U^{\mathcal{F}}} \rangle$.

Identification of the constraints on $\mathbf{E_{U'}}$ is not an easy matter in general. Investigations of the behavior of various classes of database dependencies under projection have been reported in [9], [19], and [15]. Since the representation of such constraints is not an issue for the problems considered in this paper, it will not be pursued further.

In the notation of Summary 2.2, it is easy to see that for $\mathbf{U}_1, \mathbf{U}_2 \subseteq \mathbf{U}$, $\mathbf{U}_1 \subseteq \mathbf{U}_2$ implies that $\Pi_{\mathbf{U}_1} \preceq_{\mathbf{E_U^{\mathcal{F}}}} \Pi_{\mathbf{U}_2}$. The converse, that $\Pi_{\mathbf{U}_1} \preceq_{\mathbf{E_U^{\mathcal{F}}}} \Pi_{\mathbf{U}_2}$ implies that $\mathbf{U}_1 \subseteq \mathbf{U}_2$, holds in the context of usual data dependencies, but can fail in certain situations. $\Pi_{AB} \preceq_{\mathbf{E_U^{\mathcal{F}}}} \Pi_A$ if there is only one possible value for attribute A. A less trivial example arises when a conditional functional dependency in the sense of [11] holds for $A \to B$. This means that not only does the usual FD $A \to B$ hold, but also that the value of attribute B determined for each value of attribute A is defined by the dependency itself.

Definition 3.3 (Attribute-set collections and join dependencies). An *attribute-set collection* over $\mathbf{U}$ is any set J of nonempty subsets of $\mathbf{U}$. Let $J = \{\mathbf{U}_1, \mathbf{U}_2, \ldots, \mathbf{U}_k\}$ be an attribute-set collection over $\mathbf{U}$; i.e., $\mathbf{U}_i \subseteq \mathbf{U}$ for $1 \leq i \leq k$. A database $M \in \mathsf{LDB}(\mathbf{E_U})$ satisfies the *join dependency* (or *JD*) $\bowtie[J]$ if for every sequence $\langle t_1, t_2, \ldots, t_k \rangle$ of k (not necessarily distinct) tuples for $R[\mathbf{U}]$, there is a tuple t for $R[\mathbf{U}]$ with the property that $t[\mathbf{U}_i] = t_i[\mathbf{U}_i]$ for $1 \leq i \leq k$. If $\mathbf{U} = \mathbf{U}_1 \cup \mathbf{U}_2 \cup \ldots \cup \mathbf{U}_k$, then both J and the associated join dependency $\bowtie[J]$ are called *full*. If $\bowtie[J]$ is not full, it is said to be *embedded*. Say that $\bowtie[J]$ is *entailed by* $\mathcal{F}$ if $\bowtie[J]$ holds on every $M \in \mathsf{LDB}(\mathbf{E_U^{\mathcal{F}}})$ (i.e., if $\mathcal{F} \models \bowtie[J]$).

Thus, if $\bowtie[J]$ is entailed by $\mathcal{F}$, the schema $\mathbf{E_U^{\mathcal{F}}}$ decomposes into the views in $\{\Pi_{\mathbf{U}_1}, \Pi_{\mathbf{U}_2}, \ldots, \Pi_{\mathbf{U}_k}\}$ in the precise sense that any $M \in \mathsf{LDB}(\mathbf{E_U})$ is recoverable from the k-tuple $(\pi_{\mathbf{U}_1}(M), \pi_{\mathbf{U}_2}(M), \ldots, \pi_{\mathbf{U}_k}(M))$ of view states via the reconstruction mapping which sends $\langle t_1, t_2, \ldots, t_k \rangle$ to the $\mathbf{U}$-tuple t which agrees with t_i on all attributes of the latter. This reconstruction mapping is also called the *join*.

Properties of JDs are often described in terms of associated graphs and/or hypergraphs. A full development of these ideas is not needed here, but a few definitions will prove useful. Say that $\mathbf{U}_i$ and $\mathbf{U}_j$ are *directly connected* if $\mathbf{U}_i \cap \mathbf{U}_j \neq \emptyset$. A subset $J' \subseteq J$ is *connected* if there is an ordering $\langle \mathbf{U}_{m_1}, \mathbf{U}_{m_2}, \ldots \mathbf{U}_{m_\ell} \rangle$ of the elements of J' such that each element except the first is directly connected to at least one which precedes it. A *connected block* is a maximal connected subset of J. This definition accommodates JDs with disjoint blocks. For example, if $J = \{AB, BC, CD, EF, FG, GH\}$, then $\{AB, BC, CD\}$ and $\{DE, EF, FG\}$ are maximal connected subsets. The blocks are related via the *cartesian-product* dependency $\bowtie[ABC, DEF]$.

A central focus of classical research on JDs surrounds the property of *acyclicity* of the underlying hypergraph of a JD. This property of the hypergraph of a JD has been shown to be equivalent to a long list of "desirable" properties [4]. Although such properties are not a the subject of this work, two of the equivalent characterizations of such "desirability" do arise indirectly. The first asserts that pairwise consistency implies global consistency. For this definition, assume that $\mathcal{F} = \bowtie[J]$; that is, that $\mathbf{E}_{\mathbf{U}}^{\mathcal{F}}$ is constrained by $\bowtie[J]$ alone. Call $\bowtie[J]$ *pairwise definable* if for any $M_1, M_2, \ldots, M_k \in \mathsf{LDB}(\mathbf{E}_{\mathbf{U}}^{\mathcal{F}})$, if $\pi_{\mathbf{U}_j \cap \mathbf{U}_{j'}}(M_j) = \pi_{\mathbf{U}_j \cap \mathbf{U}_{j'}}(M_{j'})$ for all $j, j' \in \{1, \ldots, k\}$, then there is an $M \in \mathsf{LDB}(\mathbf{E}_{\mathbf{U}}^{\mathcal{F}})$ with $\pi_{\mathbf{U}_i}(M_i) = \pi_{\mathbf{U}_i}(M)$ for $i \in \{1, \ldots, k\}$. (In the cases that $\mathbf{U}_j \cap \mathbf{U}_{j'} = \emptyset$, this condition is trivially satisfied.)

A second "desirable" condition involves representation of $\bowtie[J]$ by simple JDs. Specifically, the JD $\bowtie[J]$ is *binary* (or a *BJD*) if J consists of exactly two elements. Binary JDs are an alternate representation of *multivalued dependencies* or *MVDs*. Call $\bowtie[J]$ *BJD-representable* if it is equivalent to a set of binary join dependencies, called a *binary basis* for $\bowtie[J]$. Then, $\bowtie[J]$ is has an acyclic hypergraph iff it is pairwise definable and iff it has a binary basis [4, Thm. 3.4].

In accordance with customary terminology, a JD which satisfies any of these "desirable" properties will be called *acyclic*.

Definition 3.4 (Constructive join dependencies). The classification scheme of Definition 2.5 involves not only minimality and optimality of ordinary complements, but optimality of meet complements as well. As illustrated in the examples of the introduction, as well as recaptured in [14, Prop. 2.17], meet complementation is closely related to dependency preservation. Unfortunately, as noted in Definition 3.2, the explicit characterization of view dependencies is a very difficult issue in general. To sidestep that issue, at least to some degree, the alternative notion of a constructive join dependency, which involves only states of the main schema $\mathbf{E}_{\mathbf{U}}^{\mathcal{F}}$, is employed. The idea is to enhance the concept of pairwise definability identified in Definition 3.3 to the case that the constraint set $\mathcal{F}$ contains not only the JD but other constraints as well.

Continuing with the context of Definition 3.3, the join dependency $\bowtie[J] = \bowtie[\mathbf{U}_1, \mathbf{U}_2, \ldots, \mathbf{U}_k]$ is said to be *constructive* (or a *CJD*) for $\mathcal{F}$ if any set of legal databases on the views $\{\Pi_{\mathbf{U}_1}, \Pi_{\mathbf{U}_2}, \ldots, \Pi_{\mathbf{U}_k}\}$ which are pairwise consistent define a legal database of the main schema. Formally, $\bowtie[J]$ is a CJD for $\mathcal{F}$ if for any $M_1, \ldots M_k \in \mathsf{LDB}(\mathbf{E}_\mathbf{U}^{\mathcal{F}})$ with $\pi_{\mathbf{U}_j \cap \mathbf{U}_{j'}}(M_j) = \pi_{\mathbf{U}_j \cap \mathbf{U}_{j'}}(M_{j'})$ for all $j, j', \in \{1, \ldots, k\}$, there is an $M \in \mathsf{LDB}(\mathbf{E}_\mathbf{U}^{\mathcal{F}})$ with $\pi_{\mathbf{U}_i}(M_i) = \pi_{\mathbf{U}_i}(M)$ for $i \in \{1, \ldots, k\}$.

Think of $\pi_{\mathbf{U}_i}(M_i)$ as a local database on the schema of $\Pi_{\mathbf{U}_i}$. Thus, the constraints of $\Pi_{\mathbf{U}_i}$ are recaptured implicitly via a database, rather than via an explicit representation. This construction recaptures the essence of dependency preservation by requiring that any collection of view databases which agree on their common columns must arise from a single database of the main schema. If a cover of the dependencies in $\mathbf{E}_\mathbf{U}^{\mathcal{F}}$ were not embeddable, there would be view states which would not be so combinable.

It is easy to see that constructibility recaptures the situations of the examples of Sec. 1. In particular, $\bowtie[ABC, CD]$ is a CJD for $\mathcal{F}_0$ and $\mathcal{F}_2$, but not for $\mathcal{F}_1$ or $\mathcal{F}_3$. However, $\bowtie[ABC, BCD]$ is a CJD for $\mathcal{F}_1$.

It is important to observe that, unlike pairwise definability, constructibility is a property of the entire set $\mathcal{F}$ of constraints, and not just a JD. Nevertheless, the constructibility condition excludes cyclic JDs, even those induced by FDs [2, Sec. 7].

Definition 3.5 (Type classification of Π-complements). If $J = \{\mathbf{U}_1, \mathbf{U}_2\}$ is an attribute-set collection over $\mathbf{U}$ consisting of exactly two elements, so that $\bowtie[J]$ is a BJD which holds on $\mathbf{E}_\mathbf{U}^{\mathcal{F}}$, then it is immediate that $\{\Pi_{\mathbf{U}_1}, \Pi_{\mathbf{U}_2}\}$ forms a complementary pair, called a Π-*complementary pair*, with $\Pi_{\mathbf{U}_1}$ and $\Pi_{\mathbf{U}_2}$ called Π-*complements*. The notions of *minimal* and *optimal* Π-complement are obtained in the natural way by specializing the definitions of Summary 2.2 with $\mathcal{V} = \Pi\text{-Views}\langle \mathbf{E}_\mathbf{U}^{\mathcal{F}} \rangle$.

If $\bowtie[J]$ is furthermore a CJD with respect to $\mathcal{F}$, then $\{\Pi_{\mathbf{U}_1}, \Pi_{\mathbf{U}_2}\}$ necessarily forms a meet-complementary pair. This follows immediately from [14, Prop. 2.14]. Such a meet complementary pair of Π-views is called a $\wedge\Pi$-*complementary pair*, and Γ_1 and Γ_2 are called $\wedge\Pi$-*complements* of each other. Minimal and optimal $\wedge\Pi$-complements for a Π-view Γ are defined by taking $\mathcal{V}$ to be the set $\mathsf{MeetSet}\langle \Gamma; \Pi\text{-Views}\langle \mathbf{E}_\mathbf{U}^{\mathcal{F}} \rangle \rangle$ of all Π-views of $\mathbf{E}_\mathbf{U}^{\mathcal{F}}$ which are also $\wedge\Pi$-complements of Γ.

Definition 3.6 (The natural order on attribute-set collections). If J consists of more than two elements, then complementary views may still be obtained from $\bowtie[J]$ by partitioning J into two disjoint sets. To show this, first recall that there is a natural order on full attribute-set collections over $\mathbf{U}$, given by $J_1 \leq J_2$ iff for each $\mathbf{W}_1 \in J_1$ there is a $\mathbf{W}_2 \in J_2$ such that $\mathbf{W}_2 \subseteq \mathbf{W}_1$ [5, Sec. 3]. This ordering induces a natural implication order on full JDs, which is made explicit in the following.

Lemma 3.7 (Full JD implication via $\preceq$). Let J_1 and J_2 be full attribute-set collections over $\mathbf{U}$. Then $\bowtie[J_1] \models \bowtie[J_2]$ iff $J_2 \leq J_1$.

Proof. The "only if" direction is a special case of a standard inference rule for JDs, called the *covering rule* [6]. The "if" part is obtained easily by applying the specialization of the classical chase inference procedure to full join dependencies [25, Cor. 5.3]. The details are straightforward and left to the reader. $\square$

Proposition 3.8 (Complementary pairs from JDs). *Let J be a full attribute-set collection over $\mathbf{U}$ with $\mathcal{F} \models \bowtie[J]$, and let $\{J_1, J_2\}$ be a partition of J; i.e., $J_1 \cup J_2 = J$ and $J_1 \cap J_2 = \emptyset$. Define $\mathbf{P}_i = \bigcup J_i$ for $i \in \{1, 2\}$.*

(a) $\{\Pi_{\mathbf{P}_1}, \Pi_{\mathbf{P}_2}\}$ forms a complementary pair of views of $\mathbf{E}_{\mathbf{U}}^{\mathcal{F}}$.

(b) If $\bowtie[J]$ is furthermore a CJD with respect to $\mathcal{F}$, then $\{\Pi_{\mathbf{P}_1}, \Pi_{\mathbf{P}_2}\}$ forms a meet-complementary pair of views of $\mathbf{E}_{\mathbf{U}}^{\mathcal{F}}$.

Proof. Part (a) follows immediately from Lemma 3.7. For (b), suppose that $J = \{\mathbf{U}_1, \mathbf{U}_2, \ldots, \mathbf{U}_k\}$. Let $M_1', M_2' \in \mathsf{LDB}(\mathbf{E}_{\mathbf{U}}^{\mathcal{F}})$ with $\pi_{\mathbf{P}_1 \cap \mathbf{P}_2}(M_1') = \pi_{\mathbf{P}_1 \cap \mathbf{P}_2}(M_2')$, and for $i \in \{1, \ldots, k\}$, define $M_i = M_1'$ if $\mathbf{U}_i \subseteq \mathbf{P}_1$ and $M_i = M_2'$ if $\mathbf{U}_i \subseteq \mathbf{P}_2$. If $\mathbf{U}_i \subseteq \mathbf{P}_1 \cap \mathbf{P}_2$, then choose M_i arbitrarily as M_1' or M_2'. Then, in particular, $\pi_{\mathbf{U}_i \cap \mathbf{U}_j}(M_1') = \pi_{\mathbf{U}_i \cap \mathbf{U}_j}(M_2')$ for any $i, j \in \{1, \ldots, k\}$. Since $\bowtie[J]$ is assumed to be constructive, there is an $M \in \mathsf{LDB}(\mathbf{E}_{\mathbf{U}}^{\mathcal{F}})$ with $\pi_{\mathbf{U}_i}(M_i) = M$ for $i \in \{1, \ldots, k\}$. From this it follows that $\pi_{\mathbf{P}_i}(M_i') = M$ for $i \in \{1, 2\}$, as required. $\qquad \square$

Definition 3.9 (Redundancy and governing JDs). Proposition 3.8 says nothing about the optimality of the complements. For the decomposition identified by Proposition 3.8 to yield optimal Π-complements of a given type i (for $i \in \{0, 1, 2, 3\}$), it is necessary to establish further conditions on the join dependency which governs the decomposition.

There are two distinct ways in which redundancy may arise. First of all, if $\mathbf{U}_i \subsetneq \mathbf{U}_j$ (i.e., if $\mathbf{U}_i$ is a proper subset of $\mathbf{U}_j$) for (necessarily distinct) i and j, then $\mathbf{U}_i$ may be removed from J without altering the semantics of $\bowtie[J]$. This form is called *trivial redundancy*, and is a strictly set-theoretic property of the set J itself. Call the set J *reduced* if for no distinct i, j is it the case that $\mathbf{U}_i \subsetneq \mathbf{U}_j$. This is tantamount to requiring that J form an *antichain* [8, 1.3] under set inclusion. It is always a trivial matter to require that J be reduced, and this will be done from now on.

There are two far less trivial, semantic forms of (non-)redundancy. Let $\bowtie[J]$ be a full and reduced JD on $\mathbf{E}_{\mathbf{U}}^{\mathcal{F}}$ which is entailed by $\mathcal{F}$.

(a) Call $\bowtie[J]$ *JD-essential* on $\mathbf{E}_{\mathbf{U}}^{\mathcal{F}}$ if it is acyclic and for any full JD φ on $\mathbf{E}_{\mathbf{U}}^{\mathcal{F}}$ with $\mathcal{F} \models \varphi$ and $\varphi \models \bowtie[J]$, it must be the case that $\varphi = \bowtie[J]$.

(b) Call $\bowtie[J]$ *JD-covering* on $\mathbf{E}_{\mathbf{U}}^{\mathcal{F}}$ if for any full JD φ on $\mathbf{E}_{\mathbf{U}}^{\mathcal{F}}$, it must be the case that $\bowtie[J] \models \varphi$.

Thus, $\bowtie[J]$ is JD-essential if it is not implied by any stronger JD which holds on $\mathbf{E}_{\mathbf{U}}^{\mathcal{F}}$, while it is JD-governing if it implies all other full JDs which hold on $\mathbf{E}_{\mathbf{U}}^{\mathcal{F}}$. In particular, if $\bowtie[J]$ is JD-covering, then it is also JD-essential.

There are analogous notions for CJDs. Let $\bowtie[J]$ be a full and reduced CJD on $\mathbf{E}_{\mathbf{U}}^{\mathcal{F}}$ which is entailed by $\mathcal{F}$.

(a') Call $\bowtie[J]$ *CJD-essential* on $\mathbf{E}_{\mathbf{U}}^{\mathcal{F}}$ if for any full CJD φ on $\mathbf{E}_{\mathbf{U}}^{\mathcal{F}}$ with $\mathcal{F} \models \varphi$ and $\varphi \models \bowtie[J]$, it must be the case that $\varphi = \bowtie[J]$.

(b') Call $\bowtie[J]$ *CJD-covering* on $\mathbf{E}_{\mathbf{U}}^{\mathcal{F}}$ if for any full CJD φ on $\mathbf{E}_{\mathbf{U}}^{\mathcal{F}}$, it must be the case that $\bowtie[J] \models \varphi$.

Now it is possible to define types of non-redundancy for JDs and CJDs which correspond to the types of optimality for complements which are given in Table 2. These are shown as types of *governing* in Table 3.

Table 3. Types of semantic non-redundancy

n for type-n-governing JD	Form of non-redundancy	
	JD-	CJD-
0	covering	—
1	—	covering
2	essential	covering
3	covering	covering

For example, the JD $\bowtie[J]$ is *type 0 governing* (on $\mathbf{E}_{\mathbf{U}}^{\mathcal{F}}$) if it is JD-covering, and it is *type 2 governing* if it is a CJD which is JD-essential and CJD-covering.

Example 3.10. Consider again the four schemata of Sec. 1. The dependency $\bowtie[ABC, CD]$ is both JD-covering and CJD-covering on $\mathbf{E}_0$, and hence it is governing of type i on $\mathbf{E}_0$ for all $i \in \{0, 1, 2, 3\}$.

This same dependency is not JD-essential on $\mathbf{E}_1$, since both $\bowtie[AB, BC, CD]$ and $\bowtie[AB, BD, CD]$ hold on $\mathbf{E}_1$ and each implies $\bowtie[ABC, CD]$. Indeed both $\bowtie[AB, BC, CD]$ and $\bowtie[AB, BD, CD]$ are JD-essential, so neither can be JD-covering. The JD $\bowtie[ABC, BCD]$ is CJD-optimal, but cannot be JD-essential, since it is implied by $\bowtie[AB, BC, CD]$. Thus $\bowtie[ABC, BCD]$ is governing of type 1 on $\mathbf{E}_1$, but for no other type.

The JD $\bowtie[AB, BC, CD]$ is both JD-essential and CJD-optimal on $\mathbf{E}_2$. However, it is not JD-optimal, since $\bowtie[AB, BD, CD]$ is also JD-essential. Thus, it is governing of types 1 and 2 on $\mathbf{E}_2$, but not of types 0 or 3.

Each of the six JDs $\bowtie[AB, BC, CD]$, $\bowtie[AB, BD, CD]$, $\bowtie[AC, BC, BD]$, $\bowtie[AC, BD, CD]$, $\bowtie[AD, BC, CD]$, and $\bowtie[AD, BD, CD]$, is both JD-essential and CJD-essential on $\mathbf{E}_3$, and so none can be JD-governing or CJD-governing. This schema has no governing JD or CJD.

Definition 3.11 (The join-reconstruction property). The types of Definition 3.9 provide the proper characterizations via JDs to ensure the corresponding types of optimality, provided one further condition is imposed, that of *join reconstruction*. Although it is natural to think that when a schema is decomposed into projections, reconstruction must be defined by the join, this need not always be the case. For example, let $\mathbf{E}_4$ be the universal schema with the single relation schema $R[ABC]$, constrained by two rather unconventional dependencies. The first is $\psi_{41} = (\forall x)(\forall y)(\neg R(x, y, x))$, which states the the A and C values of a tuple must not be the same. The second is a conditional join dependency which takes this restriction into account: $\psi_{42} = (\forall x)(\forall y)(\forall z)((R(x, y, z') \wedge R(x', y, z) \wedge (x \neq z)) \Rightarrow R(x, y, z))$. In other words, the usual join dependency $\bowtie[AB, BC]$ holds conditionally, for all pairs of tuples which would not result in a tuple which would be illegal under constraint ψ_{41}. Nevertheless, the decomposition of $\mathbf{E}_4$ into its AB and BC projections is lossless. The reconstruction mapping is a conditional join which ignores pairs of view tuples which would result in a tuple t with $t[A] = t[C]$. In particular, it is not the usual join.

It is not the purpose of this paper to investigate this phenomenon in detail. The above example is included to illustrate that it must not simply be assumed that reconstruction of projections must be defined by the join. Suffice to say that it is possible to show that this non-join sort of reconstruction cannot occur within the context of common database dependencies which are defined by Horn sentences [9], [17, Def. 21]. For this paper, this difficulty will simply be assumed away. Say that a universal schema $\mathbf{E}_{\mathbf{U}}^{\mathcal{F}}$ has the *join-reconstruction property* if for every lossless decomposition of that schema into projections, the reconstruction mapping is necessarily the join.

Notation 3.12 (Join-reconstruction property assumed). Unless stated specifically to the contrary, for the rest of this section, assume that $\mathbf{E}_{\mathbf{U}}^{\mathcal{F}}$ has the join-reconstruction property.

Lemma 3.13 (Optimal complementary pairs from JDs). *Let J be a full attribute-set collection over $\mathbf{U}$, let $i \in \{0, 1, 2, 3\}$, and assume that $\bowtie[J]$ is governing of type i relative to Π-Views$\langle\mathbf{E}_{\mathbf{U}}^{\mathcal{F}}\rangle$. Then for every partition $\{J_1, J_2\}$ of J, $\{\Pi_{\bigcup J_1}, \Pi_{\bigcup J_2}\}$ forms an optimal complementary pair of type i relative to Π-Views$\langle\mathbf{E}_{\mathbf{U}}^{\mathcal{F}}\rangle$.*

Proof. The requirement that $\mathbf{E}_{\mathbf{U}}^{\mathcal{F}}$ have the join-reconstruction property limits the reconstruction mapping to the join. From Lemma 3.7 follows directly that smaller optimal complements must arise from JDs and CJDs which are larger in the ordering $\leq$ of Definition 3.6. The optimality then follows directly using the concepts of Definition 3.9 and Table 3.   □

Definition 3.14 (The Π-basis of a view relative to J). It is easy to extend the result of Lemma 3.13 to projections which are not defined by the union of some of the elements of J, thus obtaining a theory of optimal Π- and $\wedge\Pi$-complements for all Π-views on a suitable schema. Given an attribute-set collection J over $\mathbf{U}$ and any $\mathbf{U}' \subseteq \mathbf{U}$, define the elements of J *covered* by $\mathbf{U}'$ to be $\mathsf{Covered}_{\langle J; \Pi \rangle}\langle\mathbf{U}'\rangle = \{\mathbf{W} \in J \mid \mathbf{W} \subseteq \mathbf{U}'\}$. The *$\Pi$-complementary cover* to $\mathbf{U}'$ relative to J is given by $\overline{\mathsf{Covered}}_{\langle J; \Pi \rangle}\langle\mathbf{U}'\rangle = J \setminus \mathsf{Covered}_{\langle J; \Pi \rangle}\langle\mathbf{U}'\rangle$.

Theorem 3.15 (Governing implies optimal complements). *Let J be a full attribute-set collection over $\mathbf{U}$, let $i \in \{0, 1, 2, 3\}$, and assume that $\bowtie[J]$ is governing of type i relative to Π-Views$\langle\mathbf{E}_{\mathbf{U}}^{\mathcal{F}}\rangle$. Then for every $\mathbf{W} \subseteq \mathbf{U}$, the view $\Pi_{\mathbf{W}}$ has an optimal complement of type i relative to Π-Views$\langle\mathbf{E}_{\mathbf{U}}^{\mathcal{F}}\rangle$, given explicitly by $\Pi_{\mathbf{W}'}$, with $\mathbf{W}' = \bigcup \overline{\mathsf{Covered}}_{\langle J; \Pi \rangle}\langle\mathbf{W}\rangle$.*

Proof. With $\mathbf{W}' = \bigcup \overline{\mathsf{Covered}}_{\langle J; \Pi \rangle}\langle\mathbf{W}\rangle$, the view $\Pi_{\mathbf{W}'}$ is a complement of $\Pi_{\mathbf{W}}$ of the appropriate type, since $\bigcup \mathsf{Covered}_{\langle J; \Pi \rangle}\langle\mathbf{W}\rangle \subseteq \mathbf{W}$, and by Lemma 3.13, $\Pi_{\mathsf{Covered}_{\langle J; \Pi \rangle}\langle\mathbf{W}\rangle}$ and $\Pi_{\mathbf{W}'}$ are each (optimal) complements of one another of type i. On the other hand, an application of Lemma 3.7 shows that any Π-complement of $\Pi_{\mathbf{W}}$ must include at least the attributes included in the members of $\overline{\mathsf{Covered}}_{\langle J; \Pi \rangle}\langle\mathbf{W}\rangle$, whence the characterization of the complement holds.   □

Example 3.16. Continue with the discussion of Example 3.10 of the four schemata of Sec. 1. The optimality properties which have already been presented directly in Definition 2.5 may now be verified formally using Lemma 3.13.

Because the dependency $\bowtie[ABC, CD]$ is governing of all four types on $\mathbf{E}_0$, $\{\Pi_{ABC}^{\mathbf{E}_0}, \Pi_{CD}^{\mathbf{E}_0}\}$ forms an optimal complementary pair of type i for all four types relative to Π-Views$\langle \mathbf{E}_0 \rangle$. It is optimal regardless of whether or not dependency preservation is required.

The dependency $\bowtie[ABC, BCD]$ is CJD-optimal on $\mathbf{E}_1$, but is not even JD-essential, so $\{\Pi_{ABC}^{\mathbf{E}_1}, \Pi_{BCD}^{\mathbf{E}_1}\}$ forms an optimal complementary pair of type 1, but for no other types. In other words, it is optimal for dependency preservation, but not generally.

On $\mathbf{E}_2$, $\bowtie[ABC, CD]$ is governing of types 1 and 2, so $\{\Pi_{ABC}^{\mathbf{E}_2}, \Pi_{CD}^{\mathbf{E}_2}\}$ forms an optimal complementary pair of types 1 and 2, but not for types 0 or 3. In other words, it is optimal for dependency preservation, and, additionally, it is essential (i.e., minimal) amongst full JDs on $\mathbf{E}_2$.

On $\mathbf{E}_3$, $\bowtie[AB, BC, CD]$ is both JD- and CJD-essential, but not governing for any of the four types, and so $\{\Pi_{ABC}^{\mathbf{E}_3}, \Pi_{CD}^{\mathbf{E}_3}\}$ does not form an optimal complementary pair in any of these senses. Indeed, $\{\Pi_{ABC}^{\mathbf{E}_3}, \Pi_{BD}^{\mathbf{E}_3}\}$ and $\{\Pi_{ABD}^{\mathbf{E}_3}, \Pi_{CD}^{\mathbf{E}_3}\}$ form alternate minimal complementary pairs relative to Π-Views$\langle \mathbf{E}_3 \rangle$. As shown in Example 3.10, it has six distinct JDs, each of which is both JD-essential and CJD-essential.

Example 3.17. Let $\mathbf{E}_5$ be the universal relational schema whose only relation symbol is $R[ABCDE]$, constrained by the FDs $\mathcal{F}_5 = \{B \to C, C \to D, D \to E\}$. Arguing in a fashion similar to that for $\mathbf{E}_2$, it is not difficult to see that $\bowtie[AB, BC, CD, DE]$ is governing of types 1 and 2, but not of types 0 or 3, on the schema $\mathbf{E}_3$.

Let $J_1 = \{AB, DE\}$ and $\mathbf{P}_1 = \bigcup J_1 = ABDE$. In the notation of Proposition 3.8 and Lemma 3.13, J_2 must be $\{BC, CD\}$, and so $\mathbf{P}_2 = \bigcup J_2 = BCD$. Thus, the $\wedge\Pi$-complement of $\Pi_{ABDE}^{\mathbf{E}_5}$ is $\Pi_{BCD}^{\mathbf{E}_5}$, and vice-versa. Note that the embedded join dependency $\bowtie[AB, DE]$ is not satisfied in the schema of $\Pi_{ABDE}^{\mathbf{E}_5}$. There is no requirement that J_1 and J_2 in Proposition 3.8 and Theorem 3.15 satisfy any embedded join constraints.

The use of this schema to illustrate key points continues in Example 3.21 below.

Theorem 3.15 establishes that if $\mathbf{E}_{\mathbf{U}}^{\mathcal{F}}$ is governed by a JD of type i, then all projections have optimal complements of that type. It is also possible to establish a sort of converse, which states that if all projections have optimal complements of a given type, then the schema must be governed by a JD of that type. The only qualification is that the set of all JDs which are generated by the projections and their complements must be equivalent to a single JD; that is, it must be BJD representable. The details are sketched below.

Discussion 3.18 (Further properties of representation via BJDs). Recall from Definition 3.3 that one of the "desirable" properties of a JD $\bowtie[J]$ is that it be representable by a set of BJDs. There is a further refinement of this idea which will prove useful. Let $\varphi_1 = \bowtie[\mathbf{U}_{11}, \mathbf{U}_{12}]$ and $\varphi_2 = \bowtie[\mathbf{U}_{21}, \mathbf{U}_{22}]$ be BJDs. Say that $\{\varphi_1, \varphi_2\}$ has the *subset property* if at least one of the following four conditions holds:

$$\mathbf{U}_{11} \subseteq \mathbf{U}_{21} \text{ and } \mathbf{U}_{22} \subseteq \mathbf{U}_{12} \qquad \mathbf{U}_{11} \subseteq \mathbf{U}_{22} \text{ and } \mathbf{U}_{21} \subseteq \mathbf{U}_{12}$$
$$\mathbf{U}_{21} \subseteq \mathbf{U}_{11} \text{ and } \mathbf{U}_{12} \subseteq \mathbf{U}_{22} \qquad \mathbf{U}_{22} \subseteq \mathbf{U}_{11} \text{ and } \mathbf{U}_{12} \subseteq \mathbf{U}_{21}$$

In other words, φ_1 and φ_2 have an asymmetry relationship in that one element of φ_1 is at least as large as one of the elements of φ_2, and the other element of φ_2 is at least as large as the remaining element of φ_1. The set S of BJDs on $\mathbf{E}_{\mathbf{U}}^{\mathcal{F}}$ has the *subset property* if every pair of elements from S has the property. The key result is that if $\bowtie[J]$ is equivalent to a set of BJDs, then it is equivalent to a set of BJDs with the subset property [13, Thm. 6].

For $i \in \{0, 1, 2, 3\}$, call a BJD $\bowtie[\mathbf{W}_1, \mathbf{W}_2]$ *optimal of type i* relative to Π-Views$\langle \mathbf{E}_{\mathbf{U}}^{\mathcal{F}} \rangle$ on $\mathbf{E}_{\mathbf{U}}^{\mathcal{F}}$ if $\{\Pi_{\mathbf{W}_1}, \Pi_{\mathbf{W}_2}\}$ is an optimal pair of type i relative to Π-Views$\langle \mathbf{E}_{\mathbf{U}}^{\mathcal{F}} \rangle$.

Call the BJD $\bowtie[\mathbf{W}_1, \mathbf{W}_2]$ *primary* relative to $\bowtie[J]$ if there is a partition $\{J_1, J_2\}$ of J with the property that for $i \in \{1, 2\}$, $\mathbf{W}_i = \bigcup J_i$ and for each connected block B of J, the subset of B which is part of J_i is itself connected. Put another way, this last condition means that the the embedded join dependency $\bowtie[J_i]$ holds on $\Pi_{\mathbf{W}_i}$.

Call a binary basis B of $\bowtie[J]$ *primary* if it consists of BJDs with the subset property and with the additional property that each $\varphi \in B$ is primary relative to $\bowtie[J]$.

Lemma 3.19 (Optimal complements and BJDs). *Let J be a full attribute-set collection over $\mathbf{U}$, and assume that $\bowtie[J]$ is acyclic and reduced.*

(a) *$\bowtie[J]$ has a primary basis relative to $\bowtie[J]$.*

(b) *If $\bowtie[J]$ is JD-essential (resp. JD-governing), then it has a primary basis relative to $\bowtie[J]$ with the further property that for each $\bowtie[\mathbf{W}_1, \mathbf{W}_2]$ in that basis, $\{\Pi_{\mathbf{W}_1}, \Pi_{\mathbf{W}_2}\}$ is a minimal (resp. optimal) complementary pair relative to Π-Views$\langle \mathbf{E}_{\mathbf{U}}^{\mathcal{F}} \rangle$.*

(c) *If $\bowtie[J]$ is constructive, then every full JD φ with $\bowtie[J] \models \varphi$ is constructive as well.*

(d) *For $i \in \{0, 1, 2, 3\}$, if $\bowtie[J]$ is type i governing on $\mathbf{E}_{\mathbf{U}}^{\mathcal{F}}$, then it has a primary basis consisting of optimal complementary pairs of type i relative to Π-Views$\langle \mathbf{E}_{\mathbf{U}}^{\mathcal{F}} \rangle$.*

(e) *If S is a primary basis of $\bowtie[J]$ with the property that every $\varphi \in S$ is constructive, then $\bowtie[J]$ is constructive as well.*

(f) *If S is a binary basis of $\bowtie[J]$ consisting of optimal complementary pairs of type i relative to Π-Views$\langle \mathbf{E}_{\mathbf{U}}^{\mathcal{F}} \rangle$, then $\bowtie[J]$ is governing of type i on $\mathbf{E}_{\mathbf{U}}^{\mathcal{F}}$.*

Proof outline. To show (a), let $B_1, \ldots, B_\ell$ denote the connected blocks of $\bowtie[J]$. For each such block B_i, let $\langle \mathbf{U}_{i1}, \ldots, \mathbf{U}_{i\ell_i} \rangle$ denote an ordering of its elements with the property that each element except the first is connected to at least one element which precedes it in the ordering. Let $\langle n_1, \ldots, n_\ell \rangle$ denote a sequence of ℓ numbers, with $0 \leq n_i \leq \ell_i$ for each i and at least one of the numbers not zero.

Define $K_{\langle n_1,\ldots,n_\ell\rangle}$ to be the subset of J consisting of the first n_i elements of B_i for each i, and define $K'_{\langle n_1,\ldots,n_\ell\rangle} = J \setminus K_{\langle n_1,\ldots,n_\ell\rangle}$. It is straightforward to verify that the set of all BJDs of the form $\bowtie[\bigcup K_{\langle n_1,\ldots,n_\ell\rangle}, \bigcup K'_{\langle n_1,\ldots,n_\ell\rangle}]$ is a primary basis for $\bowtie[J]$.

Keeping Lemma 3.7 in mind, the proof of (b) is a simple verification.

Again keeping Lemma 3.7 in mind, part (c) follows directly from the definition of constructive.

Part (d) is a consequence of (b) and (c).

The details of the proof of (e) depend upon the algorithm of [13]; the idea is as follows. Let $\bowtie[\mathbf{W}_1, \mathbf{W}_2] \in S$, and let $M_1, M_2 \in \mathsf{LDB}(\mathbf{E}_{\mathbf{U}}^{\mathcal{F}})$ with $\pi_{\mathbf{W}_1 \cap \mathbf{W}_2}(M_1) = \pi_{\mathbf{W}_1 \cap \mathbf{W}_2}(M_2)$. By the definition of constructive, there is an $M \in \mathsf{LDB}(\mathbf{D})$ with $\pi_{\mathbf{W}_i}(M_i) = \pi_{\mathbf{W}_i}(M)$ for $i \in \{1,2\}$. Now, owing to the subset condition, applying a second $\bowtie[\mathbf{W}_3, \mathbf{W}_4] \in S$ will result in a split of only one of $\mathbf{W}_1$ and $\mathbf{W}_2$. Assume, say, that $\mathbf{W}_1 \subseteq \mathbf{W}_3$ and $\mathbf{W}_4 \subseteq \mathbf{W}_2$. The consequence of combining these two JDs is then $\bowtie[\mathbf{W}_1, \mathbf{W}_2 \cap \mathbf{W}_3, \mathbf{W}_4]$; i.e., $\mathbf{W}_2$ is split into $\mathbf{W}_2 \cap \mathbf{W}_3$ and $\mathbf{W}_4$, while $\mathbf{W}_1$ is not split. Now, letting $\mathbf{W}_{23}$ denote $\mathbf{W}_2 \cap \mathbf{W}_3$, if $M_1, M_{23}, M_4 \in \mathsf{LDB}(\mathbf{E}_{\mathbf{U}}^{\mathcal{F}})$ with the property that $\pi_{\mathbf{W}_j \cap \mathbf{W}_{j'}}(M_j) = \pi_{\mathbf{W}_j \cap \mathbf{W}_{j'}}(M_{j'})$ for $j, j' \in \{1, 23, 4\}$, then an $M \in \mathsf{LDB}(\mathbf{E}_{\mathbf{U}}^{\mathcal{F}})$ with the property that $\pi_{\mathbf{W}_i}(M_i) = \pi_{\mathbf{W}_i}(M)$ for $i \in \{1, 23, 4\}$ may be constructed in steps. First, construct an $M_2 \in \mathsf{LDB}(\mathbf{E}_{\mathbf{U}}^{\mathcal{F}})$ with the property that $\pi_{\mathbf{W}_i}(M_i) = \pi_{\mathbf{W}_i}(M_2)$ for $i \in \{23, 4\}$, and then combine that M_2 with M_1 to obtain an M which agrees with each of M_1, M_{23}, and M_4 on the associated projections. Continue on with further primary BJDs in an inductive fashion. The details of this construction are left to the reader.

Finally, (f) follows from the previous assertions. $\square$

The converse of Theorem 3.15, which follows from Lemma 3.19, as the following.

Theorem 3.20 (Optimal complements imply governing). *Let $i \in \{0, 1, 2, 3\}$, and assume that for every $\mathbf{W} \subseteq \mathbf{U}$, $\Pi_{\mathbf{W}}$ has an optimal complement of type i on $\mathbf{E}_{\mathbf{U}}^{\mathcal{F}}$ relative to Π-Views$\langle \mathbf{E}_{\mathbf{U}}^{\mathcal{F}}\rangle$. Assume further that the set of all BJDs of the form $\bowtie[\mathbf{W}_1, \mathbf{W}_2]$ for which $\{\Pi_{\mathbf{W}_1}, \Pi_{\mathbf{W}_2}\}$ is an optimal complementary pair of type i relative to Π-Views$\langle \mathbf{E}_{\mathbf{U}}^{\mathcal{F}}\rangle$ is equivalent to a single join dependency. Then that JD is type i governing on $\mathbf{E}_{\mathbf{U}}^{\mathcal{F}}$.*

Observe that in Theorem 3.20 it is necessary to assume that the BJDs generate a single join dependency. This corresponds to assuming that there is a governing JD which is acyclic. Of course, there are cases which lie outside of this framework, but it is unclear whether they ever occur in real modelling situations.

To conclude the investigation, the idea of working with views which are sets of projections, rather than single projections, is examined briefly. First, a motivating example is discussed.

Example 3.21. Continue with the schema $\mathbf{E}_5$ of Example 3.17; i.e., with $J = \{AB, BC, CD, DE\}$. Let let $\mathbf{U}' = ABE$. Then $\mathsf{Covered}_{\langle J;\Pi\rangle}\langle \mathbf{U}'\rangle = \{AB\}$, and so $\overline{\mathsf{Covered}}_{\langle J;\Pi\rangle}\langle \mathbf{U}'\rangle = BC \cup CD \cup DE = BCDE$, whence the optimal complement of $\Pi_{ABE}^{\mathbf{E}_5}$ of types 1 and 2 relative to Π-Views$\langle \mathbf{E}_5\rangle$ must be $\Pi_{BCDE}^{\mathbf{E}_5}$.

On the other hand, if $\mathbf{U}' = BCE$, then $\mathsf{Covered}_{\langle J;\Pi \rangle}\langle \mathbf{U}' \rangle = \{BC\}$, and so $\overline{\mathsf{Covered}}_{\langle J;\Pi \rangle}\langle \mathbf{U}' \rangle = AB \cup CD \cup DE = ABCDE = \mathbf{U}$, i.e., the optimal complements of both types relative to Π-Views$\langle \mathbf{E}_5 \rangle$ is Π_{ABCDE}, which is the identity view. With that complement, no updates at all are possible under the constant-complement strategy [3] [14]. This drawback may be remedied, at least to some degree, by working with views which are defined by sets of projections instead of single projections. A brief presentation of this extension follows.

Definition 3.22 ($\bigvee \Pi$-views). A *joined Π-view*, or $\bigvee \Pi$-*view*, is defined by a set of projections, rather than by just a single projection. Continue with the context of a full attribute-set collection J on $\mathbf{E}_\mathbf{U}^{\mathcal{F}}$, and let $J' \subseteq J$. The $\bigvee \Pi$-view defined by J', denoted $\Pi_{J'} = (\mathbf{E}_{J'}, \pi_{J'})$, has in its schema one relation $R_\mathbf{W}[\mathbf{W}]$ for each $\mathbf{W} \in J'$. The view morphism $\pi_{J'}$ sends an instance of the universal relation $R[\mathbf{U}]$ to each of its projections defined by J'. More formally, this view is the product of the set $\{\Pi_\mathbf{W}^{\mathbf{E}_\mathbf{U}} \mid \mathbf{W} \in J'\}$ of views, as elaborated in [16, 3.4]. The set of all $\bigvee \Pi$-views on $\mathbf{E}_\mathbf{U}^{\mathcal{F}}$ is denoted $\bigvee \Pi$-Views$\langle \mathbf{E}_\mathbf{U}^{\mathcal{F}} \rangle$.

For $i \in \{0, 1, 2, 3\}$, the notions of optimal complement of type i, as well as optimal complementary pairs of type i, relative to $\bigvee \Pi$-Views$\langle \mathbf{E}_\mathbf{U}^{\mathcal{F}} \rangle$ are defined as the natural extensions of the corresponding notions relative to Π-Views$\langle \mathbf{E}_\mathbf{U}^{\mathcal{F}} \rangle$.

Since the notation to describe such schemata fully becomes cumbersome, the idea will instead be illustrated by example, using $\mathbf{E}_5$ of Example 3.17 and Example 3.21 as the main schema. For $J' = \{AB, CD\}$, $\Pi_{J'}^{\mathbf{E}_5} = \Pi_{\{AB,CD\}}^{\mathbf{E}_5}$ has two relation symbols $R_{AB}[AB]$ and $R_{CD}[CD]$. For $M \in \mathsf{LDB}(\mathbf{E}_5)$, the view mapping $\pi_{J'}^{\mathbf{E}_5} = \pi_{\{AB,CD\}}^{\mathbf{E}_5} : M \mapsto (\pi_{AB}^{\mathbf{E}_5}(M), \pi_{CD}^{\mathbf{E}_5}(M))$. This view is strictly weaker than $\Pi_{ABCD}^{\mathbf{E}_5}$; i.e., $\Pi_{\{AB,CD\}}^{\mathbf{E}_5} \prec_{\mathbf{E}_5} \Pi_{ABCD}^{\mathbf{E}_5}$, since it does not preserve information on which AB-projections are associated with which CD-projections.

On the other hand, $\Pi_{\{AB,BC\}}^{\mathbf{E}_5}$ is equivalent to $\Pi_{ABC}^{\mathbf{E}_5}$, since the embedded join dependency $\bowtie[AB, BC]$ holds on $\mathbf{E}_5$. (This is thus an example, as promised in Summary 2.1, of the same congruence defining two distinct views. Clearly, these views are equivalent in any reasonable sense.)

The key advantage of $\bigvee \Pi$-views over Π-views is that since they form a larger class, the optimal complements will be smaller in general, thus allowing larger update sets under the constant-complement strategy. For example, continuing with $\mathbf{E}_5$, as illustrated in Example 3.21 above, the optimal Π-complement of $\Pi_{BC}^{\mathbf{E}_5}$ is the identity view. On the other hand, it is easy to see that $\Pi_{\{AB,CD,DE\}}^{\mathbf{E}_5}$ is a $\bigvee \Pi$-complement of $\Pi_{BC}^{\mathbf{E}_5}$ which is strictly weaker than the identity view. Indeed, with $M = \{R(a_1, b_1, c_1, d_1, e_1), R(a_2, b_2, c_2, d_2, e_2)\}$, the update from $\{R_{BC}(b_1, c_1), R_{BC}(b_2, c_2)\}$ to $\{R_{BC}(b_1, c_2), R_{BC}(b_2, c_1)\}$ on the state of $\Pi_{BC}^{\mathbf{E}_5}$ is possible with $\bigvee \Pi$-complement $\Pi_{\{AB,CD,DE\}}^{\mathbf{E}_5}$, constant, but not with the optimal Π-complement $\Pi_{ABCDE}^{\mathbf{E}_5}$ constant.

The formalization and results for the various flavors of optimal Π-complements extend easily to the $\bigvee \Pi$-framework. Return to the general framework of $\mathbf{E}_\mathbf{U}^{\mathcal{F}}$ and an attribute-set collection J over $\mathbf{U}$. For J' any attribute-set collection over $\mathbf{U}$, define $\mathsf{Covered}_{\langle J;\bigvee\Pi\rangle}\langle J'\rangle = \{\mathbf{W} \in J \mid (\exists \mathbf{W}' \in J')(\mathbf{W} \subseteq \mathbf{W}')\}$.

The $\bigvee\Pi$-*complementary cover* to J' relative to J is given by $\overline{\mathsf{Covered}}_{\langle J;\bigvee\Pi\rangle}\langle J'\rangle = J \setminus \mathsf{Covered}_{\langle J;\Pi\rangle}\langle J'\rangle$.

The proof of the following theorem is almost identical to that of Theorem 3.15, and is left to the reader.

Theorem 3.23 (Optimal complements for $\bigvee\Pi$-views). *Let $i \in \{0, 1, 2, 3\}$. If the schema $\mathbf{E}_{\mathbf{U}}^{\mathcal{F}}$ has the join-reconstruction property and the JD $\bowtie[J]$ is governing of type i, then every $\bigvee\Pi$-view of $\mathbf{E}_{\mathbf{U}}^{\mathcal{F}}$ has an optimal complement of type i relative to Π-Views$\langle \mathbf{E}_{\mathbf{U}}^{\mathcal{F}} \rangle$. More specifically, given $J' \subseteq J$, in each case the optimal complement of $\Pi_{J'}$ of type i relative to $\bigvee\Pi$-Views$\langle \mathbf{E}_{\mathbf{U}}^{\mathcal{F}} \rangle$ is given by $\Pi_{J''}$, with $J'' = \overline{\mathsf{Covered}}_{\langle J;\Pi\rangle}\langle J'\rangle$.* □

Example 3.24 (Optimal $\bigvee\Pi$-complements). Continuing with $\mathbf{E}_5$ and the discussion at the end of Definition 3.22, the optimal complements of $\Pi_{\{BC,CE\}}^{\mathbf{E}_5}$ (which is equivalent to $\Pi_{BCE}^{\mathbf{E}_5}$), of all types, relative to $\bigvee\Pi$-Views$\langle \mathbf{E}_5 \rangle$, is identical to those of $\Pi_{BC}^{\mathbf{E}_5}$. In each case, that complement is $\Pi_{\{AB,CD,DE\}}^{\mathbf{E}_5}$ (which is equivalent to $\Pi_{\{AB,CDE\}}^{\mathbf{E}_5}$).

Also, $\Pi_{\{AB,CD\}}^{\mathbf{E}_5}$ and $\Pi_{\{BC,DE\}}^{\mathbf{E}_5}$ are each optimal complements of the other for type i for $i \in \{0, 1, 2, 3\}$, relative to $\bigvee\Pi$-Views$\langle \mathbf{E}_5 \rangle$. These views are each strictly smaller than their Π-counterparts $\Pi_{ABCD}^{\mathbf{E}_5}$ and $\Pi_{BCDE}^{\mathbf{E}_5}$.

4   Conclusions and Further Directions

A characterization of optimal complements for views defined by projections on a universal-relational schema has been developed. To cover a variety of situations, four distinct notions of optimality were identified. The characterization of optimality for each notion is rooted in notions of governing dependencies. Specifically, optimal complements of a given type exist precisely in the situation that a governing join dependency of a corresponding type exists, with "governing" meaning that all other join dependencies of that type are implied by it.

There are several key areas for further work on this subject.

Individual complements: The theory developed in Sec. 3 addresses the situation in which every Π-view or $\bigvee\Pi$-view of $\mathbf{E}_{\mathbf{U}}^{\mathcal{F}}$ has an optimal complement of a given type. However, there are cases in which some views may have optimal complements, while others do not. For example, in the context of $\mathbf{E}_2$ of Sec. 1, the view $\Pi_{AB}^{\mathbf{E}_1}$ has $\Pi_{BCD}^{\mathbf{E}_1}$ as an optimal complement of all four types relative to Π-Views$\langle \mathbf{E}_{\mathbf{U}}^{\mathcal{F}} \rangle$, even though $\Pi_{ABC}^{\mathbf{E}_1}$ has an optimal complement only of type 1. The results of Sec. 3 should be expanded to identify such individual optimal complements.

Complements in the context of normalization: The theory developed in Sec. 3 addresses only the situation of a universal relational schema as the main schema. However, in practice, such schemata exist only as part of the design process; the schemata which are used in practice are multi-relational, and often obtained from a universal schema after normalization via decomposition. If a lossless and dependency preserving normalization is employed, then the results of this paper apply equally well to the result schema. For example, if the single relation $R[ABCD]$ of $\mathbf{E}_0$ of Sec. 1 is decomposed into R_{ABC} and R_{CD}, and the two-way inclusion dependency $R_{ABC}[C] = R_{CD}[C]$ is enforced as well, then the normalized schema is isomorphic to the original one, and all of the results of the theory apply equally well to it. However, it is usually the case that the two-way inclusion dependency is replaced with a one-way *foreign-key dependency*, in this situation $R_{ABC}[C] \subseteq R_{CD}[C]$. Now, the normalized schema is no longer isomorphic to the original one, and so which views identify optimal complements of others may change. This is an important practical question which will be addressed in a forthcoming paper.

Weaker equivalence of non-isomorphic complements: Consider again the situation surrounding $\mathbf{E}_3$ of Sec. 1, which does not have optimal complements of any of the four types. Indeed, in Example 3.10 it is shown that this schema has six incomparable JDs, all of which are both JD- and CJD-essential. However, the attributes in $\{B, C, D\}$ are equivalent in the sense that $B \to C \to D \to B$. It furthermore turns out that the different minimal complements of a given schema differ only in a permutation of these elements. Thus, the complements are equivalent in a sense weaker than true isomorphism but nevertheless meaningful. The theory which characterizes such equivalence will be presented in a forthcoming paper.

A general algebraic theory of optimal complements: Although the results of Sec. 3 are focused upon universal relational schemata and views defined by projection, the underlying framework of Sec. 2 is much more general, suggesting that the kind of results developed for projections on a universal schema should in fact apply in a more abstract setting. Of particular importance are the additional kinds of decompositions identified in the normalization question above, as well as decompositions on relational schemata which involve both projection and selection, such as those of [18]. An important future direction is the formalization of such a general framework and its application to other forms of decomposition.

Rapprochement with computational approaches: In recent years, there has been renewed interest in using view complements to manage data warehouses, and a number of approaches to computing such complements has arisen, the most comprehensive of which is [21]. Although the goal of that work is much different than that of this paper, in that it develops ways to compute good complements via the manipulation of expressions in the relational algebra, there are nevertheless points of similarity which deserve further investigation.

References

1. Abiteboul, S., Hull, R., Vianu, V.: Foundations of Databases. Addison-Wesley, Reading (1995)
2. Aho, A.V., Beeri, C., Ullman, J.D.: The theory of joins in relational databases. ACM TODS 4(3), 297–314 (1979)

3. Bancilhon, F., Spyratos, N.: Update semantics of relational views. ACM Trans. Database Systems 6, 557–575 (1981)

4. Beeri, C., Fagin, R., Maier, D., Yannakakis, M.: On the desirability of acyclic database schemes. JACM 30(3), 479–513 (1983)

5. Beeri, C., Mendelzon, A.O., Sagiv, Y., Ullman, J.D.: Equivalence of relational database schemes. SIAM J. Computing 10(2), 352–370 (1981)

6. Beeri, C., Vardi, M.: On the properties of join dependencies. In: Gallaire, H., Minker, J., Nicolas, J.M. (eds.) Advances in Data Base Theory, vol. 1, pp. 25–71. Plenum Press, New York (1981)

7. Bohannon, A., Pierce, B.C., Vaughan, J.A.: Relational lenses: a language for updatable views. In: Proceedings of the Twenty-Fifth ACM SIGACT-SIGMOD-SIGART Symposium on Principles of Database Systems, Chicago, Illinois, USA, June 26-28, pp. 338–347 (2006)

8. Davey, B.A., Priestly, H.A.: Introduction to Lattices and Order, 2nd edn. Cambridge University Press, Cambridge (2002)

9. Fagin, R.: Horn clauses and database dependencies. J. Assoc. Comp. Mach. 29(4), 952–985 (1982)

10. Fagin, R.: Degrees of acyclicity for hypergraphs and relational database schemes. J. Assoc. Comp. Mach. 30(3), 514–550 (1983)

11. Fan, W., Geerts, F., Jia, X., Kementsietsidis, A.: Conditional functional dependencies for capturing data inconsistencies. ACM Trans. Database Systems 33(2) (2008)

12. Foster, J.N., Pierce, B.C., Zdancewic, S.: Updatable security views. In: Proceedings of the 22nd IEEE Computer Security Foundations Symposium, CSF 2009, Port Jefferson, New York, USA, July 8-10, pp. 60–74 (2009)

13. Goodman, N., Tay, Y.C.: A characterization of multivalued dependencies equivalent to a join dependency. Inf. Process. Lett. 18(5), 261–266 (1984)

14. Hegner, S.J.: An order-based theory of updates for closed database views. Ann. Math. Art. Intell. 40, 63–125 (2004)

15. Hegner, S.J.: The complexity of embedded axiomatization for a class of closed database views. Ann. Math. Art. Intell. 46, 38–97 (2006)

16. Hegner, S.J.: Semantic bijectivity and the uniqueness of constant-complement updates in the relational context. In: Schewe, K.-D., Thalheim, B. (eds.) SDKB 2008. LNCS, vol. 4925, pp. 172–191. Springer, Heidelberg (2008)

17. Hegner, S.J.: Internal representation of database views. J. Universal Comp. Sci. 16(20), 2956–2985 (2010)

18. Hegner, S.J.: A model of independence and overlap for transactions on database schemata. In: Catania, B., Ivanović, M., Thalheim, B. (eds.) ADBIS 2010. LNCS, vol. 6295, pp. 209–223. Springer, Heidelberg (2010)

19. Hull, R.: Finitely specifiable implicational dependency families. J. Assoc. Comp. Mach. 31(2), 210–226 (1984)

20. Lechtenbörger, J.: The impact of the constant complement approach towards view updating. In: Proceedings of the Twenty-Second ACM SIGMOD-SIGACT-SIGART Symposium on Principles of Database Systems, San Diego, California, June 09-11, pp. 49–55 (2003)

21. Lechtenbörger, J., Vossen, G.: On the computation of relational view components. ACM Trans. Database Systems 28, 175–208 (2003)

22. Ore, O.: Theory of equivalence relations. Duke Math. J. 9, 573–627 (1942)
23. Paredaens, J., De Bra, P., Gyssens, M., Van Gucht, D.: The Structure of the Relational Database Model. Springer, Heidelberg (1989)
24. Rissanen, J.: Independent components of relations. ACM Trans. Database Systems 2(4), 317–325 (1977)
25. Sciore, E.: A complete axiomatization of full join dependencies. J. Assoc. Comp. Mach. 29(2), 373–393 (1982)

Coding Theory Motivated by Relational Databases

Attila Sali

Alfréd Rényi Institute of Mathematics
Hungarian Academy of Sciences
Budapest, P.O.B.127, H-1364 Hungary
sali@renyi.hu

Abstract. In the present paper results on minimal Armstrong instances of certain integrity constraints in relational databases are surveyed that lead to coding theory type problems. First, branching dependencies are studied. Finding minimal Armstrong instances for some collections of these integrity constraints lead to a new metric space. Error correcting codes in that space have been investigated on their own right since then.

In the second part Armstrong instances of functional dependencies are investigated when the size of the domain of each attribute is bounded by a constant q. These come up naturally in real life databases, as well as in the study of higher order data model. These instances can be directly considered as q-ary codes, if tuples are taken as codewords.

1 Introduction

Interaction between combinatorics and database theory have a long history. For example, in query optimization acyclic joins, as it was stated in [1], "enjoyed a flurry of activity in the database community in the late 1970s and early 1980s". These investigations have close connections with notions of acyclicity in hypergraphs see [5,24,12,4,30].Other combinatorial studies involved problems of existence and minimal size of Armstrong instances of certain dependency systems. These included methods of extremal combinatorics, graph theory, polynomials over finite fields, finite geometries and design theory. The present paper aims to show a recent connection with theory of error correcting codes.

Arguably the most important database constraint is the collection of functional dependencies that a relational schema satisfies, in particular, the key dependencies. If R denotes the set of attributes, then $K \subseteq R$ is a *key*, if the functional dependency $K \to R$ holds. In what follows we use the terminology of the book [1].

The following problem is interesting from the point of view of schema design. Given a collection Σ of functional dependencies, what other dependencies hold in a database instance that satisfies Σ? A way of solving this problem is the construction of an *Armstrong instance* for Σ, that is a database that satisfies a functional dependency $X \to Y$ if and only if $\Sigma \models X \to Y$. Silva and Melkanoff [48] developed a design aid that for a collection of functional and multivalued

K.-D. Schewe, and B. Thalheim (Eds.): SDKB 2010, LNCS 6834, pp. 96–113, 2011.

dependencies as input presents an Armstrong instance for that set. The existence of Armstrong instance for a set of functional dependencies was proved by Armstrong [3] and Demetrovics [13]. Later Fagin [23] gave a necessary and sufficient condition for general dependencies.

Further investigations [14,15,16,18,20,17,26] concentrated on the minimum size of an Armstrong instance, since it is a good measure of the complexity of the collection of dependencies or system of minimal keys in question. A useful Armstrong relation for a constraint set should be of minimal size. Indeed, the smaller the relation, the easier it is to understand for humans, redundant tuples do not add any new information about the constraint set. Furthermore, a faint data mining connection exists as follows. If the size of an instance is smaller than that of the minimal Armstrong instance for a collection of dependencies, then that collection can be ruled out for the instance in question.

An interesting new branch of combinatorial design theory was started by a conjecture of Demetrovics, Füredi and Katona [14].

Definition 1.1. *A collection of partitions of* $\{1, 2, \ldots, n\}$ *is called* orthogonal double cover *(of* K_n*) if it satisfies the following two properties:*

1. *for any two partitions there is exactly one pair of elements, which is covered by both,*
2. *each pair of elements is covered by exactly two different partitions.*

A partition is said to cover *a pair of elements if they are in the same class of the partition.*

The following conjecture was formulated in [14]. (It was posed in other terms, since the notion of orthogonal double cover was introduced later, in [28].)

Conjecture 1.1 (Demetrovics, Katona, Füredi [14]). There exists an orthogonal double cover of the n-element set by n partitions provided $n \geq 7$.

Another conjecture was stated in the same paper. Its solution has a surprising connection to Armstrong codes that are one of the main topics of the present paper.

Conjecture 1.2 ([14]). If $n = 3r + 1$, then there exists an orthogonal double cover of the n-element set by n partitions that have one 1-element class and r of the 3-element classes.

Note that the two conjectures are independent in the sense that the solution of one of them does not imply the solution of the other.

Ganter and Gronau [27] proved that Conjecture 1.2 is true for $n \geq 13$. Later Bennett and Wu [6] verified that Conjecture 1.1 is true, as well.

Orthogonal double covers bare now a well researched area of combinatorial design theory, we just list a few papers without trying to be complete [11,27,28,32,33,34,35,38].

In the present paper two areas are discussed where database concepts and problems lead to coding theory. In Section 2 branching dependencies are studied. Finding minimal Armstrong instances for some collections of these integrity constraints lead to a new metric space. Error correcting codes in that space have been investigated on their own right since then.

In Section 3 Armstrong instances of functional dependencies are investigated when the size of the domain of each attribute is bounded by a constant q. These come up naturally in real life databases, as well as in the study of higher order data model. These instances can be directly considered as q-ary codes, that is codes over the alphabet $\{0, 1, 2, \ldots, q - 1\}$, if tuples are taken as codewords.

2   Branching Dependencies

Functional dependencies are generalized in many different ways. In this section we concentrate on a version that was introduced by Demetrovics et. al. [18]. Imagine that a database contains data of employees of some firm. Then the value of a tuple in attribute set $\{birthday, mother's\ name, family\ name\}$ does not determine the value in attribute $first\ name$ uniquely, but "almost", that is no more than six different values can be expected, taking into account the possibility of twins, triplets, etc. $Branching\ dependencies$ capture this type of implications.

Definition 2.1. *Let* $\mathbf{R} = (A_1, A_2, \ldots, A_n)$ *be a relational schema. A* (p, q)-*dependency on* $\mathbf{R}$ *is an expression of the form* $X \xrightarrow{(p.q)} y$ *where* $X \subseteq \mathbf{R}$ *and* $y \in \mathbf{R}$.

A relation $\mathbf{r}$ *over schema* $\mathbf{R}$ *satisfies* (p, q)-*dependency* $X \xrightarrow{(p.q)} y$ *if for every* $q+1$ *tuples* $t_0, t_1, \ldots, t_q$ *with* $|\{t_0[y], t_1[y], \ldots, t_q[y]\}| = q + 1$, *there exists* $x \in X$ *such that* $|\{t_0[x], t_1[x], \ldots, t_q[x]\}| \geq p + 1$.

$(1, 1)$-dependencies are $functional\ dependencies$.
Branching dependencies may look similar to $numerical\ dependencies$ defined by Grant and Minker [31], nevertheless, they are substantially different from these latter ones.

Example 2.1. Let us suppose that the database consists of the trips of an international transport truck, more precisely, the names of the countries the truck enters. For the sake of simplicity, let us suppose, that the truck goes through exactly four countries in each trip, (counting the start and endpoints, too) and does not enter a country twice during one trip. Suppose furthermore, that one country has at most five neighbors. Let A_1, A_2, A_3, A_4 denote the first, second, third and fourth country as attributes. It is easy to see that $A_1 \xrightarrow{(1,5)} A_2$, $\{A_1, A_2\} \xrightarrow{(1,4)} A_3$ and $\{A_2, A_3\} \xrightarrow{(1,4)} A_4$.
Similar situation arises when paths in bounded degree graphs are stored.

The goal of paper [18] was to collect properties of functional dependencies that are preserved directly or with some slight modification by branching dependencies. A key concept is the concept of $extension$. This is a generalization of $closures$ that are well investigated in connection with functional dependencies. Demetrovics and Katona [16] formulated the equivalence of closures on attribute sets with (full) systems of functional dependencies.

Definition 2.2. *Let Σ be a collection of (p,q)-dependencies over the schema* **R**. *Let us suppose that $1 \leq p \leq q$. The mapping $\mathcal{J}_{\Sigma pq} \colon 2^{\mathbf{R}} \to 2^{\mathbf{R}}$ is defined by*

$$\mathcal{J}_{\Sigma pq}(A) = \left\{ b \colon \Sigma \models A \xrightarrow{(p,q)} b \right\}. \tag{1}$$

Proposition 2.1. *[18] Let* **R**, Σ, p *and* q *as above. Furthermore, let $A, B \subseteq \mathbf{R}$. Then*

$$
\begin{aligned}
&(i)\ A \subseteq \mathcal{J}_{\Sigma pq}(A) \\
&(ii)\ A \subseteq B \implies \mathcal{J}_{\Sigma pq}(A) \subseteq \mathcal{J}_{\Sigma pq}(B).
\end{aligned} \tag{2}
$$

Set functions satisfying (i) and (ii) of (2) are called *extensions*.

Armstrong instances play an important role in design of databases. They can be used to test implications between constraint sets. Silva and Melkanoff gave an algorithm to find Armstrong instances in case of functional dependencies [48]. Any (full) collection of functional dependencies have Armstrong instances. However, for branching dependencies the situation is more complex. We have the following analogy.

$$
\begin{array}{cc}
\text{Functional dependencies} & \text{Branching dependencies} \\
\downarrow \uparrow & \downarrow (\uparrow\ ?) \\
\text{Closures} & \text{Extensions} \\
\downarrow & (\downarrow\ ?) \\
\text{Armstrong instances} & \text{Armstrong instances}
\end{array}
$$

An extension $\mathcal{N} \colon 2^{\mathbf{R}} \to 2^{\mathbf{R}}$ is said to be (p,q)-*representable* if there exists a collection Σ of (p,q)-dependencies over **R** that has an Armstrong instance and $\mathcal{N} = \mathcal{J}_{\Sigma pq}$.

Theorem 2.1 (Demetrovics, Katona, Sali,[18]). *Let $\mathcal{N}$ be an extension on subsets of* **R** *satisfying $\mathcal{N}(\emptyset) = \emptyset$. Then $\mathcal{N}$ is (p,q)-representable if one of the following holds.*

$$
\begin{aligned}
&(i)\ p = 1\ and\ 1 < q\ or \\
&(ii)\ p = 2\ and\ 3 < q\ or \\
&(iii)\ 2 < p\ and\ p^2 - p - 1 < q.
\end{aligned} \tag{3}
$$

The question of (p,q)-representability and the size of the minimal Armstrong instance of extensions and closures leads to beautiful and hard combinatorial problems.

Closures are special extensions. We can use some structure theory to prove the following.

Theorem 2.2 (Demetrovics, Katona, Sali,[18]). *Let $\mathcal{L}$ be a closure on* **R**. *If $p = 1$ or $p = 2$ and $p \leq q$, or $3 \leq p$ and $\left(\frac{p+1}{2}\right)^2 \leq q$, then $\mathcal{L}$ is (p,q)-representable.*

Theorem 2.2 allows $p = q$ in some cases while Theorem 2.1 does not. This is not surprising in the light of the next proposition.

Proposition 2.2. *Let* **R** *be a relational database schema,* Σ *a collection of* (p,p)-*dependencies for some* $p \geq 1$. *Then in addition to (i) and (ii) of (2),*

$$(iii)\ \mathcal{J}_{\Sigma pp}\left(\mathcal{J}_{\Sigma pp}(A)\right) = \mathcal{J}_{\Sigma pp}(A) \tag{4}$$

holds, as well for $A \subseteq \mathbf{R}$.

Thus, (p,p)-representable extensions are closures. Every closure is (p,p)-representable for $p = 1, 2$ by Theorem 2.2. It was shown in [18], that there exist a closure which is (p,p)-representable exactly for $p = 1, 2$ only. This motivates the following definition.

Definition 2.3 ([47]). *Let* $\mathcal{L}$ *be a closure on the set* **R**. *The* spectrum $\mathrm{sp}\,(\mathcal{L})$ *of* $\mathcal{L}$ *is defined as follows.*

$$q \in \mathrm{sp}\,(\mathcal{L}) \iff \mathcal{L} \text{ is } (q,q) - \text{representable} \tag{5}$$

Note that $\mathrm{sp}\,(\mathcal{L}) \subseteq \mathbb{N}$.

It is very hard to determine the spectrum of an arbitrary closure. However, for *uniform* closures given in Definition 2.4 we can give a complete characterization.

Definition 2.4. *Let* $\mathcal{C}_n^k$ *denote the following closure on* **R**:

$$\mathcal{C}_n^k(X) = \begin{cases} X & \text{if } |X| < k \\ \mathbf{R} & \text{otherwise.} \end{cases} \tag{6}$$

The result of Theorem 2.3 is quiet surprising in the following sense. If an instance R of a database schema **R** satisfies $X \xrightarrow{(p,q)} a$ for some $X \subset \mathbf{R}$ and $a \in \mathbf{R}$, furthermore the tuples of R take at least $q + 1$ distinct values in each attribute, then R satisfies $X \xrightarrow{(p-1,q-1)} a$, as well. Thus one would expect the spectrum of a closure being an interval of natural numbers. However, in [47] the following was proven.

Theorem 2.3 (Sali sr., Sali [47]). *Let* $n \geq k^2 (k - 1)$. *Then the spectrum* $\mathrm{sp}\,(\mathcal{C}_n^k)$ *of* $\mathcal{C}_n^k$ *is given by:*

$$\mathrm{sp}\,(\mathcal{C}_n^k) = \{1, 2, \ldots, k - 1\} \cup \{p \colon \exists s \in \mathbb{N}\ p + 1 - \left\lceil \frac{p+1}{s} \right\rceil = k - 1\}. \tag{7}$$

(7) gives a spectrum that consists of an interval and some "sporadic points". In particular, $\mathcal{C}_n^{10}$ is $(17,17)$-representable but neither $(16,16)$- nor $(15,15)$-representable. It is also $(18,18)$-representable, but it is not (p,p)-representable for $p > 18$.

2.1   Minimal Armstrong Instances

Let $s_{pq}(\mathcal{N})$ denote the minimum number of rows of a matrix (minimum size of a relation over schema **R**) that (p,q)-represents $\mathcal{N}$, for an extension $\mathcal{N}$. If $\mathcal{N}$ is not (p,q)-representable, then we put $s_{pq}(\mathcal{N}) = \infty$.

Proposition 2.3. *Let $\mathcal{N}$ be an extension on $\mathbf{R}$ with $\mathcal{N}(\emptyset) = \emptyset$ and let (p, q) satisfy one of $(i) - (iii)$ of (3). Assume that $|\mathbf{R}| = n$. Then*

$$s_{pq}(\mathcal{N}) \leq q(n+1)2^n. \tag{8}$$

Lemma 2.1. *Let us assume that $\mathcal{C}_n^k$ is (p, q)-representable. Then*

$$\binom{s_{pq}(\mathcal{C}_n^k)}{q+1} \geq \binom{n}{k-1}. \tag{9}$$

In some cases we could show that Lemma 9 gives the right order of magnitude. The constructions involve finite projective planes in one case (Theorem 2.4), a Hamiltonian theorem in another case [20].

Theorem 2.4 (Demetrovics, Katona, Sali [20])

$$3^{\frac{1}{3}} n^{\frac{2}{3}} + O(n^{\frac{1}{3}}) < s_{22}(\mathcal{C}_n^3) < \frac{3}{4^{\frac{1}{3}}} n^{\frac{2}{3}} + o(n^{\frac{2}{3}}). \tag{10}$$

The exact value of $s_{pq}(\mathcal{C}_n^k)$ is known in a few cases only [19] and [20].

Theorem 2.5 (Demetrovics, Katona, Sali [19,20])

$$
\begin{aligned}
&(pq1)\ s_{pq}(\mathcal{C}_n^1) = q + 1, \\
&(222)\ s_{22}(\mathcal{C}_n^2) = 2n\ \text{for } n > 5, \\
&(ppn)\ s_{pp}(\mathcal{C}_n^n) = \min\left\{\nu\ \text{integer}: \binom{\nu-1}{p} \geq n\right\}, \\
&(122)\ s_{12}(\mathcal{C}_n^2) = \min\left\{s\ \text{integer}: \binom{s}{3} \geq 2n\right\}\ \text{for } n > 452.
\end{aligned}
\tag{11}
$$

The proof of (pq1) of 11 is easy, while (222) needs some ad-hoc arguments. The lower bound in (ppn) is proven using a result of Lovász [39] on the maximum number of edges of a k-forest. The upper bound is a natural construction.

The coding theory connection comes from the proof of the upper bound (construction) in (122), which is based on

Theorem 2.6 (Demetrovics, Katona, Sali [20]). *Let $|X| = n$ and $2k > q$. The family of all q-subsets of X can be partitioned into unordered pairs (except possibly one if $\binom{n}{q}$ is odd), so that paired q-subsets are disjoint and if A_1, B_1 and A_2, B_2 are two such pairs with $|A_1 \cap A_2| \geq k$, then $|B_1 \cap B_2| < k$, provided $n > n_0(k, q)$.*

Construction of an Armstrong instance.
Let $\binom{m}{3} \geq 2n$. A matrix with m rows and n columns will be constructed that $(1,2)$-represents $\mathcal{C}_n^2$. Apply Theorem 2.6 with $q = 3$ and $k = 2$ to obtain disjoint pairs of 3-subsets of rows. There are $\lfloor \binom{m}{3}/2 \rfloor \geq n$, such pairs. Choose n of them. We construct a column from such a pair, as follows. Put 1's in the rows indexed by the first 3-set, 2's in the rows indexed by the second one, and all different entries, that are at least 3, in the other positions. If a and b are two distinct columns, then there are no 3 rows that agree in both a and b, because we used all distinct 3-subsets of rows, hence $\forall c \in \mathbf{R}: \{a,b\} \xrightarrow{(1,2)} c$.

On the other hand, if a is constructed from the pair of 3-subsets A_1, A_2 and b is constructed from B_1, B_2, then either $|A_1 \cap B_1| < 2$ or $|A_2 \cap B_2| < 2$, so there are 3 rows which contain all identical entries in column a, but all distinct ones in column b, hence $a \xcancel{\xrightarrow{(1,2)}} b$.

Theorem 2.6 is proved using the following Hamiltonian type theorem.

Theorem 2.7 (Demetrovics, Katona, Sali [20]). *Let $G_0 = (V, E_0)$ and $G_1 = (V, E_1)$ be simple graphs on the same vertex set $|V| = N$, such that $E_0 \cap E_1 = \emptyset$. The 4-tuple (x, y, z, v) is called an* alternating cycle *if (x, y) and (z, v) are in E_0 and (y, z) and (x, v) are in E_1. Let r be the minimum degree of G_0 and let s be the maximum degree of G_1. Suppose, that*

$$2r - 8s^2 - s - 1 > N, \tag{12}$$

then there is a Hamiltonian cycle in G_0 such that if (a, b) and (c, d) are both edges of the cycle, then (a, b, c, d) is not an alternating cycle.

The pairs of disjoint q-subsets are obtained from neighboring vertices of a Hamiltonian cycle of type above. G_0 and G_1 are as follows. The vertex set V consists of the q-subsets of X, $|V| = \binom{n}{q} = N$. Two q-subsets are adjacent in G_0 if their intersection is empty, while two q-subsets are adjacent in G_1 if they intersect in at least k elements.

2.2 Enomoto-Katona Space

Define
$$\gamma(\{A_1, B_1\}, \{A_2, B_2\}) = \max\{|A_1 \cap A_2| + |B_1 \cap B_2|, |A_1 \cap B_2| + |B_1 \cap A_2|\}.$$

Theorem 2.8 (Enomoto, Katona [22]). *Let $|X| = n$. The family of all k-element subsets of X can be partitioned into disjoint pairs (except possibly one if $\binom{n}{k}$ is odd), so that $\gamma(\{A_1, B_1\}, \{A_2, B_2\}) \leq k$ holds for any two such pairs $\{A_1, B_1\}$ and $\{A_2, B_2\}$, provided $n > n_0(k)$.*

The proof of Theorem 2.8 follows the line of that of Theorem 2.6, the difference is that a strengthening of Theorem 2.7 is needed, which involves weighted Hamiltonian cycles. Define $\delta_0(\{A_1, B_1\}, \{A_2, B_2\}) = 2k - \gamma(\{A_1, B_1\}, \{A_2, B_2\})$. This is a *distance* in the *space of all disjoint pairs* of k-element subsets of X. Theorem 2.8 answers a coding type question, how many elements can be chosen from this space with large pairwise distances.

In general, let Y be a finite set and $\delta(x, y) \geq 0$ a real-valued symmetric ($\delta(x, y) = \delta(y, x)$) function defined on the pairs $x, y \in Y$. Let $0 < d$ be a fixed integer. A subset $C = \{c_1, \ldots, c_m\} \subset Y$ is called a *code of distance d* if $\delta(c_i, c_j) \geq d$ holds for $i \neq j$. The following (probably too general) question can be asked.

Problem 2.1. Let Y, $\delta(x, y)$ and the real d be given. Determine the maximum size $|C|$ of a d-distance code.

The following special case of Problem 2.1 arises now naturally.

Problem 2.2. Let Y_1, $\delta_0(x, y)$ be the space with distance defined above. Determine the maximum size $|C|$ of a k-distance code.

Unfortunately, Theorem 2.8 is not a solution, since the condition on the distance permits the existence of a pair $\{A, B_1\}, \{A, B_2\}, B_1 \cap B_2 = \emptyset$, which is excluded in Theorem 2.8 by the unique usage of every k-element subset. Observe that δ can be formulated without using the auxiliary function γ. The following distance d is identical to δ.

$$d(\{A_1, B_1\}, \{A_2, B_2\}) = \min\{|A_1 - A_2| + |B_1 - B_2|, |A_1 - B_2| + |B_1 - A_2|\}. \quad (13)$$

The Enomoto-Katona space is defined as follows.

Definition 2.5. *Let $n, k \in \mathcal{N}$ with $2k \leq n$ and X be an n-set. Consider*

$$\mathcal{R} := \left\{ \{A, B\} \subseteq \binom{X}{k} \mid A \cap B = \emptyset \right\}, \quad (14)$$

consisting of all unordered pairs of disjoint k-element subsets of X. The function

$$d^{\mathcal{R}} : \mathcal{R} \times \mathcal{R} \to \{0, 1, \ldots, 2k\},$$
$$(\{A, B\}, \{S, T\}) \mapsto \min\{|A \setminus S| + |B \setminus T|, |A \setminus T| + |B \setminus S|\} \quad (15)$$

is a metric on $\mathcal{R}$. The finite metric space $(\mathcal{R}, d^{\mathcal{R}})$, called Enomoto-Katona space.

Connection with Hamming and Johnson spaces. Let Q be a finite set of cardinality $q \geq 2$ and $n \in \mathcal{N}$. The elements of Q^n are called words of length n and will be denoted by $y = (y_1, y_2, \ldots, y_n)$. The space Q^n equipped with the Hamming metric

$$d_H : Q^n \times Q^n \to \{0, 1, \ldots, n\}, (y, z) \mapsto |\{x \in \{1, 2, \ldots, n\} \mid y_x \neq z_x\}| \quad (16)$$

is called the Hamming space and $C \subseteq Q^n$ is called a code. The coding type problem in the Hamming space consists of the determination of the maximum cardinality $A_q(n, d)$ of a code with $d_H(y, z) \geq d$ for all distinct codewords y and z. It is easy to see that $d_H(y, z) > 2e$ iff the balls of radius e around y and z are disjoint.

If $q = 2$, say $Q = \{0, 1\}$, then (Q^n, d_H) is called the binary Hamming space. It can be transformed into a set-theoretical space on a finite n-set X in the following way: Let $\sigma : \{1, 2, ..., n\} \to X$ be a bijection and transform $y \in \{0, 1\}^n$ into $A := \{\sigma(x) \in X \mid y_x = 1\} \subseteq X$. The resulting metric on the power set $\mathcal{P}(X)$ of X is

$$d_H : \mathcal{P}(X) \times \mathcal{P}(X) \to \{0, 1, ..., n\}, (A, S) \mapsto |A \setminus S| + |S \setminus A|. \tag{17}$$

The weight w of a binary word $y \in \{0, 1\}^n$ is the number of components which are equal to one, i.e. $w := |\text{supp}(y)| = d_H((y_1, y_2, ..., y_n), (0, 0, ..., 0))$ with $\text{supp}(y) := \{x \in \{1, 2, ..., n\} \mid y_x = 1\}$. The maximum cardinality of a (binary) constant weight code of length n, minimum Hamming distance d and weight w is denoted by $A(n, d, w)$. Its determination is another coding type problem. For exact values of and bounds on $A(n, d, w)$ confer Agrell et al. [2] and their references. Fu et al. [25] considered equidistant constant weight codes. Let $B(n, d, w)$ denote the maximum cardinality of a (binary) constant weight code of length n and weight w with a Hamming distance of exactly d between all distinct codewords. Of cause, $B(n, d, w) \leq A(n, d, w)$.

Clearly, the space of all words of length n and constant weight w is a subspace of the binary Hamming space. Transforming it into a set-theoretical space on a finite n-set X, every word is mapped onto a w-subset of X and vice versa. The resulting metric on $\binom{X}{w} = \{A \in \mathcal{P}(X) \mid w = |A|\}$ is

$$d_H : \binom{X}{w} \times \binom{X}{w} \to \{0, 1, ..., n\}, (A, S) \mapsto |A \setminus S| + |S \setminus A|. \tag{18}$$

Since $|A \setminus S| = |S \setminus A|$ and, hence, the Hamming distance between words of constant weight is even, it can be convenient to use $d_J(A, S) := \frac{1}{2} d_H(A, S) = |A \setminus S| \in \{0, 1, ..., w\}$. The space $\left(\binom{X}{w}, d_J\right)$ is sometimes called the Johnson space. It is again easy to see that two w-subsets of X have a Johnson distance greater than $2e$ iff the balls of radius e around these subsets are disjoint.

From this point of view, the Enomoto-Katona space $(\mathcal{R}, d^\mathcal{R})$ is a generalization of the set-theoretical Johnson space.

Coding type results for the Enomoto-Katona space. A set $\mathcal{C}$ of unordered pairs of k-subsets of an n-set is an (n, k, d)–code if the distance of any two elements is at least d.

Let $C(n, k, d)$ be the maximum size of an (n, k, d)-code. $C'(n, k, d)$ denotes the same under the additional condition that a k–element subset may occur only once in the pairs $\{A, B\} \in \mathcal{C}$ as A or B. With this notation Theorem 2.8 states that $C'(n, k, k) = \lfloor \frac{1}{2} \binom{n}{k} \rfloor$. Brightwell and Katona [9] gave general upper and lower bounds for the numbers $C(n, k, d)$. It is quite natural to ask if one can choose $\lfloor \frac{1}{2} \binom{n}{k} \rfloor$ pairs with pairwise difference at least $k + 1$. The answer is negative.

Theorem 2.9 (Brightwell, Katona[9]). *Let $d \leq 2k \leq n$ be integers. Then*

$$C(n,k,d) \leq \frac{1}{2} \frac{n(n-1)\cdots(n-2k+d)}{k(k-1)\cdots\lceil\frac{d+1}{2}\rceil \cdot k(k-1)\cdots\lfloor\frac{d+1}{2}\rfloor} \tag{19}$$

holds.

It is not too hard to check that Theorem 2.9 implies that if $2 \leq k \leq n/2$ then $C(n,k,k+1) < \lfloor\frac{1}{2}\binom{n}{k}\rfloor$. Now we give a lower estimate on $C(2k,k,d)$ for some cases. The method is a modification of the method used by Sloane and Graham [29] proving lower bounds for constant weight codes.

Let $X = \{\omega_1,\ldots,\omega_{q-1}\}$ be the set of all non-zero elements of the finite field $GF(q)$. Let $d = 2\delta$ and define $\mathcal{N}_0(k,\delta)$ as the family of all k-element subsets A of X such that $\sum_{i_1<\ldots<i_\rho\in A} \omega_{i_1}\cdots\omega_{i_\rho} = 0$ holds for every integer $1 \leq \rho < \delta$.

Theorem 2.10 (Brightwell, Katona[9]). *If $2k+1$ is a prime power and $d = 2\delta$ then*

$$\frac{1}{2}|\mathcal{N}_0(k,\delta)| \leq C(2k,k,d) \tag{20}$$

holds.

The size of $\mathcal{N}_0(k,\delta)$ can be determined for small values, but we believe that it cannot be much less than

$$\frac{1}{q^{\delta-1}}\binom{2k}{k}, \tag{21}$$

since the defining sums are probably nearly equally distributed among all the $q^{\delta-1}$ possibilities. It was proved in [9] that for fixed k and d, $C(n,k,d) = \Theta(n^{2k-d+1})$, and it was conjectured that the upper bound in Theorem 2.9 is asymptotically correct. This conjecture was settled in affirmative by Bollobás, Katona and Leader in [8].

Theorem 2.11 (Bollobás, Leader, Katona[8])

$$\lim_{n\to\infty} \frac{C(n,k,d)}{n^{2k-d+1}} = \frac{1}{2} \frac{1}{k(k-1)\cdots\lceil\frac{d+1}{2}\rceil \cdot k(k-1)\cdots\lfloor\frac{d+1}{2}\rfloor}. \tag{22}$$

The Enomoto-Katona space was investigated recently by Quistorff in a pair of papers [40,41]. The *coding type problem* concerning $(\mathcal{R}, d^\mathcal{R})$ is the determination of the maximum cardinality $C(n,k,d)$ of a code with $d^\mathcal{R}(\{A,B\},\{S,T\}) \geq d$ for all distinct $\{A,B\},\{S,T\} \in \mathcal{C}$. Upper bounds on $C(n,k,d)$ are discussed in [40].

The *sphere packing problem* concerning $(\mathcal{R}, d^\mathcal{R})$ is the determination of the maximum cardinality $P(n,k,e)$ of an e-error-correcting code.

In the Hamming and in the Johnson space, a code is e-error-correcting iff all mutual distances exceed $2e$. The coding type and the sphere packing problem are less closely connected in the Enomoto-Katona space: If $d^\mathcal{R}(\{A,B\},\{S,T\}) > 2e$ for all distinct $\{A,B\},\{S,T\} \in \mathcal{C}$ then $\mathcal{C}$ is e-error-correcting but the converse statement does not hold. For example $\{\{1,2\},\{3,4\}\}$ and $\{\{1,3\},\{2,4\}\}$ are only at distance 2 from each other and nevertheless form a 1-error-correcting code. Since on the other hand, every e-error-correcting code $\mathcal{C}$ satisfies at least $d^{\mathcal{R}}(\{A, B\}, \{S, T\}) > e$ for all distinct $\{A, B\}, \{S, T\} \in \mathcal{C}$, the statement

$$C(n, k, 2e + 1) \leq P(n, k, e) \leq C(n, k, e + 1) \tag{23}$$

follows. Quistorff proved the following.

Theorem 2.12 (Quistorff [41])

- $P(n, k, e) \leq C(n, k, 2e + 1) \cdot P(2k, k, e)$.
- If $k \leq 2e$ then $P(n, k, e) \leq A(n, 4(2e + 1 - k), 2k) \cdot P(2k, k, e)$.

Theorem 2.13 (Quistorff [41]). *If e is even or $e > \frac{k}{2}$ then $C(n, k, 2e + 1) = P(n, k, e)$.*

An interesting connection between unordered pairs of subsets and equidistant constant weight codes is the following.

Theorem 2.14 (Quistorff [41]). $C(4k, 2k, 2k) = B(4k - 1, 2k, 2k - 1)$.

Quistorff gave the current best bound for the coding problem.

Theorem 2.15 (Quistorff [41]). *Let $e \in \mathbb{N}$ with $k - d + 1 \leq e \leq \min\{k, 2k - d\}$. Then*

$$C(n, k, d) \leq \frac{\binom{n}{e}}{2\binom{k}{e}} \left\lfloor \frac{\binom{n-e}{2k-d-e+1}}{\binom{k}{2k-d-e+1}} \right\rfloor. \tag{24}$$

3   Armstrong Codes

All papers cited in the Introduction assumed that the *domain* of each attribute is unbounded, countably infinite. However, in the study of *Higher Order Data model* [36,43,44,45] the question of bounded domains arises naturally. In fact, if a minimal key system contains only *counter attributes*, then the possible number of tuples in an Armstrong instance is bounded from above. Another reason to consider bounded domains comes from real life databases. In many cases the domain of an attribute is a well defined finite set, for example in car rental, the class of cars can take values from the set {subcompact, compact, mid-size, full-size, SUV, sports-car, van}. Same kind of finiteness may occur in the case of job assignments, schedules, etc.

Thalheim [49] investigated the maximum number of minimal keys in the case of bounded domains and showed that having restrictions on the sizes of domains makes a significant difference.

It is natural to ask what can be said about Armstrong instances if attribute A_i has a domain of size q. The main question of this section was introduced in [45] and investigated in papers [37,46]. Let $\mathcal{K}_n^k$ denote the collection of all k-subsets of an n-element attribute set $\mathbf{R}$.

Definition 3.1. *Let $q > 1$ and $k > 1$ be given natural numbers. Let $f(q, k)$ be the maximum such n that there exists an Armstrong instance for $\mathcal{K}_n^k$ being the system of minimal keys.*

It is clear that for a meaningful Armstrong instance we need at least two distinct symbols, so $q > 1$ is necessary. On the other hand the minimal Armstrong instance for $\mathcal{K}_n^1$ uses only two symbols for arbitrary n [16], hence $f(q,k)$ is well defined only for $k > 1$.

Definition 3.2. *Let $\mathcal{K}$ be a Sperner system of minimal keys.*

$$\mathcal{K}^{-1} = \{A \subset \mathbf{R}:\ \nexists K \in \mathcal{K} \text{ such that } K \subseteq A \text{ and } A \text{ is maximal subject to this condition}\}$$

is the collection of maximal antikeys corresponding to $\mathcal{K}$.

The following basic fact is known [16].

Proposition 3.1. $\mathbf{A}$ *is an Armstrong instance for $\mathcal{K}$ iff the following two properties hold:*

(**K**) *There are no two rows of $\mathbf{A}$ that agree in all positions for any $K \in \mathcal{K}$ and*
(**A**) *For every $A \in \mathcal{K}^{-1}$ there exist two rows of $\mathbf{A}$ that agree in all positions of A.*

It is helpful to view an Armstrong instance for $\mathcal{K}_n^k$ as minimal key system using at most q symbols as a q-ary code $\mathcal{C}$ of length n, where codewords are the tuples, or rows of the instance. Using $(\mathcal{K}_n^k)^{-1} = \mathcal{K}_n^{k-1}$ we obtain

(**md**) $\mathcal{C}$ has minimum Hamming-distance at least $n - k + 1$ by (**K**).
(**di**) For any set of $k - 1$ coordinates there exist two codewords that agree exactly there by (**A**).

A $k - 1$-set of coordinate can be considered as a 'direction', so in $\mathcal{C}$ the minimum distance is *attained in all directions*. Such a code $\mathcal{C}$ is called *Armstrong-instance type code* of parameters (q, k, n), or *Armstrong(q, k, n)-code* for short. For example, the rows of the $k+1 \times k+1$ identity matrix form an Armstrong$(2, k, k+1)$-code, so Armstrong codes **do** exist.

Remark 3.1. Let $q > 1$ and $k > 1$ be given natural numbers. Then $f(q,k)$ is the maximum n such that there exists an Armstrong(q, k, n)-code.

In the following q is considered to be fixed, while k is let to increase without bound. That is, we consider the size of the domain as a fixed finite number, while the sizes of keys increase.

Bounds on Armstrong codes. The following lower and upper bounds were proved in [37].

Theorem 3.1 (G.O.H. Katona, K.-D. Schewe, Sali [37])

1. *Given $q > 4$, there is k_0 such that for every $k > k_0$ and for every $n < \frac{1}{2}k \log q$ we have $n \leq f(q,k)$.*
2. *There exists k_0 and $c > 1$ constants, that for $k > k_0$, and $\lfloor ck \rfloor \leq f(2,k)$.*

3. *Let $q > 1$ and $k > 2$ be integers. Then*

$$f(q,k) \leq q(k-1)\left(1 + \frac{q-1}{\sqrt{\frac{2(qk-q-k+2)^{k-1}}{(k-1)!}} - q}\right) \tag{25}$$

holds.

4. *If $5 \leq k$ and $2 \leq q$ then the upper bound in (25) can be improved to*

$$f(q,k) \leq q(k-1) \tag{26}$$

with the following exceptions: $(k,q) = (5,2), (5,3), (5,4), (5,5), (6,2)$.

The lower bounds were given by greedy construction. The main advantage of the second lower bound is that it gives a constant larger than 1, while the identity matrix construction does not. In order to prove the upper bounds two estimates on n were given that are functions of the number of codewords: $a_{q,k}(m)$ being a decreasing, while $b_{q,k}(m)$ being an increasing function of m. Therefore, if α is the solution of the equation

$$a_{q,k}(m) = b_{q,k}(m) \tag{27}$$

in m then $a_{q,k}(\alpha) = b_{q,k}(\alpha)$ is a universal (independent of m) upper bound for n. The paper [37] also contains an exact and an almost exact bound.

Proposition 3.2. $f(q,2) = \binom{q+1}{2}$ *and* $f(q,3) \leq 3q - 1$.

Interestingly enough, the theorem of Ganter et.al. [27] on special type of *orthogonal double covers* of Conjecture 1.2 gives a lower bound for $f(q,3)$. The Armstrong instance provided there has $r + 1$ symbols in every column, and has $3r + 1$ columns. That is, $q = r + 1$ and $n = 3q - 2$. We believe that this is the right answer, since that is a solution of the minimum representation of $\mathcal{C}_n^3$. Nevertheless, the proof of Proposition 3.2 has no room for for improvement.

Conjecture 3.1. $f(q,3) = 3q - 2$

Using heavy artillery. It was clear that the lower bound given in Theorem 3.1 can be improved, but constructions are hard to come by. On the other hand, the upper bound (26) seems nice enough to be sharp. However, both were improved in [46].

Theorem 3.2 (Székely, Sali [46]). *For $k > k_0(q)$ we have*

$$\frac{\sqrt{q}}{e}k < f(q,k) < (q - \log q)k. \tag{28}$$

The idea of the upper bound is to embed an Armstrong(q, k, n)-code into an $n' = (q - 1)n$-dimensional space as a spherical code and use existing bounds for the size spherical codes of given minimum distance. On the other hand, an old result of Demetrovics and Katona [16] gives a lower bound for the size of an Armstrong(q, k, n)-code. Comparing the two estimates results in the lower bound for c, where $k - 1 = cn$.

It is not hard to see that if k is fixed and an Armstrong(q, k, n)-code exists for some $k < n$, then Armstrong(q, k, n')-codes also exist for all $k < n' < n$. Let $\mathcal{C}$ be an Armstrong(q, k, n)-code of size $m = |\mathcal{C}|$. Let $\ell = k - 1$. Using (**di**) and the argument of [16],

$$\binom{n}{\ell} \leq \binom{m}{2} \tag{29}$$

is obtained. Let $s: \{0, 1, \ldots, q - 1\} \to \mathbb{R}^{q-1}$ be a bijective mapping of the q symbols to the vertices of a regular simplex centered at the origin. Extend this mapping to codewords by juxtaposition of coordinates of vectors that are images of symbols of codewords under s. Thus each codeword of $\mathcal{C}$ is mapped to a vector from $\mathbb{R}^{(q-1)n}$ and we normalize them so they are unit vectors. Let $\mathcal{D}$ be the spherical code obtained. Using the minimum distance of $\mathcal{C}$ we obtain that $\mathcal{D}$ has minimum angle ϕ with $\cos\phi = \frac{\ell q - n}{(q-1)n}$ and $\sin(\frac{\phi}{2}) = \sqrt{\frac{q(n-k+1)}{2(q-1)n}}$. By (29) and the upper bound of Rankin [42]

$$A(n, \phi) \leq \sqrt{\frac{\pi}{2} n^3 \cos\phi} \left(\sqrt{2}\sin(\frac{\phi}{2})\right)^{-n} (1 + o(1)) \tag{30}$$

on the maximum size of a spherical code in n dimension with minimum angle ϕ. Applying that $m \leq A((q-1)n, \phi)$ we obtain

$$\sqrt{2\binom{n}{\ell}} < m \leq \sqrt{\frac{\pi}{2}(q-1)^3 n^3 \frac{\ell q - n}{(q-1)n}} \left(\sqrt{\frac{q(n-k+1)}{(q-1)n}}\right)^{-(q-1)n} (1 + o(1)). \tag{31}$$

Writing $\ell = cn$ and using the approximation of $\binom{n}{cn}$ (31) yields

$$\sqrt{2}\left(\frac{1}{c^c(1-c)^{1-c}}\right)^{\frac{n}{2}} < \sqrt{\frac{\pi}{2}(q-1)n\sqrt{(cq-1)n}} \left(\sqrt{\frac{q-1}{q(1-c)}}\right)^{(q-1)n}. \tag{32}$$

Now, (32) can only hold for large enough n if

$$\frac{1}{c^c(1-c)^{1-c}} < \left(\frac{q-1}{q(1-c)}\right)^{q-1}. \tag{33}$$

It is easy to see that for $c = \frac{1}{q}$ LHS>1 and RHS=1 in (33). However, that only gives the upper bound established in [37]. With considerably more effort it can be shown that LHS>RHS in (33) for $c = \frac{1}{q - \log q}$, as well.

Lovász Local Lemma, that is a probabilistic construction is used to prove the lower bound.

3.1 Binary Armstrong-Codes

Using simulated annealing Andries Brouwer found extremal examples of binary Armstrong codes. A. Keszler showed in her diploma thesis using computer that Armstrong$(2, n-2, n)$-codes do not exist for $n \leq 8$, the case $n = 9$ is extremal.

Proposition 3.3 (Brouwer [10]). *Armstrong(2, 7, 9)- and Armstrong(2, 7, 10)-codes exist.*

Take the unique Steiner system S(3,4,10) and delete a point and add the all-0 vector. This is an Armstrong$(2, 7, 9)$-code. Take the unique S(3,4,10) and the all-0 vector. This is an Armstrong$(2, 7, 10)$-code.

Armstrong(2, n − 2, n)-codes for large n

Proposition 3.4 (Blokhuis [7]). *There exists Armstrong(2, n−2, n)-codes for any n > 19.*

Proof. First we partition the triplets from an n-set into n collections with the property that two triplets in the same collection intersect in at most 1 point. The triplet $\{p, q, r\}$ goes into collection $\mathcal{T}_i$ iff $p+q+r \equiv i \pmod{n}$. Let $c_0, c_1, \ldots, c_{n-1}$ be vectors formed from n rows of a (0,1)-Hadamard matrix of smallest possible order that is at least n by taking the first n coordinates of each, respectively. Since $n \geq 20$, the vectors c_i have pairwise Hamming distance at least 9. Our code $\mathcal{C}$ consists of the codewords $c_0, c_1, \ldots, c_{n-1}$, and for every $T \in \mathcal{T}_i$ the codeword $c_i + t$ where t is the characteristic vector of triple T.   ☐

This "skeleton-code" approach can be extended for Armstrong$(2, k, n)$-codes where $n - k = m$ is small. If $m = 3$, we can partition the quadruplets of an n-set into n classes that two quadruplets in the same collection intersect in at most 2 elements by putting quadruple $\{p, q, r, a\}$ in collection $p + q + r + s$ (mod n). Using Hadamard matrices, we can find n codewords of mutual distance 12 if $n = 24$ or $n \geq 26$. For general m we can prove the following.

Theorem 3.3 (Blokhuis [7]). *Let $n - k = 2m$ or $n - k = 2m - 1$ and $m > 1$. Then an Armstrong(2, k, n)-code exists if $n \geq 8m \log m$.*

Proof. We apply the skeleton-code method. That is the $n - k + 1$-tuples (subsets) of the n-set are partitioned into A classes $\mathcal{T}_i$ $(i = 0, 1, \ldots, A - 1)$ so that the symmetric difference of two tuples in the same class is at least $n - k + 1$. Then A codewords $c_0, c_1, \ldots, c_{A-1}$ of length n are selected of pairwise distance at least $3(n - k + 1)$. The Armstrong$(2, k, n)$-code $\mathcal{C}$ will consists of the codewords $c_0, c_1, \ldots, c_{A-1}$, and for every $T \in \mathcal{T}_i$ the codeword $c_i + t$ where t is the characteristic vector of $n - k + 1$-tuple T. If T and T' are $n - k + 1$-tuples of the same class $\mathcal{T}_i$, then the distance of $c_i + t$ and $c_i + t'$ is exactly the size of the symmetric difference of T and T', that is at least $n - k + 1$. If T and T' are of different classes, say $T \in \mathcal{T}_i$ and $T' \in \mathcal{T}_j$, then the distance of $c_i + t$ and $c_j + t'$ is at least $3(n - k + 1) - |T| - |T'| \geq n - k + 1$. Thus the minimum distance of code $\mathcal{C}$ is $n - k + 1$ that is attained in every $n - k + 1$-tuple of coordinates T between codewords c_i and $c_i + t$, that is $\mathcal{C}$ is an Armstrong$(2, k, n)$-code.

In order to find the partition of the $n - k + 1$-tuples, let p be the smallest prime number not less than n. (It is known that $p \leq n + n^{3/5}$.) Let $n - k + 1 = 2m + 1$, (the $n - k = 2m - 1$ case is similar). The $2m + 1$-tuple $\underline{a} = (a_1, a_2, \ldots, a_{2m+1})$ is mapped to $(\sigma_1(\underline{a}), \sigma_2(\underline{a}), \ldots, \sigma_m(\underline{a})) \in \mathbb{F}_p^m$, where $\sigma_i(\underline{a})$ is the ith symmetric function. We claim that if two $2m + 1$-tuples mapped to the same m-tuple mod p, then they differ in at least $m + 1$ positions, so the symmetric difference of them is at least $n - k + 1$. Indeed, let $\underline{a} = (a_1, a_2, \ldots, a_{2m+1})$ and $\underline{b} = (b_1, b_2, \ldots, b_{2m+1})$ be mapped to the same m-tuple, that is assume that $\sigma_i(\underline{a}) = \sigma_i(\underline{b}$ for $i = 1, 2, \ldots, m$. Consider the polynomials $a(x) = \prod_{i=1}^{2m+1}(x - a_i)$ and $b(x) = \prod_{i=1}^{2m+1}(x - b_i)$. Then by the agreement of the symmetric functions $a(x) - b(x)$ is of degree m. On the other hand, $c(x) = \prod_{c \in \underline{a} \cap \underline{b}}(x - c) \mid a(x) - b(x)$. This implies that the degree of $c(x)$ is at most m, so the tuples $\underline{a}$ and $\underline{b}$ differ in at least $m + 1$ positions. A partition class of the $n - k + 1$-tuples consists of those that map to the same m-tuple   mod p. The number of the latter vectors is p^m, so we need that many codewords of length n of pairwise distance at least $3(n - k + 1) = 3(2m + 1)$. Now, if $M < p^m$ codewords, then the spheres of radius $3(2m + 1)$ around them cover at most $Mn^{3(2m+1)}$ points, so if $p^m n^{3(2m+1)} < 2^n$, then we can find a skeleton code using a simple greedy argument. This latter inequality is true if $n \geq 8m \log m$. $\square$

4   Conclusions

We surveyed a new direction in the interaction of Database Theory and Combinatorics. We showed through examples how database questions lead top problems belonging to Coding Theory. The first area discussed was the investigation of minimum Armstrong instances of branching dependencies. Here the main interesting point was that constructions traditionally involving combinatorial design theory now lead to a new metric space and codes with given minimum distance in that space. This metric is already included in the list of known distances [21]. Further research in this area would include new bounds on codes in the Enomoto-Katona space. From the database direction, results on minimal Armstrong instances of branching dependency systems are of interest.

The second topic discussed in this survey was the concept of Armstrong-codes. These come up naturally if the domains of attributes in a relational schema are bounded. In this case the existence of Armstrong-instances is the main question. Function $f(q, k)$ was introduced, as the largest number of attributes in a relational schema where each attribute has a q-element domain and every k element attribute set is a minimal key. Lower and upper bounds were obtained, but they are far from each other. Further research should close the gap in the bounds, in particular constructions extremal Armstrong-codes are of interest. Up to now, very few explicit constructions are known, the lower bounds are probabilistic.

References

1. Abiteboul, S., Hull, R., Vianu, V.: Foundations of Databases. Addison-Wesley, Reading (1995)
2. Agrell, E., Vardy, A., Zeger, K.: Upper bounds for constant-weight codes. IEEE Transactions on Information Theory 46, 2373–2395 (2000)
3. Armstrong, W.W.: Dependency structures of database relationships. Information Processing, 580–583 (1974)

4. Ausiello, G., D'Atri, A., Moscarini, M.: Chordality properties on graphs and minimal conceptual connections in semantic data models. Journal of Computer and System Sciences 33(2), 179–202 (1986)
5. Beeri, C., Fagin, R., Maier, D., Yannakakis, M.: On the desirability of acyclic database schemes. J. ACM 30, 479–513 (1983)
6. Bennett, F.E., Wu, L.: On minimum matrix representation of closure operations. Discrete Applied Mathematics 26(1), 25–40 (1990)
7. Blokhuis, A., Sali, A.: Paper in preparation
8. Bollobás, B., Katona, G.O.H., Leader, I.: Paper in preparation
9. Brightwell, G., Katona, G.O.H.: A new type of coding theorem. Studia Sci. Math. Hungar. 38, 139–147 (2001)
10. Brouwer, A.E.: Personal communication (2008)
11. Bryant, D.E., Khodkar, A.: On orthogonal double covers of graphs. Designs, Codes and Cryptography 13, 103–105 (1998) 10.1023/A:1008283627078
12. D'Atri, A., Moscarini, M.: On the recognition and design of acyclic databases. In: Proceedings of the 3rd ACM SIGACT-SIGMOD Symposium on Principles of Database Systems PODS 1984, pp. 1–8. ACM, New York (1984)
13. Demetrovics, J.: On the equivalence of candidate keys with Sperner systems. Acta Cybernetica 4, 247–252 (1979)
14. Demetrovics, J., Füredi, Z., Katona, G.O.H.: Minimum matrix reperesentation of closure operetions. Discrete Applied Mathematics 11, 115–128 (1985)
15. Demetrovics, J., Gyepesi, G.: A note on minimum matrix reperesentation of closure operetions. Combinatorica 3, 177–180 (1983)
16. Demetrovics, J., Katona, G. O. H.: Tempero, E.: Extremal combinatorial problems in relational data base. In:FCT 1981. LNCS, vol. 117, pp. 110–119. Springer, Heidelberg (1981)
17. Demetrovics, J., Katona, G.O.H.: A survey of some combinatorial results concerning functional dependencies in databases. Annals of Mathematics and Artificial Intelligence 7, 63–82 (1993)
18. Demetrovics, J., Katona, G.O.H., Sali, A.: The characterization of branching dependencies. Discrete Applied Mathematics 40, 139–153 (1992)
19. Demetrovics, J., Katona, G.O.H., Sali, A.: Representations of branching dependencies. Acta Sci. Math. (Szeged) 60, 213–223 (1995)
20. Demetrovics, J., Katona, G.O.H., Sali, A.: Design type problems motivated by database theory. Journal of Statistical Planning and Inference 72, 149–164 (1998)
21. Deza, M.-M., Deza, E.: Dictionary of distances. Elsevier, Amsterdam (2006)
22. Enomoto, H., Katona, G.O.H.: Pairs of disjoint q-element subsets far from each other. Electronic Journal of Combinatorics 8, # R7 (2001)
23. Fagin, R.: Horn clauses and database dependencies. Journal of the Association for Computing Machinery 29(4), 952–985 (1982)
24. Fagin, R.: Degrees of acyclicity for hypergraphs and relational database schemes. J. ACM 30, 514–550 (1983)
25. Fu, F.-W., Kløve, T., Luo, Y., Wei, V.: On equidistant constant weight codes. Discrete Applied Mathematics 128, 157–164 (2003)
26. Füredi, Z.: Perfect error-correcting databases. Discrete Applied Mathematics 28, 171–176 (1990)
27. Ganter, B., Gronau, H.-D.O.F.: On two conjectures of Demetrovics, Füredi and Katona concerning partitions. Discrete Mathematics 88, 149–155 (1987)
28. Ganter, B., Gronau, H.-D.O.F., Mullin, R.C.: On orthogonal double covers of K_n. Ars Combinatoria 37, 209–221 (1994)

29. Graham, R., Sloane, N.: Lower bounds for constant weight code. IEEE Trans. Inform. Theory 26, 37–43 (1980)
30. Grahne, G., Räihä, K.-J.: Characterizations for acyclic database schemes. In: Preparata, F., Kanellakis, P. (eds.) Advances in Computing Research, p. 1941. JAI Press Inc., Greenwich (1986)
31. Grant, J., Minker, J.: Normalization and axiomatization for numerical dependencies. Information and Control 65, 1–17 (1985)
32. Gronau, H.-D.O.F., Grttmller, M., Hartmann, S., Leck, U., Leck, V.: On orthogonal double covers of graphs. Designs, Codes and Cryptography 27, 49–91 (2002) 10.1023/A:1016546402248
33. Gronau, H.-D.O.F., Schmidmeier, M.: Orthogonal covers by multiplication graphs. Discrete Applied Mathematics 157(9), 2048–2056 (2009); Optimal Discrete Structures and Algorithms - ODSA 2006
34. Hartmann, S., Leck, U.: Self-orthogonal decompositions of graphs into matchings. Electronic Notes in Discrete Mathematics 23, 5–11 (2005); Workshop on Graph Asymmetries
35. Hartmann, S., Leck, U., Leck, V.: More orthogonal double covers of complete graphs by hamiltonian paths. Discrete Mathematics 308(12), 2502–2508 (2008)
36. Hartmann, S., Link, S., Schewe, K.-D.: Weak functional dependencies in higher-order datamodels. In: Seipel, D., Turull-Torres, J.M. (eds.) FoIKS 2004. LNCS, vol. 2942. Springer, Heidelberg (2004)
37. Katona, G.O.H., Sali, A., Schewe, K.-D.: Codes that attain minimum distance in all possible directions. Central Eruopean J. of Math. 6, 1–11 (2008)
38. Leck, U., Leck, V.: Orthogonal double covers of complete graphs by trees of small diameter. Discrete Applied Mathematics 95(1-3), 377–388 (1999)
39. Lovász, L.: Toplogical and algebraic methods in graph theory. In: Graph Theory and Related Topics: Proc. Conf. Univ. Waterloo, Ontario 1977. Academic Press, New York (1979)
40. Quistorff, J.: New upper bounds on enomoto-katona's coding type problem. Studia Sci. Math. Hungar. 42, 61–72 (2005)
41. Quistorff, J.: Combinatorial problems in the enomoto-katona space. Studia Sci. Math. Hungar. 46, 121–139 (2009)
42. Rankin, R.: The closest packing of spherical caps in n dimensions. Proceedings of the Glagow Mathematical Society 2, 145–146 (1955)
43. Sali, A.: Minimal keys in higher-order datamodels. In: Seipel, D., Turull-Torres, J.M. (eds.) FoIKS 2004. LNCS, vol. 2942, Springer, Heidelberg (2004)
44. Sali, A., Schewe, K.-D.: Counter-free keys and functional dependencies in higher-order datamodels. Fundamenta Informaticae 70, 277–301 (2006)
45. Sali, A., Schewe, K.-D.: Keys and Armstrong databases in trees with restructuring. Acta Cybernetica 18, 529–556 (2008)
46. Sali, A., Székely, L.A.: On the existence of armstrong instances with bounded domains. In: Hartmann, S., Kern-Isberner, G. (eds.) FoIKS 2008. LNCS, vol. 4932, pp. 151–157. Springer, Heidelberg (2008)
47. Sali sr, A., Sali, A.: Generalized dependencies in relational databases. Acta Cybernetica (Szeged) 13, 431–438 (1998)
48. Silva, A., Melkanoff, M.: A method for helping discover the dependencies of a relation. In: Gallaire, H., Minker, J., Nicolas, J.-M. (eds.) Advances in Data Base Theory, vol. 1. Plenum Publishing, New York (1981)
49. Thalheim, B.: The number of keys in relational and nested relational databases. Discrete Applied Mathematics 40, 265–282 (1992)

A Proof System with Bounded Non-determinism in Database Transformations

Qing Wang

University of Otago, Dunedin, New Zealand
`qing.wang@otago.ac.nz`

Abstract. Database Abstract State Machines (DB-ASMs) provide a universal computation model for database transformations that encompass queries and updates. In this paper we present a proof system for DB-ASMs. It is shown that the proof system for DB-ASMs is sound. As DB-ASMs are restricted by allowing quantifiers over only the database part of a state which is a finite structure, we can formalise non-determinism of DB-ASMs by utilising a modal operator [ ] for an update set or multiset generated by a DB-ASM rule. In doing so, we lay down a solid foundation for the completeness proof of the proof system proposed for DB-ASMs in this paper.

1 Introduction

Abstract State Machine (ASM) [1] is a universal computation model with flexible levels of abstraction. In past years the logical foundations for ASMs have been well studied from several perspectives [3,4,7,9,10]. In particular, Stärk and Nanchen [10] developed a logic complete for *hierarchical ASMs* (i.e., ASMs that do not contain recursive rule definitions). This logic differs from other logics for ASMs in at least two respects: (i) the consistency of updates has been accounted for in the reasoning part of the logic; (ii) modal operators can be eliminated by using some logical equivalences. Inspired by the sequential ASM thesis capturing sequential algorithms [5], the authors of [8,13,14] developed a variant of ASMs for modelling database transformations, called *database Abstract State Machines* (DB-ASMs). It has been shown that DB-ASMs satisfy five postulates for database transformations and all computations stipulated by these five postulates for database transformations can be simulated, step by step, by a DB-ASM. These results were formalised into the DB-ASM thesis [13] which provides a unifying theoretical framework for the studies of database transformations encompassing both queries and updates.

The DB-ASM thesis introduces non-determinism into database transformations. Non-determinism becomes important in database transformations when we are faced with object creation in certain data models, as discussed intensively in [11,12]. Furthermore, the degree of non-determinism in a class of database transformations is also one of critical factors determining the upper bound of the expressiveness of associated languages. In DB-ASMs, only non-deterministic

K.-D. Schewe, and B. Thalheim (Eds.): SDKB 2010, LNCS 6834, pp. 114–133, 2011.

choice among finite answers to a query in database transformations is permitted by the inclusion of choice rules.

Due to the presence of choice rules in DB-ASMs, the most challenging problem in formalising a logic for DB-ASMs is the handling of non-deterministic update sets associated with a DB-ASM rule. Stärk and Nanchen [10] discussed various problems they encountered when they tried to formalise non-determinism into the logic for ASMs. They stated:

> Unfortunately, the formalisation of consistency cannot be applied directly to non-deterministic ASMs. The formula $Con(R)$ (as defined in Sect. 8.1.2 of [1]) expresses the property that the *union of all possible* update sets of R in a given state is consistent. This is clearly not what is meant by consistency. Therefore, in a logic for ASMs with **choose** one had to add $Con(R)$ as an atomic formula to the logic.

However, we observe that this statement is not universally true. For update sets or multisets that contain only finite updates, they can be made explicit in the formulae of a logic to capture non-deterministic transitions. Then, the formalisation of consistency as defined in Sect. 8.1.2 of [1] can still be applied to such an explicitly specified update set Δ yielded by a rule. Therefore, in this paper we present an approach to solve the problem of non-determinism in formalising the logic for DB-ASMs. The underlying assumption of this approach is the finiteness of update sets and multisets, which can be assured by the definition of DB-ASMs. Because DB-ASMs are restricted to have quantifiers over only the database part of a state which is a finite structure, update sets (or multisets) yielded by a DB-ASM rule are thus restricted to be finite. Moreover, less-than-or-equal (denoted as $\leq$) and membership (denoted as $\in$) in the logic for DB-ASMs are used as predicates under a fixed interpretation. It means that a second-order variable is always bound to an update set or an update multiset that must be finite.

The rest of the paper is structured as follows. In Section 2 we briefly recall the definition of DB-ASMs. In Section 3 we define the syntax and semantics of the logic for DB-ASMs, along with the formalisation of a proof system. Then we discuss the soundness of the logic for DB-ASMs in Section 4 and conclude the paper in Section 5.

2   Database Abstract State Machines

In this section we recall *database Abstract State Machines* (DB-ASMs) [13]. Every state of a DB-ASM is a meta-finite structure [2], consisting of two parts: the database part and algorithmic part linked by a finite number of bridge functions that interpret elements in the database part by elements in the algorithmic part. A signature Υ of states is a set of function symbols, each associated with a fixed arity. Υ comprises a sub-signature Υ_{db} for the database part, a sub-signature Υ_a for the algorithmic part and bridge functions $\{f_1, \ldots, f_\ell\}$. A state over Υ consists of a base set B that is the union of two subsets B_{db} and B_a for the database and algorithmic parts, respectively, together with interpretations of function symbols in Υ. For every state over Υ, the restriction to Υ_{db} results in a finite structure. A function symbol is *dynamic* if the function is changeable.

Let S be a state of a DB-ASM M over Υ, $f \in \Upsilon_{db}$ be a dynamic function symbol of arity n and $a_1, ..., a_n, b$ be elements in the base set of S. Then $f(a_1, ..., a_n)$ is called a *location* of M. An *update* of M is a pair (ℓ, b), where ℓ is a location and b is called the *update value* of ℓ. The interpretation of ℓ in S is called the *content* of ℓ in S, denoted by $val_S(\ell)$. An *update set* is a set of updates; an *update multiset* is a multiset of updates. Let D, D' and D'' be the domains. Then a *location operator* $\rho = (f_\alpha, \odot, f_\beta)$ consisting of a unary function $f_\alpha : D \to D'$, a commutative and associative binary operation $\odot$ over D', and a unary function $f_\beta : D' \to D''$, which define $\rho(b) = f_\beta(f_\alpha(a_1) \odot \cdots \odot f_\alpha(a_n))$ for a multiset $b = \{\!\{a_1, ..., a_n\}\!\}$. By assigning location operators to a location, a collection of update values to the location can be aggregated into a single value.

An update set Δ is *consistent* if any two updates in Δ to the same location must have the same update value. If S is a state of a DB-ASM M and Δ is a consistent update set for the signature of M, then there exists a unique state $S' = S + \Delta$ resulting from updating S with Δ: we simply have

$$
val_{S+\Delta}(\ell) \;\; = \;\; \begin{cases} b & \text{if } (\ell, b) \in \Delta \\ val_S(\ell) & \text{else} \end{cases}
$$

A variable assignment ζ for state S is a finite function which assigns elements in the base set of S to a finite number of variables. If ζ is a variable assignment, then $\zeta[x_1 \mapsto b_1, \ldots, x_k \mapsto b_k]$ is another variable assignment defined by

$$
\zeta[x_1 \mapsto b_1, \ldots, x_k \mapsto b_k](x) = \begin{cases} b_i & \text{if } x = x_i (i = 1, \ldots, k) \\ \zeta(x) & \text{else} \end{cases}
$$

For convenience, we use the notation $val_{S,\zeta}(t)$ for the interpretation of term t in a state S under a variable assignment ζ. If r is a DB-ASM rule (we will define it in Definition 1) and S is a meta-finite state over signature Υ of r, we associate a set $\Delta(r, S)$ of update sets and a set $\ddot{\Delta}(r, S)$ of update multisets with r and S, respectively. DB-ASM rules may involve variables, so we use the notation $\Delta(r, S, \zeta)$ for a set of update sets that depends on a variable assignment ζ, and analogously $\ddot{\Delta}(r, S, \zeta)$ for a set of update multisets. We also refer to *database variables* as variables that must be interpreted by elements in B_{db}. The notation $var(t)$ is used to denote the set of variables occurring in a term t. Furthermore, similar to formulae we can define the set $fr(r)$ of free variables appearing in a DB-ASM rule r, with variables being bound by forall and choice rules. A rule r is called *closed* iff $fr(r) = \emptyset$.

Definition 1. The set $\mathcal{R}$ of *DB-ASM rules* over a signature $\Upsilon = \Upsilon_{db} \cup \Upsilon_a \cup \{f_1, \ldots, f_\ell\}$ and associated sets of update sets are defined as follows:

- If $t_0, \ldots, t_n$ are terms over Υ, and f is a dynamic n-ary function symbol in Υ, then $f(t_1, \ldots, t_n) := t_0$ is a rule r in $\mathcal{R}$ called *assignment rule* with

$fr(r) = \bigcup\limits_{i=0}^{n} var(t_i)$, where $var(t_i)$ is the set of variables occurring in the terms t_i $(i = 0, \ldots, n)$. For a state S over Υ and a variable assignment ζ for $fr(r)$ we obtain

$$\Delta(r, S, \zeta) = \{\{(f(a_1, \ldots, a_n), a_0)\}\}$$

with $a_i = val_{S,\zeta}(t_i)$ $(i = 0, \ldots, n)$, and

$$\ddot{\Delta}(r, S, \zeta) = \{\!\{(f(a_1, \ldots, a_n), a_0)\}\!\}$$

- If φ is a Boolean term and $r' \in \mathcal{R}$ is a DB-ASM rule, then **if** φ **then** r' **endif** is a rule r in $\mathcal{R}$ called *conditional rule* with $fr(r) = fr(\varphi) \cup fr(r')$. For a state S over Υ and a variable assignment ζ for the variables in $fr(r)$, we obtain

$$\ddot{\Delta}(r, S, \zeta) = \begin{cases} \ddot{\Delta}(r', S, \zeta) & \text{if } val_{S,\zeta}(\varphi) = true \\ \emptyset & \text{else} \end{cases}$$

and

$$\Delta(r, S, \zeta) = \begin{cases} \Delta(r', S, \zeta) & \text{if } val_{S,\zeta}(\varphi) = true \\ \emptyset & \text{else} \end{cases}$$

- If φ is a Boolean term with only database variables, $\{x_1, \ldots, x_k\} \subseteq fr(\varphi)$ and $r' \in \mathcal{R}$ is a DB-ASM rule, then **forall** $x_1, \ldots, x_k$ **with** φ **do** r' **enddo** is a rule r in $\mathcal{R}$ called *forall rule* with $fr(r) = fr(r') \cup fr(\varphi) - \{x_1, \ldots, x_k\}$. For a state S over Υ and a variable assignment ζ for the variables in $fr(r)$, let $\mathcal{B} = \{(b_1, \ldots, b_k) \mid val_{S,\zeta[x_1 \mapsto b_1, \ldots, x_k \mapsto b_k]}(\varphi) = true\}$, and $\mathfrak{M}$ denote the set of mappings α from $\mathcal{B}$ to $\bigcup\{\Delta(r', S, \zeta[x_1 \mapsto b_1, \ldots, x_k \mapsto b_k]) \mid (b_1, \ldots, b_k) \in \mathcal{B}\}$ with $\alpha(b_1, \ldots, b_k) \in \Delta(r', S, \zeta[x_1 \mapsto b_1, \ldots, x_k \mapsto b_k])$. Then each $\alpha \in \mathfrak{M}$ defines an update set $\Delta_\alpha = \bigcup\{\alpha(b_1, \ldots, b_k) \mid (b_1, \ldots, b_k) \in \mathcal{B}\}$, from which we obtain

$$\Delta(r, S, \zeta) = \{\Delta_\alpha \mid \alpha \in \mathfrak{M}\}.$$

Analogously, let $\ddot{\mathfrak{M}}$ denote the set of mappings $\ddot{\alpha}$ from $\mathcal{B}$ to $\bigcup\{\ddot{\Delta}(r', S, \zeta[x_1 \mapsto b_1, \ldots, x_k \mapsto b_k]) \mid (b_1, \ldots, b_k) \in \mathcal{B}\}$ with $\ddot{\alpha}(b_1, \ldots, b_k) \in \ddot{\Delta}(r', S, \zeta[x_1 \mapsto b_1, \ldots, x_k \mapsto b_k])$. Then each $\ddot{\alpha} \in \ddot{\mathfrak{M}}$ defines an update multiset $\ddot{\Delta}_{\ddot{\alpha}} = \biguplus\{\ddot{\alpha}(b_1, \ldots, b_k) \mid (b_1, \ldots, b_k) \in \mathcal{B}\}$, which finally gives

$$\ddot{\Delta}(r, S, \zeta) = \{\ddot{\Delta}_{\ddot{\alpha}} \mid \ddot{\alpha} \in \ddot{\mathfrak{M}}\}.$$

- If $r_1, \ldots, r_n$ are rules in $\mathcal{R}$, then the rule r defined as **par** $r_1 \ldots r_n$ **endpar** is a rule in $\mathcal{R}$, called *parallel rule* with $fr(r) = \bigcup\limits_{i=1}^{n} fr(r_i)$. For a state S over Υ and a variable assignment ζ for the variables in $fr(r)$ we obtain

$$\Delta(r, S, \zeta) = \{\Delta_1 \cup \cdots \cup \Delta_n \mid \Delta_i \in \Delta(r_i, S, \zeta) \text{ for } i = 1, \ldots, n\}$$

and

$$\ddot{\Delta}(r, S, \zeta) = \{\ddot{\Delta}_1 \uplus \cdots \uplus \ddot{\Delta}_n \mid \ddot{\Delta}_i \in \ddot{\Delta}(r_i, S, \zeta) \text{ for } i = 1, \ldots, n\}.$$

- If φ is a Boolean term with only database variables, $\{x_1, \ldots, x_k\} \subseteq fr(\varphi)$ and $r' \in \mathcal{R}$ is a DB-ASM rule, then **choose** $x_1, \ldots, x_k$ **with** φ **do** r' **enddo** is a rule r in $\mathcal{R}$ called *choice rule* with $fr(r) = fr(r') \cup fr(\varphi) - \{x_1, \ldots, x_k\}$. For a state S over Υ and a variable assignment ζ for the variables in $fr(r)$ let $\mathcal{B} = \{(b_1, \ldots, b_k) \mid val_{S, \zeta[x_1 \mapsto b_1, \ldots, x_k \mapsto b_k]}(\varphi) = true\}$. Then we obtain

$$\Delta(r, S, \zeta) = \bigcup \{\Delta(r', S, \zeta[x_1 \mapsto b_1, \ldots, x_k \mapsto b_k]) \mid (b_1, \ldots, b_k) \in \mathcal{B}\}.$$

and

$$\ddot{\Delta}(r, S, \zeta) = \bigcup \{\ddot{\Delta}(r', S, \zeta[x_1 \mapsto b_1, \ldots, x_k \mapsto b_k]) \mid (b_1, \ldots, b_k) \in \mathcal{B}\}.$$

- If r_1, r_2 are rules in $\mathcal{R}$, then the rule r defined as **seq** $r_1 ; r_2$ **endseq** is a rule in $\mathcal{R}$, called *sequence rule* with $fr(r) = fr(r_1) \cup fr(r_2)$. For a state S over Υ and a variable assignment ζ for the variables in $fr(r)$, we obtain

$$\Delta(r, S, \zeta) = \{\Delta_1 \oslash \Delta_2 \mid \Delta_1 \in \Delta(r_1, S, \zeta) \text{ and } \Delta_2 \in \Delta(r_2, S + \Delta_1, \zeta)\}$$

with update sets defined as

$$\Delta_1 \oslash \Delta_2 = \Delta_2 \cup \{(\ell, v) \in \Delta_1 \mid \neg \exists v'.(\ell, v') \in \Delta_2\},$$

and

$$\ddot{\Delta}(r, S, \zeta) = \{\ddot{\Delta}_1 \oslash \ddot{\Delta}_2 \mid \ddot{\Delta}_1 \in \ddot{\Delta}(r_1, S, \zeta) \text{ and } \ddot{\Delta}_2 \in \ddot{\Delta}(r_2, S + AsSet(\ddot{\Delta}_1), \zeta)\}$$

with update multisets defined as

$$\ddot{\Delta}_1 \oslash \ddot{\Delta}_2 = \ddot{\Delta}_2 \uplus \{\!\{(\ell, v) \in \ddot{\Delta}_1 \mid \neg \exists v'.(\ell, v') \in \ddot{\Delta}_2\}\!\}.$$

- If $r' \in \mathcal{R}$ is a DB-ASM rule and θ is a location function that assigns location operators ρ to locations interpreted by terms t with $var(t) \subseteq fr(r')$, then **let** $\theta(t) = \rho$ **in** r' **endlet** is a rule $r \in \mathcal{R}$ called *let rule* with $fr(r) = fr(r')$. For a state S over Υ and a variable assignment ζ for the variables in $fr(r)$ let $\ddot{\Delta}(r', S, \zeta) = \{\ddot{\Delta}_1, \ldots, \ddot{\Delta}_n\}$ with update multisets $\ddot{\Delta}_i = \ddot{\Delta}_i^{(t)} \uplus \ddot{\Delta}_i^-$ such that the first of these two multisubsets contains the updates to locations $val_{S, \zeta}(t)$, while the second one contains updates to all other locations. Define

$$\ddot{\Delta}_i^{(r)} = \{(\ell, a) \mid \ell = val_{S, \zeta}(t), a = \theta(t)(\{\!\{a_1, \ldots, a_k \mid (\ell, a_i) \in \ddot{\Delta}_i^{(t)}\}\!\})\} \uplus \ddot{\Delta}_i^-$$

and

$$\Delta_i^{(r)} = \{(\ell, a) \mid \ell = val_{S, \zeta}(t), a = \theta(t)(\{\!\{a_1, \ldots, a_k \mid (\ell, a_i) \in \ddot{\Delta}_i^{(t)}\}\!\})\} \cup \Delta_i^-,$$

with $\Delta_i^- = \{(\ell, a) \mid (\ell, a) \in \ddot{\Delta}_i^-\}$. This finally gives

$$\ddot{\Delta}(r, S, \zeta) = \{\ddot{\Delta}_1^{(r)}, \ldots, \ddot{\Delta}_n^{(r)}\} \quad \text{and} \quad \Delta(r, S, \zeta) = \{\Delta_1^{(r)}, \ldots, \Delta_n^{(r)}\}.$$

Only assignment rules "create" updates in update sets and multisets, only choice rules introduce non-determinism and let rules let updates to the same location collapse to a single update by means of location operators, whereas all other rules only rearrange these updates into different sets and multisets, respectively.

Definition 2. A *database Abstract State Machine* (DB-ASM) M over a signature Υ consists of

- a set $\mathcal{S}_M$ of states over Υ closed under isomorphisms,
- non-empty subsets $\mathcal{I}_M \subseteq \mathcal{S}_M$ of initial states, and $\mathcal{F}_M \subseteq \mathcal{S}_M$ of final states, both also closed under isomorphisms,
- a closed DB-ASM rule r_M over Υ, and
- a binary relation δ_M over $\mathcal{S}_M$ determined by r_M such that

$$\{S_{i+1} \mid (S_i, S_{i+1}) \in \delta_M\} = \{S_i + \Delta \mid \Delta \in \Delta(r_M, S_i)\}$$

holds.

Example 1. Suppose that we have the following DB-ASM rule
$$\textbf{forall } x \textbf{ with } \exists y. R(x,x,y)$$
$$\textbf{do}$$
$$\textbf{let } \theta(f(x)) = \textbf{sum in}$$
$$\textbf{forall } y \textbf{ with } R(x,x,y)$$
$$\textbf{do } f(x) := 1 \textbf{ enddo}$$
$$\textbf{endlet}$$
$$\textbf{enddo}$$
using **sum** as a shortcut for the location operator $(id, +, id)$. If the state contains the tuples $R(a_3,a_3,a_5), R(a_3,a_3,a_6), R(a_4,a_4,a_7), R(a_5,a_5,a_4), R(a_5,a_5,a_9)$, $R(a_5,a_5,a_5), R(a_6,a_7,a_3)$, then first the update multisets $\{\!\{(f(a_3),1),(f(a_3),1)\}\!\}$, $\{\!\{(f(a_4),1)\}\!\}, \{\!\{(f(a_5),1),(f(a_5),1),(f(a_5),1)\}\!\}$ are produced by means of the forall rules, which are then collapsed to the update set $\{(f(a_3),2),(f(a_4),1),$ $(f(a_5),3)\}$ using the **sum**-operator in the let rule. Thus, for x such that there are tuples $R(x,x,y)$ in the database, then the number of such tuples is counted and assigned to $f(x)$.

3   A Logical Formalisation

We formalise the logic for DB-ASMs based on a logic of meta-finite structures [2] that characterises states of a database transformation.

3.1   Syntax

Let us fix a countable set $\mathcal{X}_{FO} = \{x_1, x_2, ...\}$ of database variables. For simplicity, $\overline{x}, \overline{y},...$ are used to denote tuples of variables in $\mathcal{X}_{FO}$.

Definition 3. *Let* $\Upsilon = \Upsilon_{db} \cup \Upsilon_a \cup \{f_1, \ldots f_\ell\}$ *be a signature of states and* $\{\rho_1, \ldots, \rho_m\} \subseteq \Upsilon_a$ *be a set of location operators. Then the terms and formulae for DB-ASMs over signature* Υ *are inductively defined as follows.*

1. *The set* $\mathcal{T}$ *of terms is constituted by the sets* $\mathcal{T}_{db}$ *and* $\mathcal{T}_a$ *of terms over the database and algorithmic parts called* database terms *and* algorithmic terms, *respectively (i.e.,* $\mathcal{T} = \mathcal{T}_{db} \cup \mathcal{T}_a$), *such that*

   (a) $x \in \mathcal{T}_{db}$, *where* $x \in \mathcal{X}_{FO}$ *and* $fr(x) = \{x\}$;

   (b) $f(t_1, \ldots, t_n) \in \mathcal{T}_{db}$, *where* $f \in \Upsilon_{db}$ *is a n-ary function symbol,* $\{t_1, \ldots, t_n\} \subseteq \mathcal{T}_{db}$, *and* $fr(f(t_1, \ldots, t_n)) = \bigcup_{1 \leq j \leq n} fr(t_j)$;

   (c) $f(t_1, \ldots, t_n) \in \mathcal{T}_a$, *where* $f \in \{f_1, \ldots f_\ell\}$ *is a n-ary function symbol,* $\{t_1, \ldots, t_n\} \subseteq \mathcal{T}_{db}$ *and* $fr(f(t_1, \ldots, t_n)) = \bigcup_{1 \leq j \leq n} fr(t_j)$;

   (d) $f(t_1, \ldots, t_n) \in \mathcal{T}_a$, *where* $f \in \Upsilon_a - \{\rho_1, \ldots, \rho_m\}$ *is a n-ary function symbol,* $\{t_1, \ldots, t_n\} \subseteq \mathcal{T}_a$, *and* $fr(f(t_1, \ldots, t_n)) = \bigcup_{1 \leq j \leq n} fr(t_j)$;

   (e) $\rho_{\overline{x}}(t | \varphi(\overline{x}, \overline{y})) \in \mathcal{T}_a$, *where* $t \in \mathcal{T}_a$, $\rho \in \{\rho_1, \ldots, \rho_m\}$, $\varphi(\overline{x}, \overline{y}) \in \Phi$ *is a formula defined in the following with* $fr(t) \subseteq fr(\varphi(\overline{x}, \overline{y}))$ *and* $fr(\rho_{\overline{x}}(t | \varphi(\overline{x}, \overline{y}))) = \overline{y}$.

2. *The set* Φ *of formulae is generated by applying the following rules:*

$$\varphi := \varphi_a \,|\, \neg\varphi \,|\, \varphi_1 \wedge \varphi_2 \,|\, \forall x.\varphi \,|\, \exists x.\varphi \,|\, \exists X.\varphi \,|\, \forall X.\varphi \,|\,$$
$$upd(r, \Delta) \,|\, upm(r, \ddot{\Delta}) \,|\, \Delta(f, \overline{t}, t_0) \,|\, \ddot{\Delta}(f, \overline{t}, t_0, t') \,|\, def(r) \,|\, [\Delta]\varphi$$

where x *is a database variable and* φ_a *is an atomic formula which can be*

   - $t_1 = t_2$ *for either* $t_1, t_2 \in \mathcal{T}_{db}$ *or* $t_1, t_2 \in \mathcal{T}_a$, *and* $fr(t_1 = t_2) = fr(t_1) \cup fr(t_2)$;
   - $P_1(t_1, \ldots, t_n)$ *for n-ary predicate symbol* $P_1 \in \Upsilon_{db}$, $t_i \in \mathcal{T}_{db}$ $(i = 1, \ldots, n)$, *and* $fr(P_1(t_1, \ldots, t_n)) = \bigcup_{1 \leq j \leq n} fr(t_j)$;
   - $P_2(t_1, \ldots, t_n)$ *for n-ary predicate symbol* $P_2 \in \Upsilon_a$, $t_i \in \mathcal{T}_a$ $(i = 1, \ldots, n)$, *and* $fr(P_2(t_1, \ldots, t_n)) = \bigcup_{1 \leq j \leq n} fr(t_j)$;

The formulae $\exists X.\varphi$ and $\forall X.\varphi$ are second-order formulae in which X is a second-order variable bound to an update set Δ or an update multiset $\ddot{\Delta}$. The predicates $upd(r, \Delta)$ and $upm(r, \ddot{\Delta})$ describe an update set Δ and an update multiset $\ddot{\Delta}$ generated by a rule r, respectively. When applying forall and parallel rules of a DB-ASM, updates produced in parallel computations may be identical and thus need the multiset semantics. For this reason, both predicates $upd(r, \Delta)$ and $upm(r, \ddot{\Delta})$ are included in the logic. The formula $\Delta(f, \overline{t}, t_0)$ describes that an update $(f(\overline{t}), t_0)$ exists in an update set Δ, while $\ddot{\Delta}(f, \overline{t}, t_0, t')$ describes that an update $(f(\overline{t}), t_0)$ is the t'th occurrence in an update multiset $\ddot{\Delta}$. The predicate $def(r)$ is used to formulate the definedness property of a rule r of M, meaning that a rule r is defined iff r generates at least one update set. Instead of introducing modal operators $[\,]$ and $\langle\,\rangle$ for a rule r, i.e., the formulae $[r]\varphi$ and $\langle r\rangle\varphi$ expressing the evaluation of φ over a state after executing the rule r on the current state, we use $[\Delta]\varphi$ to express the evaluation of φ over a state after executing the update set Δ on the current state.

We use the notations ρ-*term* referring to a term in the form of $\rho_{\overline{x}}(t|\varphi(\overline{x},\overline{y}))$ and *pure term* referring to a term defined by only applying Rules (1).(a)-(1).(d) (i.e., terms that do not contain any formulae and ρ-terms). A formula is *pure* if it does not contain the formulae $\exists X.\varphi$, $\forall X.\varphi$, $\mathrm{upd}(r,\Delta)$, $\mathrm{upm}(r,\ddot{\Delta})$, $\Delta(f,\overline{t},t_0)$, $\ddot{\Delta}(f,\overline{t},t_0,t')$, $\mathrm{def}(r)$ and $[\Delta]\varphi$. A formula or a term is *static* if it does not contain any dynamic function symbols. The formulae occurring in conditional, forall and choice rules of a DB-ASM must be pure. By Rule 1.(e), ρ-terms are built upon formulae, and by Rule 2, ρ-terms can also be used for constructing formulae, so formulae and terms can be iteratively created in the logic for DB-ASMs. The expressions $\psi_1 \vee \psi_2$, $\psi_1 \Rightarrow \psi_2$, $\psi_1 \Leftrightarrow \psi_2$ and $\forall \overline{x}.\varphi$ may be used as shortcuts in the standard way.

3.2 Semantics

We use the notation $[\overline{x} \mapsto \overline{a}]$ as a shorthand for $[x_1 \mapsto a_1, \ldots, x_n \mapsto a_n]$.

Definition 4. *Let S be a state of signature Υ with the base set $B = B_{db} \cup B_a$, $\mathbb{F}_{dyn}$ be the set of all dynamic function symbols in signature Υ and ζ be a variable assignment. The semantics of the logic for DB-ASMs over Υ can be defined by*

Terms

- $val_{S,\zeta[x\mapsto a]}(x) = a$ for $a \in B_{db}$;
- $val_{S,\zeta}(f(t_1,\ldots,t_n)) = f(val_{S,\zeta}(t_1),\ldots,val_{S,\zeta}(t_n))$ and for $i = 1,\ldots,n$
  - if $f \in \Upsilon_{db}$, then $val_{S,\zeta}(t_i)$ and $f(val_{S,\zeta}(t_1),\ldots,val_{S,\zeta}(t_n)) \in B_{db}$;
  - if $f \in \Upsilon_a$, then $val_{S,\zeta}(t_i)$ and $f(val_{S,\zeta}(t_1),\ldots,val_{S,\zeta}(t_n)) \in B_a$;
  - if $f \in \{f_1,\ldots,f_\ell\}$, then $f(val_{S,\zeta}(t_1),\ldots,val_{S,\zeta}(t_n)) \in B_a$ and $val_{S,\zeta}(t_i) \in B_{db}$;
- $val_{S,\zeta[\overline{y}\mapsto \overline{b}]}(\rho_{\overline{x}}(t|\varphi(\overline{x},\overline{y}))) =$

$$\begin{cases} \rho(\{val_{S,\zeta[\overline{y}\mapsto \overline{b},\overline{x}\mapsto \overline{a}]}(t)|\ \text{for all } \overline{a} \text{ such that } [\![\varphi(\overline{x},\overline{y})]\!]_{S,\zeta[\overline{y}\mapsto \overline{b},\overline{x}\mapsto \overline{a}]} = true\}) \\ \qquad \text{if there exists at least one } \overline{a} \text{ such that } [\![\varphi(\overline{x},\overline{y})]\!]_{S,\zeta[\overline{y}\mapsto \overline{b},\overline{x}\mapsto \overline{a}]} = true; \\ \bot \quad \text{otherwise.} \end{cases}$$

Formulae

- $[\![t_1 = t_2]\!]_{S,\zeta} = \begin{cases} true & \text{if } val_{S,\zeta}(t_1) = val_{S,\zeta}(t_2); \\ false & \text{otherwise.} \end{cases}$

- $[\![P_i(t_1,...,t_n)]\!]_{S,\zeta} = \begin{cases} true & \text{if } (val_{S,\zeta}(t_1),...,val_{S,\zeta}(t_n)) \in P_i; \\ false & \text{otherwise.} \end{cases}$ *(i=1,2)*

- $[\![\exists X.\varphi]\!]_{S,\zeta} = \begin{cases} true & \text{if } [\![\varphi]\!]_{S,\zeta[X\mapsto P]} = true \text{ for some finite} \\ & \quad P \subseteq \mathbb{F}_{dyn} \times B^n \times B \text{ or} \\ & \quad P \subseteq \mathbb{F}_{dyn} \times B^n \times B \times \mathbb{N} \ (n \text{ is determined by} X), \\ false & \text{otherwise} \end{cases}$

$$- [\![\forall X.\varphi]\!]_{S,\zeta} = \begin{cases} true & if\ [\![\varphi]\!]_{S,\zeta[X \mapsto P]} = true\ for\ all\ finite \\ & P \subseteq \mathbb{F}_{dyn} \times B^n \times B\ or \\ & P \subseteq \mathbb{F}_{dyn} \times B^n \times B \times \mathbb{N}\ \ (n\ is\ determined\ by X), \\ false & otherwise \end{cases}$$

$$- [\![upd(r, \Delta)]\!]_{S,\zeta} = \begin{cases} true & if\ val_{S,\zeta}(\Delta) \in \Delta(r, S, \zeta), \\ false & otherwise \end{cases}$$

$$- [\![upm(r, \ddot{\Delta})]\!]_{S,\zeta} = \begin{cases} true & if\ val_{S,\zeta}(\ddot{\Delta}) \in \ddot{\Delta}(r, S, \zeta), \\ false & otherwise \end{cases}$$

$$- [\![\Delta(f, \bar{t}, t_0)]\!]_{S,\zeta} = \begin{cases} true & if\ (f, val_{S,\zeta}(\bar{t}), val_{S,\zeta}(t_0)) \in val_{S,\zeta}(\Delta), \\ false & otherwise \end{cases}$$

$$- [\![\ddot{\Delta}(f, \bar{t}, t_0, t')]\!]_{S,\zeta} = \begin{cases} true & if\ (f, val_{S,\zeta}(\bar{t}), val_{S,\zeta}(t_0), n) \in val_{S,\zeta}(\ddot{\Delta}) \\ & for\ some\ n \in \mathbb{N}\ and\ val_{S,\zeta}(t') < n, \\ false & otherwise \end{cases}$$

$$- [\![def(r)]\!]_{S,\zeta} = \begin{cases} true & if\ \Delta(r, S, \zeta) \neq \emptyset, \\ false & otherwise \end{cases}$$

$$- [\![[\Delta]\varphi]\!]_{S,\zeta} = \begin{cases} true & if\ [\![\varphi]\!]_{S+\Delta,\zeta} = true\ for\ each\ state\ after\ applying \\ & \Delta \in \Delta(r, S, \zeta)\ over\ state\ S \\ false & otherwise \end{cases}$$

The semantics for first-order formulae $\neg\varphi$, $\varphi_1 \wedge \varphi_2$, $\exists x.\varphi$ and $\forall x.\varphi$ is defined as usual. As variables in the logic are restricted to range over only B_{db}, the finiteness condition on the database part of a state implies that elements in a multiset $\{\!\!\{val_{S,\zeta[\bar{y} \mapsto \bar{b}, \bar{x} \mapsto \bar{a}]}(t)|$ for all $\bar{a}$ such that $[\![\varphi(\bar{x}, \bar{y})]\!]_{S,\zeta[\bar{y} \mapsto \bar{b}, \bar{x} \mapsto \bar{a}]} = true\}\!\!\}$ must be finite. The following example shows that the logic for DB-ASMs can be applied in aggregate computing of database applications.

Example 2. Let us consider a state containing a relation schema AUTHORSHIP = {PubID,UnitID,PersonID,Order} in the database part, and the location operators *max* and *sum* existing in the algorithmic part. Then we can express the following two aggregate queries in the logic for DB-ASMs.

Q_1: Calculate the total number of publications in the database.

$$sum_{x_1}(1|\exists x_2, x_3, x_4.\text{AUTHORSHIP}(x_1, x_2, x_3, x_4))$$

Q_2: Find the author who has published the maximal number of publications in the database.

$$max_{x_3}(sum_{x_1}(1|\exists x_2, x_4.\text{AUTHORSHIP}(x_1, x_2, x_3, x_4))$$
$$|\exists y_1, y_2, y_4.\text{AUTHORSHIP}(y_1, y_2, x_3, y_4))$$

3.3 Consistency and Update Sets

In [10] Stärk and Nanchen used a predicate $\mathrm{Con}(r)$ as an abbreviation for the statement that the rule r is defined and consistent. As a rule r in their work was considered to be deterministic, there was no ambiguity with the reference to the update set associated with r, i.e., a defined rule r is consistent iff the update set generated by r is consistent. However, in the case of the logic for DB-ASMs, the presence of non-determinism makes the situation a bit complicated.

Let r be a DB-ASM rule and Δ be an update set. Then $\mathrm{con}(r, \Delta)$ is an abbreviation of the following formula, representing that the update set Δ generated by the rule r is consistent.

$$\mathrm{con}(r, \Delta) \equiv \mathrm{upd}(r, \Delta) \wedge \bigwedge_{f \in \mathbb{F}_{dyn}} \forall \overline{x}, y, y'.(\Delta(f, \overline{x}, y) \wedge \Delta(f, \overline{x}, y') \Rightarrow y = y')$$

Since the rule r may be non-deterministic, it is possible that rule r may yield an update set Δ in one case and a different update set in another case. So sometimes it would be more convenient to use the formula $\mathrm{con}(\Delta)$ as well, which is the abbreviation defined as

$$\mathrm{con}(\Delta) \equiv \bigwedge_{f \in \mathbb{F}_{dyn}} \forall \overline{x}, y, y'.(\Delta(f, \overline{x}, y) \wedge \Delta(f, \overline{x}, y') \Rightarrow y = y')$$

A rule r is said to be *weakly consistent* (denoted as $\mathrm{wcon}(r)$) iff r is defined and at least one update set generated by r is consistent such that $\mathrm{wcon}(r) \equiv \mathrm{def}(r) \wedge \exists \Delta.\mathrm{con}(r, \Delta)$. A rule r is said to be *strongly consistent* (denoted as $\mathrm{scon}(r)$) iff r is defined and every update set generated by r is consistent such that $\mathrm{scon}(r) \equiv \mathrm{def}(r) \wedge \forall \Delta.(\mathrm{upd}(r, \Delta) \Rightarrow \mathrm{con}(r, \Delta))$. In the case that a rule r is deterministic, the weak notion of consistency coincides with the strong notion of consistency.

We also introduce two abbreviations $\mathrm{inv}(\Delta, f, \overline{x})$ and $\mathrm{inv}(\ddot{\Delta}, f, \overline{x})$ asserting that the update set Δ and multiset $\ddot{\Delta}$ do not have any update to the location of the function symbol f at the argument $\overline{x}$, respectively, such that

- $\mathrm{inv}(\Delta, f, \overline{x}) \equiv \forall y.\neg\Delta(f, \overline{x}, y).$
- $\mathrm{inv}(\ddot{\Delta}, f, \overline{x}) \equiv \forall y, z.\neg\ddot{\Delta}(f, \overline{x}, y, z).$

For the modal expressions $[r]\varphi$ and $\langle r \rangle \varphi$ with the following semantics:

- $$[[r]\varphi]_{S,\varsigma} = \begin{cases} true & \text{if } [\varphi]_{S+\Delta,\varsigma} = true \text{ for all consistent } \Delta \in \Delta(r, S, \varsigma), \\ false & \text{otherwise} \end{cases}$$

- $$[\langle r \rangle \varphi]_{S,\varsigma} = \begin{cases} false & \text{if } [\varphi]_{S+\Delta,\varsigma} = false \text{ for all consistent } \Delta \in \Delta(r, S, \varsigma), \\ true & \text{otherwise} \end{cases}$$

they can be treated as the shortcuts in the logic for DB-ASMs such that $[r]\varphi \equiv \forall \Delta.(\mathrm{upd}(r, \Delta) \Rightarrow [\Delta]\varphi)$ and $\langle r \rangle \varphi \equiv \exists \Delta.(\mathrm{upd}(r, \Delta) \wedge [\Delta]\varphi)$. If Δ is inconsistent, then the formula $[\Delta]\varphi$ is interpreted as *true*. The reason for this is that there is no successor states to the current state after applying an inconsistent update set over it. In doing so, the formula $[\Delta]\varphi$ in the logic for DB-ASMs can be treated in a very similar way to the formula $[r]\varphi$ in the logic for ASMs [10].

3.4 Axioms and Inference Rules

Let r_1 and r_2 be two DB-ASM rules. Then r_1 and r_2 are *equivalent* (denoted as $r_1 \simeq r_2$) if, for all states and variable assignments, $\forall \Delta.(\mathrm{upd}(r_1, \Delta) \Leftrightarrow \mathrm{upd}(r_2, \Delta))$.

Let M be a DB-ASM. Then a formula φ is said to be *implied* by a set Ψ of formulae w.r.t. M (denoted as $\Psi \models_M \varphi$) if for all states S and variable assignments ζ of M, the following condition is satisfied:

- If $[\![\psi]\!]_{S,\zeta} = true$ for every $\psi \in \Psi$, then $[\![\varphi]\!]_{S,\zeta} = true$.

A formula φ is said to be *derived* from a set Ψ of formulae w.r.t. M (denoted as $\Psi \vdash_M \varphi$) if φ is derivable by successively applying a set of axioms and inference rules. To simplify the expression, we skip M in the following discussion. With the use of modal operator $[\,]$ for an update set Δ (i.e., $[\Delta]$), the logic for DB-ASMs becomes a multi-modal logic. We may use it to reason about properties of a database transformation over different states of a run. The set of axioms and inference rules of the logic for DB-ASMs is defined in the following.

- The axioms **D1-D7** assert the properties of $\mathrm{def}(r)$.

  D1 $\mathrm{def}(f(\bar{t}) := t_0)$

  D2 $\mathrm{def}(\textbf{if } \varphi \textbf{ then } r \textbf{ endif}) \Leftrightarrow \neg\varphi \vee (\varphi \wedge \mathrm{def}(r))$

  D3 $\mathrm{def}(\textbf{forall } \bar{z} \textbf{ with } \varphi \textbf{ do } r \textbf{ enddo}) \Leftrightarrow \forall \bar{z}.(\varphi \Rightarrow \mathrm{def}(r))$

  D4 $\mathrm{def}(\textbf{par } r_1...r_n \textbf{ endpar}) \Leftrightarrow \mathrm{def}(r_1) \wedge \cdots \wedge \mathrm{def}(r_n)$

  D5 $\mathrm{def}(\textbf{choose } \bar{z} \textbf{ with } \varphi \textbf{ do } r \textbf{ enddo}) \Leftrightarrow \exists \bar{z}.(\varphi \wedge \mathrm{def}(r)) \vee \forall \bar{z}.(\neg\varphi)$

  D6 $\mathrm{def}(\textbf{seq } r_1 \ r_2 \textbf{ endseq}) \Leftrightarrow \mathrm{def}(r_1) \wedge (\mathrm{wcon}(r_1) \Rightarrow \langle r_1 \rangle \mathrm{def}(r_2))$

  D7 $\mathrm{def}(\textbf{let } \theta(t) = \rho \textbf{ in } r \textbf{ endlet}) \Leftrightarrow \mathrm{def}(r)$

- The axioms **U1-U7** assert the properties of $\mathrm{upd}(r, \Delta)$.

  U1 $\mathrm{upd}(f(\bar{t}) := t_0, \Delta) \Leftrightarrow \Delta(f, \bar{t}, t_0) \wedge \forall \bar{x}, y.(\bar{x} \neq \bar{t} \vee y \neq t_0 \Rightarrow \neg\Delta(f, \bar{x}, y)) \wedge$
  $\bigwedge\limits_{f \neq f' \wedge f \in \mathbb{F}_{dyn} \wedge f' \in \mathbb{F}_{dyn},} \forall \bar{x}, y.\neg\Delta(f', \bar{x}, y)$

  U2 $\mathrm{upd}(\textbf{if } \varphi \textbf{ then } r \textbf{ endif}, \Delta) \Leftrightarrow (\varphi \wedge \mathrm{upd}(r, \Delta)) \vee (\neg\varphi \wedge \bigwedge\limits_{f \in \mathbb{F}_{dyn}} \forall \bar{x}, y.\neg\Delta(f, \bar{x}y))$

  U3 $\mathrm{upd}(\textbf{forall } \bar{z} \textbf{ with } \varphi \textbf{ do } r \textbf{ enddo}, \Delta) \Leftrightarrow \mathrm{def}(\textbf{forall } \bar{z} \textbf{ with } \varphi \textbf{ do } r$
  $\textbf{enddo}) \wedge (\Delta = \bigcup\limits_{\bar{z}}(\Delta'|\varphi \wedge \mathrm{upd}(r, \Delta')) \vee (\neg\varphi \wedge \bigwedge\limits_{f \in \mathbb{F}_{dyn}} \forall \bar{x}, y.\neg\Delta(f, \bar{x}, y)))$

  U4 $\mathrm{upd}(\textbf{par } r_1 \ldots r_n \textbf{ endpar}, \Delta) \Leftrightarrow \mathrm{def}(\textbf{par } r_1 \ldots r_n \textbf{ endpar}) \wedge$
  $\bigwedge\limits_{i=1}^{n} \exists \Delta_i.\mathrm{upd}(r_i, \Delta_i) \wedge \bigwedge\limits_{f \in \mathbb{F}_{dyn}} \forall \bar{x}, y.(\Delta(f, \bar{x}, y) \Leftrightarrow \bigvee\limits_{i=1}^{n} \Delta_i(f, \bar{x}, y))$

  U5 $\mathrm{upd}(\textbf{choose } \bar{z} \textbf{ with } \varphi \textbf{ do } r \textbf{ enddo}, \Delta) \Leftrightarrow \exists \bar{z}.(\varphi \wedge \mathrm{upd}(r, \Delta))$
  $\vee (\forall \bar{z}.\neg\varphi \wedge \bigwedge\limits_{f \in \mathbb{F}_{dyn}} \forall \bar{x}, y.\neg\Delta(f, \bar{x}, y))$

  U6 $\mathrm{upd}(\textbf{seq } r_1 \ r_2 \textbf{ endseq}, \Delta) \Leftrightarrow \exists \Delta_1, \Delta_2.\mathrm{upd}(r_1, \Delta_1) \wedge [\Delta_1]\mathrm{upd}(r_2, \Delta_2)$
  $\bigwedge\limits_{f \in \mathbb{F}_{dyn}} \forall \bar{x}, y.(\Delta(f, \bar{x}, y) \Leftrightarrow (\Delta_1(f, \bar{x}, y) \wedge ([\Delta_1]\mathrm{def}(r_2) \wedge \mathrm{inv}(\Delta_2, f, \bar{x})))$
  $\vee (\mathrm{con}(\Delta_1) \wedge [\Delta_1]\Delta_2(f, \bar{x}, y)))$

U7 $\text{upd}(\textbf{let } \theta(t) = \rho \textbf{ in } r \textbf{ endlet}, \Delta) \Leftrightarrow \exists \ddot{\Delta}.\text{upm}(r, \ddot{\Delta}) \wedge \bigwedge\limits_{f \in \mathbb{F}_{dyn}} \forall \overline{x}, y.(\Delta(f, \overline{x}, y)$

$\Leftrightarrow (f(\overline{x}) \neq t \wedge \exists z. \ddot{\Delta}(f, \overline{x}, y, z)) \vee (f(\overline{x}) = t \wedge y = \rho_{y'}(y' | \exists z. \ddot{\Delta}(f, \overline{x}, y', z)))$

- The axioms **G1-G7** assert the properties of $\text{upm}(r, \ddot{\Delta})$.

G1 $\text{upm}(f(\overline{t}) := t_0, \ddot{\Delta}) \Leftrightarrow \ddot{\Delta}(f, \overline{t}, t_0, 0) \wedge \forall \overline{x}, y, z.(\ddot{\Delta}(f, \overline{x}, y, z) \Rightarrow \overline{x} = \overline{t} \wedge y = t_0 \wedge z = 0) \wedge \bigwedge\limits_{f \neq f' \wedge f \in \mathbb{F}_{dyn} \wedge f' \in \mathbb{F}_{dyn}} \forall \overline{x}, y, z. \neg \ddot{\Delta}(f', \overline{x}, y, z)$

G2 $\text{upm}(\textbf{if } \varphi \textbf{ then } r \textbf{ endif}, \ddot{\Delta}) \Leftrightarrow (\varphi \wedge \text{upm}(r, \ddot{\Delta})) \vee$
$(\neg \varphi \wedge \bigwedge\limits_{f \in \mathbb{F}_{dyn}} \forall \overline{x}, y, z. \neg \ddot{\Delta}(f, \overline{x}, y, z))$

G3 $\text{upm}(\textbf{forall } \overline{z} \textbf{ with } \varphi \textbf{ do } r \textbf{ enddo}, \ddot{\Delta}) \Leftrightarrow \text{def}(\textbf{forall } \overline{z} \textbf{ with } \varphi \textbf{ do } r$
$\textbf{enddo}) \wedge (\ddot{\Delta} = \biguplus\limits_{\overline{z}} (\ddot{\Delta}' | \varphi \wedge \text{upm}(r, \ddot{\Delta}')) \vee (\neg \varphi \wedge \bigwedge\limits_{f \in \mathbb{F}_{dyn}} \forall \overline{x}, y, z'. \neg \ddot{\Delta}(f, \overline{x}, y, z')))$

G4 $\text{upm}(\textbf{par } r_1 \ldots r_n \textbf{ endpar}, \ddot{\Delta}) \Leftrightarrow \text{def}(\textbf{par } r_1 \ldots r_n \textbf{ endpar}) \wedge$
$\bigwedge\limits_{f \in \mathbb{F}_{dyn}} \forall \overline{x}, y, w'.(\ddot{\Delta}(f, \overline{x}, y, w') \Leftrightarrow w' < \sum_{w^i_{max}} (w^i_{max} + 1 | \bigvee\limits_{i=1}^{n} \ddot{\Delta}_i(f, \overline{x}, y, w^i_{max})$
$\wedge \forall w.(\ddot{\Delta}_i(f, \overline{x}, y, w) \Rightarrow w \leq w^i_{max}))) \wedge \bigwedge\limits_{i=1}^{n} \exists \ddot{\Delta}_i.\text{upm}(r_i, \ddot{\Delta}_i)$

G5 $\text{upm}(\textbf{choose } \overline{z} \textbf{ with } \varphi \textbf{ do } r \textbf{ enddo}, \ddot{\Delta}) \Leftrightarrow \exists \overline{z}.(\varphi \wedge \text{upm}(r, \ddot{\Delta}))$
$\vee (\forall \overline{z}. \neg \varphi \wedge \bigwedge\limits_{f \in \mathbb{F}_{dyn}} \forall \overline{x}, y, z. \neg \ddot{\Delta}(f, \overline{x}, y, z))$

G6 $\text{upm}(\textbf{seq } r_1 \ r_2 \textbf{ endseq}, \ddot{\Delta}) \Leftrightarrow \exists \ddot{\Delta}_1, \ddot{\Delta}_2, \Delta_1.\text{upm}(r_1, \ddot{\Delta}_1) \wedge \Delta_1 = AsSet(\ddot{\Delta}_1)$
$\wedge [\Delta_1]\text{upm}(r_2, \ddot{\Delta}_2) \wedge \bigwedge\limits_{f \in \mathbb{F}_{dyn}} \forall \overline{x}, y, w.(\ddot{\Delta}(f, \overline{x}, y, w) \Leftrightarrow (\ddot{\Delta}_1(f, \overline{x}, y, w) \wedge$
$([\Delta_1]\text{def}(r_2) \wedge \text{inv}(\ddot{\Delta}_2, f, \overline{x}))) \vee (\text{con}(\Delta_1) \wedge [\Delta_1]\ddot{\Delta}_2(f, \overline{x}, y, w)))$

G7 $\text{upm}(\textbf{let } \theta(t) = \rho \textbf{ in } r \textbf{ endlet}, \ddot{\Delta}) \Leftrightarrow \exists \ddot{\Delta}'.\text{upm}(r, \ddot{\Delta}') \wedge$
$\bigwedge\limits_{f \in \mathbb{F}_{dyn}} \forall \overline{x}, y, z.(\ddot{\Delta}(f, \overline{x}, y, z) \Leftrightarrow (f(\overline{x}) \neq t \wedge \ddot{\Delta}'(f, \overline{x}, y, z))$
$\vee (f(\overline{x}) = t \wedge y = \rho_{y'}(y' | \exists z. \ddot{\Delta}'(f, \overline{x}, y', z))))$

- Axiom **M1** and Rules **M2-M3** are from the axiom system K of modal logic, which is the weakest normal modal logic system [6]. Axiom **M1** is called *Distribution Axiom* of K and Rule **M2** is called *Necessitation Rule* of K. Rule **M3** is the inference rule called *Modus Ponens* in classical logic.

M1 $[\Delta](\varphi \Rightarrow \psi) \Rightarrow [\Delta]\varphi \Rightarrow [\Delta]\psi$

M2 $\varphi \vdash [\Delta]\varphi$

M3 $\varphi, \varphi \Rightarrow \psi \vdash \psi$

- Axiom **M4** asserts that, if an update set Δ is not consistent, then there is no successor state after applying Δ over the current state and thus $[\Delta]\varphi$ is interpreted as true for any formula φ. Since applying an update set Δ over the current state is deterministic, Axiom **M5** describes the deterministic accessibility relation in terms of $[\Delta]$.

M4 $\neg\mathrm{con}(\Delta) \Rightarrow [\Delta]\varphi$

M5 $\neg[\Delta]\varphi \Leftrightarrow [\Delta]\neg\varphi$

- Axiom **M6** is also called *Barcan Axiom*, saying that all states in a run of a database transformation have the same base set, and thus the quantifiers in all states always range over the same set of elements.

   M6 $\forall x.[\Delta]\varphi \Rightarrow [\Delta]\forall x.\varphi$

- Axioms **M7** and **M8** assert that the interpretation of static and pure formulae is the same in all states of a database transformation, which is not affected by the execution of any DB-ASM rule r.

   M7 $\mathrm{con}(r, \Delta) \wedge \varphi \Rightarrow [\Delta]\varphi$ for static and pure φ

   M8 $\mathrm{con}(r, \Delta) \wedge [\Delta]\varphi \Rightarrow \varphi$ for static and pure φ

- Axiom **A1** asserts that, if a consistent update set Δ does not contain any update to the location $f(\overline{x})$, then the content of the location $f(\overline{x})$ in a successor state after applying the update set Δ is the same as its content in the current state. Axiom **A2** asserts that, if a consistent update set Δ does contain an update which updates the content of the location $f(\overline{x})$ to y, then the content of the location $f(\overline{x})$ in the successor state after applying the update set Δ is equal to y. Axioms **A3** and **A4** say that, if a DB-ASM rule r yields an update set Δ, then the rule r is defined and there must exist an update in the update set Δ, respectively. Axiom **A5** says that, if a DB-ASM rule r yields an update multiset, then the rule r also yields an update set.

   A1 $\mathrm{con}(\Delta) \wedge \mathrm{inv}(\Delta, f, \overline{x}) \wedge f(\overline{x}) = y \Rightarrow [\Delta]f(\overline{x}) = y$

   A2 $\mathrm{con}(\Delta) \wedge \Delta(f, \overline{x}, y) \Rightarrow [\Delta]f(\overline{x}) = y$

   A3 $\mathrm{upd}(r, \Delta) \Rightarrow \mathrm{def}(r)$

   A4 $\mathrm{upd}(r, \Delta) \Rightarrow \exists f, \overline{x}, y.\Delta(f, \overline{x}, y)$

   A5 $\mathrm{upm}(r, \ddot{\Delta}) \Rightarrow \exists \Delta.\mathrm{upd}(r, \Delta)$

- The following are axiom schemes from classical logic.

   P1 $\varphi \Rightarrow (\psi \Rightarrow \varphi)$

   P2 $(\varphi \Rightarrow (\psi \Rightarrow \chi)) \Rightarrow ((\varphi \Rightarrow \psi) \Rightarrow (\varphi \Rightarrow \chi))$

   P3 $(\neg\varphi \Rightarrow \neg\psi) \Rightarrow (\psi \Rightarrow \varphi)$

- Axiom **EG**, called *Existential Generalisation* in classical logic, says that some static term t satisfying a pure formula φ implies that there exists some element satisfying φ. Axiom **UI**, called *Universal Instantiation* in classical logic, says that a pure formula φ satisfied by all elements implies that there exists some static term t satisfying φ.

   EG $\varphi[t/x] \Rightarrow \exists x.\varphi$ if φ is pure, t is static and x ranges over B_{db}

   UI $\forall x.\varphi \Rightarrow \varphi[t/x]$ if φ is pure, t is static and x ranges over B_{db}

- The following are the equality axioms from first-order logic with equality. Axiom **EQ1** asserts the reflexivity property, Axiom **EQ2** asserts the substitutions for functions, Axiom **EQ3** asserts the substitutions for predicates and Axiom **EQ4** asserts the substitutions for ρ-terms. Again, terms occurring in the axioms are restricted to be static, which do not contain any dynamic function symbols.

EQ1 $t = t$ for static term t

EQ2 $t_1 = t_{n+1} \wedge ... \wedge t_n = t_{2n} \Rightarrow f(t_1, ..., t_n) = f(t_{n+1}, ..., t_{2n})$ for any function f and static terms t_i $(i = 1, ..., 2n)$

EQ3 $t_1 = t_{n+1} \wedge ... \wedge t_n = t_{2n} \Rightarrow p(t_1, ..., t_n) = p(t_{n+1}, ..., t_{2n})$ for any predicate P and static terms t_i $(i = 1, ..., 2n)$

EQ4 $t_1 = t_2 \wedge (\varphi_1(\overline{x}, \overline{y}) \Leftrightarrow \varphi_2(\overline{x}, \overline{y})) \Rightarrow \rho_{\overline{x}}(t_1 | \varphi_1(\overline{x}, \overline{y})) = \rho_{\overline{x}}(t_2 | \varphi_2(\overline{x}, \overline{y}))$ for pure formulae $\varphi_i(\overline{x}, \overline{y})$ and static terms t_i $(i = 1, 2)$

- The following axiom is taken from dynamic logic, asserting that executing a sequence rule equals to executing the rules sequentially.

DY1 $[\textbf{seq}\ r_1\ r_2\ \textbf{endseq}]\varphi \Leftrightarrow [r_1][r_2]\varphi$

- Axiom **E** is the extensionality axiom.

E $r_1 \simeq r_2 \Rightarrow \forall \Delta.\mathrm{upd}(r_1, \Delta) \Leftrightarrow \mathrm{upd}(r_2, \Delta)$

4 Soundness

We prove the soundness of the proof system by deriving valid properties of other systems.

Lemma 1. *The following modal axioms and rules used in the logic for ASMs [10] are derivable in the logic for DB-ASMs* [1].

(1) $[r](\varphi \Rightarrow \psi) \Rightarrow [r]\varphi \Rightarrow [r]\psi$

(2) $\varphi \vdash [r]\varphi$

(3) $\neg wcon(r) \Rightarrow [r]\varphi$

(4) $[r]\varphi \Leftrightarrow \neg[r]\neg\varphi$

Remark 1. The logic for ASMs [10] is deterministic by excluding the choice rule, whereas the logic for DB-ASMs includes the choice rule. Therefore, the formula $\mathrm{Con}(R)$ used by **Axiom 5** (i.e., $\neg\mathrm{Con}(R) \Rightarrow [R]\varphi$) in the logic for ASMs [10] indeed corresponds to the weak version of the consistency (i.e., $wcon(r)$) in the context of the logic for DB-ASMs.

Lemma 2. *The following properties are derivable in the logic for DB-ASMs.*

(5) $con(r, \Delta) \wedge [\Delta]f(\overline{x}) = y \Rightarrow \Delta(f, \overline{x}, y) \vee (inv(\Delta, f, \overline{x}) \wedge f(\overline{x}) = y)$

(6) $con(r, \Delta) \wedge [\Delta]\varphi \Rightarrow \neg[\Delta]\neg\varphi$

(7) $[\Delta]\exists x.\varphi \Rightarrow \exists x.[\Delta]\varphi$

(8) $[\Delta]\varphi_1 \wedge [\Delta]\varphi_2 \Rightarrow [\Delta](\varphi_1 \wedge \varphi_2)$

---

[1] Property (3) and Property (4) are valid only under the assumption that the rule r is defined and deterministic.

Proof. Property (5) is derivable by applying Axioms **A1** and **A2**. Property (6) is a straightforward result of Axiom **M5**. Property (7) can be derived by applying Axioms **M5** and **M6**. For Property (8), it is derivable by using Axioms **M1-M3**.

Lemma 3. *The following properties in [4] are also derivable in the logic for DB-ASMs.*

- $\overline{x} = \overline{t} \Rightarrow (y = t_0 \Leftrightarrow [f(\overline{t}) := t_0]f(\overline{x}) = y)$
- $\overline{x} \neq \overline{t} \Rightarrow (y = f(x) \Leftrightarrow [f(\overline{t}) := t_0]f(\overline{x}) = y)$

However, the principles 41 and 42 mentioned in [10] are not derivable in our logic. In DB-ASMs, two parallel computations may produce an update multiset in which there are identical updates to a location assigned with a location operator. Therefore, the following statement is not true.

$$[\mathbf{par}\ r\ r\ \mathbf{endpar}]\varphi \Leftrightarrow [r]\varphi$$

Example 3. Let S be a state. Suppose that firing a DB-ASM rule r over S yields an update multiset $\ddot{\Delta}_1 = \{\!\{(f_1, a, 3, 0), (f_1, a, 3, 1), (f_2, a, 1, 0)\}\!\}$, then firing the DB-ASM rule **par** r r **endpar** over S would yield $\ddot{\Delta}_2 = \{\!\{(f_1, a, 3, 0), (f_1, a, 3, 1),$ $(f_2, a, 1, 0), (f_1, a, 3, 2), (f_1, a, 3, 3), (f_2, a, 1, 1)\}\!\}$. If $\theta(f_1(a)) = \Pi$ and $\theta(f_2(a)) = \bot$ where $\Pi = (id, \times, id)$ for the binary multiplication function $\times$ and the identity function id, then

- applying rule r over S may lead to the update set $\Delta_1 = \{(f_1, a, 9), (f_2, a, 1)\}$ such that
  - $f_1^{S+\Delta_1}(a) = \Pi(3, 3) = 9$, and
  - $f_2^{S+\Delta_1}(a) = 1$.
- applying rule **par** r r **endpar** over S may lead to the update set $\Delta_2 = \{(f_1, a, 81), (f_2, a, 1)\}$ such that
  - $f_1^{S+\Delta_2}(a) = \Pi(3, 3, 3, 3) = 81$, and
  - $f_2^{S+\Delta_2}(a) = 1$.

Following the approach of defining the predicate joinable in [10], we define the predicate joinable over two DB-ASM rules as follows. As DB-ASM rules are allowed to be non-deterministic, the predicate joinable(r_1, r_2) means that there exists a pair of update sets without conflicting updates, which are yielded by rules r_1 and r_2, respectively. Then, based on the use of predicate joinable, the properties in Lemma 4 are all derivable.

$$\text{joinable}(r_1, r_2) :\equiv \exists \Delta_1, \Delta_2.(\text{upd}(r_1, \Delta_1) \wedge \text{upd}(r_2, \Delta_2) \wedge$$
$$\bigwedge_{f \in \mathbb{F}_{dyn}} \forall \overline{x}, y, y'.(\Delta_1(f, \overline{x}, y) \wedge \Delta_2(f, \overline{x}, y') \Rightarrow y = y'))$$

Lemma 4. *The following properties for weak consistency are derivable in the logic for DB-ASMs.*

(9) wcon$(f(\overline{t}) := t_0)$

(10) wcon(**if** φ **then** r **endif**) $\Leftrightarrow \neg\varphi \vee (\varphi \wedge \text{wcon}(r))$

(11) wcon(**forall** $\overline{z}$ **with** φ **do** r **enddo**) $\Leftrightarrow \forall\overline{z}.(\varphi \Rightarrow \text{wcon}(r) \wedge$
$\quad \forall\overline{z}'.(\varphi[\overline{z}'/\overline{z}] \Rightarrow \text{joinable}(r, r[\overline{z}'/\overline{z}])))$

(12) wcon(**par** $r_1 \ldots r_n$ **endpar**) $\Leftrightarrow \text{wcon}(r_1) \wedge \ldots \wedge \text{wcon}(r_n) \wedge$
$\quad \bigwedge_{1 \leq i \neq j \leq n} \text{joinable}(r_i, r_j)$

(13) wcon(**choose** $\overline{z}$ **with** φ **do** r **enddo**) $\Leftrightarrow \exists\overline{z}.(\varphi \wedge \text{wcon}(r)) \vee \forall\overline{z}.(\neg\varphi)$

(14) wcon(**seq** r_1 r_2 **endseq**) $\Leftrightarrow \text{def}(r_1) \wedge \exists\Delta_1.\text{con}(r_1, \Delta_1) \wedge [\Delta_1]\text{wcon}(r_2)$

(15) wcon(**let** $\theta(t) = \rho$ **in** r **endlet**) $\Leftrightarrow \exists\Delta_1, \Delta_2.(\text{def}(r) \wedge \text{upd}(r, \Delta_1) \wedge \text{con}(\Delta_2) \wedge$
$\quad \bigvee_{f \in \mathbb{F}_{dyn}} \forall\overline{x}, y.(\Delta_1(f, \overline{x}, y) \wedge f(\overline{x}) \neq t \Leftrightarrow \Delta_2(f, \overline{x}, y)))$

Property (17) in Lemma 5 asserts that formula φ' is interpreted to be true after applying the rule **choose** $\overline{z}$ **with** φ **do** r **enddo** iff it is true in all successor states or it is true in the current state if there is no any successor state.

Lemma 5. *The following properties for the formula* $[r]\varphi$ *are derivable in the logic for DB-ASMs.*

(16) $[\textbf{if } \varphi \textbf{ then } r \textbf{ endif}]\varphi' \Leftrightarrow (\varphi \wedge [r]\varphi') \vee (\neg\varphi \wedge \varphi')$

(17) $[\textbf{choose } \overline{z} \textbf{ with } \varphi \textbf{ do } r \textbf{ enddo}]\varphi' \Leftrightarrow \forall\overline{z}.(\varphi \Rightarrow [r]\varphi') \vee \forall\overline{z}.(\neg\varphi \Rightarrow \varphi')$

The properties in Lemma 6 state that a parallel composition is commutative and associative while a sequential composition is associative.

Lemma 6. *The following properties for parallel and sequential compositions are derivable in the logic for DB-ASMs.*

(18) **par** r_1 r_2 **endpar** $\simeq$ **par** r_2 r_1 **endpar**

(19) **par** (**par** r_1 r_2 **endpar**) r_3 **endpar** $\simeq$ **par** r_1 (**par** r_2 r_3 **endpar**) **endpar**

(20) **seq** (**seq** r_1 r_2 **endseq**) r_3 **endseq** $\simeq$ **seq** r_1 (**seq** r_2 r_3 **endseq**) **endseq**

Lemma 7. *The extensionality axiom for transition rules in [10] is derivable in the logic for DB-ASMs.*

(21) $r_1 \simeq r_2 \Rightarrow ([r_1]\varphi \Leftrightarrow [r_2]\varphi)$

Based on the above derivable properties, we have the following theorem for the soundness of the proof system.

Theorem 1. *Let* M *be a DB-ASM and* Φ *a set of sentences. If* $\Phi \vdash_M \varphi$, *then* $\Phi \models_M \varphi$.

5   Conclusion

In this paper we proposed a logic for DB-ASMs. By utilising a modal operator [ ] for an update set, the logic for DB-ASMs can capture bounded non-determinism, which solved the problems left in [10,15]. We showed the soundness of the proof system in this paper, and will continue to explore the completeness of the proof system in the future work.

References

1. Börger, E., Stärk, R.F.: Abstract State Machines: A Method for High-Level System Design and Analysis. Springer, Heidelberg (2003)
2. Grädel, E., Gurevich, Y.: Metafinite model theory. Information and Computation 140(1), 26–81 (1998)
3. Groenboom, R., de Renardel Lavalette, G.: Reasoning about dynamic features in specification languages - a modal view on creation and modification. In: Proceedings of the International Workshop on Semantics of Specification Languages (SoSL), pp. 340–355. Springer, Heidelberg (1994)
4. Groenboom, R., de Renardel Lavalette, G.: A formalization of evolving algebras. In: Proceedings of Accolade 1995 (1995); Dutch Research School in Logic
5. Gurevich, Y.: Sequential abstract state machines capture sequential algorithms. ACM Transactions on Computational Logic 1(1), 77–111 (2000)
6. Hughes, G., Cresswell, M.: A new introduction to modal logic. Burns & Oates (1996)
7. de Renardel Lavalette, G.: A logic of modification and creation. In: Logical Perspectives on Language and Information. CSLI publications, Stanford (2001)
8. Schewe, K.-D., Wang, Q.: A customised ASM thesis for database transformations. Acta Cybernetica 19(4), 765–805 (2010)
9. Schönegge, A.: Extending Dynamic Logic for Reasoning about Evolving Algebras. Technical Report 49/95, Universität Karlsruhe, Fakultät für Informatik (1995)
10. Stärk, R., Nanchen, S.: A logic for abstract state machine. Journal of Universal Computer Science 7(11) (2001)
11. Van den Bussche, J.: Formal Aspects of Object Identity in Database Manipulation. PhD thesis, University of Antwerp (1993)
12. Van den Bussche, J., Van Gucht, D.: Semi-determinism (extended abstract). In: Proceedings of the Eleventh ACM SIGACT-SIGMOD-SIGART Symposium on Principles of Database Systems, pp. 191–201. ACM Press, New York (1992)
13. Wang, Q.: Logical Foundations of Database Transformations for Complex-Value Databases. Logos Verlag, Berlin (2010)
14. Wang, Q., Schewe, K.-D.: Axiomatization of database transformations. In: Proceedings of the 14th International ASM Workshop (2007)
15. Wang, Q., Schewe, K.-D.: Towards a Logic for Abstract MetaFinite State Machines. In: Hartmann, S., Kern-Isberner, G. (eds.) FoIKS 2008. LNCS, vol. 4932, pp. 365–380. Springer, Heidelberg (2008)

APPENDIX

A   Proof of Lemma 1

Each property in Lemma 1 can be proven as follows:

Proof for Property (1)

- By $[r]\varphi = \forall\Delta.(\text{upd}(r,\Delta) \Rightarrow [\Delta]\varphi)$, we have
$$[r](\varphi \Rightarrow \psi) \wedge [r]\varphi = \forall\Delta.(\text{upd}(r,\Delta) \Rightarrow [\Delta](\varphi \Rightarrow \psi))\wedge$$
$$\forall\Delta.(\text{upd}(r,\Delta) \Rightarrow [\Delta]\varphi).$$

- By the axioms from classical logic, we have
  $[r](\varphi \Rightarrow \psi) \wedge [r]\varphi = \forall\Delta.(\mathrm{upd}(r, \Delta) \Rightarrow ([\Delta](\varphi \Rightarrow \psi) \wedge [\Delta]\varphi)).$
- Then by Axiom **M1**: $[\Delta](\varphi \Rightarrow \psi) \Rightarrow [\Delta]\varphi \Rightarrow [\Delta]\psi$, we can get
  $\forall\Delta.(\mathrm{upd}(r, \Delta) \Rightarrow ([\Delta](\varphi \Rightarrow \psi) \wedge [\Delta]\varphi)) \Rightarrow \forall\Delta.(\mathrm{upd}(r, \Delta) \Rightarrow [\Delta]\psi).$

Therefore, $[r](\varphi \Rightarrow \psi) \Rightarrow [r]\varphi \Rightarrow [r]\psi$ is derivable.

Proof for Property (2)

As discussed before, each DB-ASM rule is defined. Thus, for a DB-ASM rule r, we assume that $\Delta(r, S, \zeta) = \{\Delta_1, ..., \Delta_n\}$.

- By Rule **M2**: $\varphi \vdash [\Delta]\varphi$, we have $\varphi \vdash [\Delta_i]\varphi$ $(i = 1, ..., n)$ for all update sets $\{\Delta_1, .., \Delta_n\}$ generated by r, i.e., $\varphi \vdash \forall\Delta.(\mathrm{upd}(r, \Delta) \Rightarrow [\Delta]\varphi)$.
- By the definition that $[r]\varphi = \forall\Delta.(\mathrm{upd}(r, \Delta) \Rightarrow [\Delta]\varphi)$, we can get $\varphi \vdash [r]\varphi$.

Therefore, $\varphi \vdash [r]\varphi$ is derivable.

Proof for Property (3)

- By $\mathrm{wcon}(r) \Leftrightarrow \mathrm{def}(r) \wedge \exists\Delta.\mathrm{con}(r, \Delta)$ and the fact that $\mathrm{def}(r)$ is trivial for a DB-ASM rule r, we have $\neg\mathrm{wcon}(r) \Leftrightarrow \neg\exists\Delta.\mathrm{con}(r, \Delta)$.
- By $\mathrm{con}(r, \Delta) \Leftrightarrow (\mathrm{upd}(r, \Delta) \wedge \mathrm{con}(\Delta))$, we have $\neg\mathrm{wcon}(r) \Leftrightarrow \neg\exists\Delta.(\mathrm{upd}(r, \Delta) \wedge \mathrm{con}(\Delta))$.
- Since a rule r in [10] is deterministic and a DB-ASM rule is always defined, we get $\neg\mathrm{wcon}(r) \Leftrightarrow \neg\mathrm{con}(\Delta)$.
- By Axiom **M4**: $\neg\mathrm{con}(\Delta) \Rightarrow [\Delta]\varphi$ and the fact that a defined rule r in [10] yields exactly one update set Δ, we get $\neg\mathrm{wcon}(r) \Rightarrow [r]\varphi$.

Therefore, $\neg\mathrm{wcon}(r) \Rightarrow [r]\varphi$ is derivable if a rule r is defined and deterministic.

Proof for Property (4)

- By $[r]\varphi = \forall\Delta.(\mathrm{upd}(r, \Delta) \Rightarrow [\Delta]\varphi)$, we have $\neg[r]\neg\varphi = \exists\Delta.(\mathrm{upd}(r, \Delta) \wedge \neg[\Delta]\neg\varphi)$.
- By Axiom **M5**: $\neg[\Delta]\varphi \Leftrightarrow [\Delta]\neg\varphi$, we have $\neg[r]\neg\varphi = \exists\Delta.(\mathrm{upd}(r, \Delta) \wedge [\Delta]\varphi)$.
- When the rule is defined and deterministic, it means that the interpretation of the formula $\forall\Delta.(\mathrm{upd}(r, \Delta) \Rightarrow [\Delta]\varphi)$ coincides the interpretation of the formula $\exists\Delta.(\mathrm{upd}(r, \Delta) \wedge [\Delta]\varphi)$.

Therefore, $[r]\varphi \Leftrightarrow \neg[r]\neg\varphi$ is derivable if a rule r is defined and deterministic.

B   Proof of Lemma 4

It is not difficult to prove the properties in Lemma 4, except for Property (11). For this reason, we present the proof for Property (11) in the following.

$\mathrm{wcon}(\textbf{forall } \bar{z} \textbf{ with } \varphi \textbf{ do } r \textbf{ enddo})$

$\Leftrightarrow(\texttt{Apply the definition of } \mathrm{wcon}.)$

$\mathrm{def}(\textbf{forall } \bar{z} \textbf{ with } \varphi \textbf{ do } r \textbf{ enddo}) \wedge \exists\Delta.\mathrm{con}(\textbf{forall } \bar{z} \textbf{ with } \varphi \textbf{ do } r \textbf{ enddo}, \Delta)$

$\Leftrightarrow$(Apply **D3**.)

$\forall \bar{z}.(\varphi \Rightarrow def(r)) \wedge \exists\Delta.con(\textbf{forall } \bar{z} \textbf{ with } \varphi \textbf{ do } r \textbf{ enddo}, \Delta)$

$\Leftrightarrow$(Apply the definition of *con*.)

$\forall \bar{z}.(\varphi \Rightarrow def(r)) \wedge \exists\Delta.(upd(\textbf{forall } \bar{z} \textbf{ with } \varphi \textbf{ do } r \textbf{ enddo}, \Delta)\wedge$

$$\forall \bar{x}, y, y'. \bigwedge_{f\in\mathbb{F}_{dyn}} (\Delta(f, \bar{x}, y) \wedge \Delta(f, \bar{x}, y') \Rightarrow y = y'))$$

$\Leftrightarrow$(Apply **U3**. Here we can neglect *def*(**forall** $\bar{z}$ **with** φ **do** r **enddo**), as it already appears in the first part of the conjunction.)

$$\forall \bar{z}.(\varphi \Rightarrow def(r) \wedge \exists\Delta.((\Delta = \bigcup_{\bar{z}'}\{\Delta' \mid \varphi[\bar{z}'/\bar{z}] \wedge upd(r[\bar{z}'/\bar{z}], \Delta')\})\wedge$$

$$\forall \bar{x}, y, y'. \bigwedge_{f\in\mathbb{F}_{dyn}} (\Delta(f, \bar{x}, y) \wedge \Delta(f, \bar{x}, y') \Rightarrow y = y')))$$

(Here we got many update sets Δ'. The union Δ of these update sets satisfies the consistency property $\forall \bar{x}, y, y'. \bigwedge_{f\in\mathbb{F}_{dyn}}(\Delta(f, \bar{x}, y) \wedge \Delta(f, \bar{x}, y') \Rightarrow y = y')$. This implies that also each Δ' satifies the same condition. In addition, as consistency holds for the union, we cannot have conflicting updates in different update sets, which gives $\forall \bar{x}, y, y'. \bigwedge_{f\in\mathbb{F}_{dyn}}(\Delta_1(f, \bar{x}, y) \wedge \Delta_2(f, \bar{x}, y') \Rightarrow y = y')$, if Δ_1, Δ_2 are two update sets appearing in the union. Conversely, if we have this mutual consistency condition, the union is consistent.)

$\Leftrightarrow$

$$\forall \bar{z}.(\varphi \Rightarrow def(r) \wedge \exists\Delta_1(upd(r, \Delta_1)\wedge$$

$$\forall \bar{x}, y, y'. \bigwedge_{f\in\mathbb{F}_{dyn}} (\Delta_1(f, \bar{x}, y) \wedge \Delta_1(f, \bar{x}, y') \Rightarrow y = y'))\wedge$$

$$\forall \bar{z}'.(\varphi[\bar{z}'/\bar{z}] \Rightarrow def(r[\bar{z}'/\bar{z}]) \wedge \exists\Delta_2(upd(r[\bar{z}'/\bar{z}], \Delta_2)\wedge$$

$$\forall \bar{x}, y, y'. \bigwedge_{f\in\mathbb{F}_{dyn}} (\Delta_2(f, \bar{x}, y) \wedge \Delta_2(f, \bar{x}, y') \Rightarrow y = y'))\wedge$$

$$\forall \bar{x}, y, y'. \bigwedge_{f\in\mathbb{F}_{dyn}} (\Delta_1(f, \bar{x}, y) \wedge \Delta_2(f, \bar{x}, y') \Rightarrow y = y')))$$

$\Leftrightarrow$(Apply again the definition of *con*. In addition, apply the definition of *joinable*.)

$\forall \bar{z}.(\varphi \Rightarrow def(r) \wedge \exists\Delta_1.con(r, \Delta_1) \wedge \forall\bar{z}'.(\varphi[\bar{z}'/\bar{z}] \Rightarrow def(r[\bar{z}'/\bar{z}])\wedge$

$\exists\Delta_2.con(r[\bar{z}'/\bar{z}], \Delta_2) \wedge joinable(r, r[\bar{z}'/\bar{z}])))$

$\Leftrightarrow$(Apply the definition of *wcon*.)

$\forall \bar{z}.(\varphi \Rightarrow wcon(r) \wedge \forall\bar{z}'.(\varphi[\bar{z}'/\bar{z}] \Rightarrow joinable(r, r[\bar{z}'/\bar{z}])))$

C   Proof of Lemma 5

The properties in Lemma 5 can be proven based on the logical equivalence $[r]\varphi \equiv \forall\Delta.(\text{upd}(r,\Delta) \Rightarrow [\Delta]\varphi)$ as follows.

Proof for Property (16)

We have $[\textbf{if } \varphi \textbf{ then } r \textbf{ endif}]\varphi' \Leftrightarrow \forall\Delta.(\text{upd}(\textbf{if } \varphi \textbf{ then } r \textbf{ endif},\Delta) \Rightarrow [\Delta]\varphi')$. Then by Axiom **U2**, we have $[\textbf{if } \varphi \textbf{ then } r \textbf{ endif}]\varphi' \Leftrightarrow \forall\Delta.(((\varphi\wedge\text{upd}(r,\Delta))\vee (\neg\varphi \wedge \bigwedge\limits_{f\in\mathbb{F}_{dyn}} \forall\overline{x},y.\neg\Delta(f,\overline{x},y))) \Rightarrow [\Delta]\varphi')$. By $(\varphi_1 \vee \varphi_2 \Rightarrow \varphi) \Leftrightarrow ((\varphi_1 \Rightarrow \varphi) \vee (\varphi_2 \Rightarrow \varphi))$, we have $[\textbf{if } \varphi \textbf{ then } r \textbf{ endif}]\varphi' \Leftrightarrow \forall\Delta.(((((\varphi\wedge\text{upd}(r,\Delta)) \Rightarrow [\Delta]\varphi'))\vee((\neg\varphi\wedge \bigwedge\limits_{f\in\mathbb{F}_{dyn}} \forall\overline{x},y.\neg\Delta(f,\overline{x},y)) \Rightarrow [\Delta]\varphi')) \Leftrightarrow (\varphi\wedge[r]\varphi')\vee(\neg\varphi\wedge\varphi')$.

Proof for Property (17)

Using the same approach as in the proof for Property (16), we have $[\textbf{choose } \overline{z} \textbf{ with } \varphi \textbf{ do } r \textbf{ enddo}]\varphi' \Leftrightarrow \forall\Delta.(\text{upd}(\textbf{choose } \overline{z} \textbf{ with } \varphi \textbf{ do } r \textbf{ enddo},\Delta) \Rightarrow [\Delta]\varphi')$. Then by Axiom **U5**, we have $[\textbf{choose } \overline{z} \textbf{ with } \varphi \textbf{ do } r \textbf{ enddo}]\varphi' \Leftrightarrow \forall\Delta.(\text{def}(\textbf{choose } \overline{z} \textbf{ with } \varphi \textbf{ do } r \textbf{ enddo}) \wedge\exists\overline{z}.(\varphi\wedge \text{upd}(r,\Delta))\vee(\forall\overline{z}.\neg\varphi\wedge \bigwedge\limits_{f\in\mathbb{F}_{dyn}} \forall\overline{x},y.\neg\Delta(f,\overline{x},y))) \Rightarrow [\Delta]\varphi')$. Then by $(\varphi_1 \vee \varphi_2 \Rightarrow \varphi) \Leftrightarrow ((\varphi_1 \Rightarrow \varphi) \vee (\varphi_2 \Rightarrow \varphi))$, we can prove that $[\textbf{choose } \overline{z} \textbf{ with } \varphi \textbf{ do } r \textbf{ enddo}]\varphi' \Leftrightarrow\forall\overline{z}.(\varphi \Rightarrow [r]\varphi') \vee \forall\overline{z}.(\neg\varphi \Rightarrow \varphi')$.

Author Index